SHEPPARD'S BOOK DEALERS
IN EUROPE

SHEPPARD'S
BOOK DEALERS
IN EUROPE

A DIRECTORY OF
ANTIQUARIAN AND SECONDHAND
BOOK DEALERS ON THE
CONTINENT OF EUROPE

TENTH EDITION

RICHARD
JOSEPH
PUBLISHERS

First Edition published 1967
Tenth Edition published 1997

RICHARD JOSEPH PUBLISHERS LIMITED
UNIT 2, MONKS WALK
FARNHAM, SURREY GU9 8HT
ENGLAND
TEL: (01252) 734347
FAX: (01252) 734307
E-MAIL: RJOE01@AOL.COM

I.S.S.N. 0963-0171
I.S.B.N. 1 872699 46 4

MADE IN ENGLAND

Printed and bound by
Professional Book Supplies Ltd., Abingdon, Oxford.

Editor's Note. Whilst every care is taken to ensure that the
information given in this Directory is as accurate and
complete as possible, the Publishers cannot accept any
responsibility for any inaccuracies that occur or for any
relevant information that was not available to the Publishers
or its professional advisers at the time of going to press.

CONTENTS

ALPHABETICAL INDEX

DISPLAYED ADVERTISEMENT INDEX

SPECIALITY INDEX
to the Geographical Directory of Dealers

This index lists dealers under specific subject headings. The following list has been created from the subjects provided by dealers' entry forms.

7

SPECIALITY INDEX

INTRODUCTION

The tenth edition of this title is published this month, and contains a number of improvements which should greatly benefit the user and enhance trade between dealers and collectors throughout the geographical continent of Europe.

This edition lists 1,541 dealers from twenty-four countries; 1,072 with complete information supplied to us which represents a twenty per cent increase on the last edition. In addition, we have included 469 dealers whom we know to have been trading throughout the period of research for this edition but have not returned their free dealer questionnaire. These are shown as single line entries only. All dealers who merited a single line entry in the last edition and have either not advertised in the trade (during our research) or returned their questionnaire, have been dropped. Thus dealers, who thought that just having their name included will help their business, will be disappointed.

The improvements include a dealer's E-Mail address and those credit cards which are accepted as a method of payment. Otherwise, the information remains the same as shown in the last edition. The number of dealers with E-Mail communications links total 79 (or 7% of the total replies received). This is equal to the percentage of dealers in the current British Isles edition but less than the 10.7% of dealers in the North American directory. The number of dealers who accept credit cards in this edition is 162 (15%, compared to 17% in the British Isles).

During the last two years, the term 'book town' has become better known and more such book towns have been established. However, we note that many dealers in Redu (Belgium) now only open at the weekends and during holidays. Those intending to visit Redu should check opening times before setting off. Other book towns listed include Becherel and Montolieu (France) and Bredevoort on the Dutch/German border.

The format of the contents follows the convention as in other Sheppard directories; the prime index is the geographical index, followed by the Business and Proprietor Indexes.

Before the Speciality Index, we show for the first time, an index of dealers by their E-Mail number; thus making it easier for those using this new method of communication. The number of classifications in the Speciality Index is now 400, an increase of forty on the last edition. Two classifications have been broken down into more detail. The heading of Music, includes sections covering Folk, Jazz, Music Hall and Opera and under Sport, there are subjects such as Fencing, Field Sports, Horse Racing and Hunting. These will make the task of locating books on these subjects easier.

Lastly, we show all dealers who offer a booksearch service and those stocking books in large print.

Anyone wishing to be included in the next edition should write to Mrs M. Goulding at Richard Joseph Publishers Ltd., Unit 2 Monks Walk, Farnham, Surrey GU9 8HT.

R. Joseph
January 1997

USE OF THE DIRECTORY

This directory is divided into four sections. The first is the *Geographical Directory of Dealers*, in which full details, where supplied, are given for each business or private dealer. These are listed alphabetically by town in which the shop or business premises are located. The details, as supplied by dealers, are presented in the following manner:

Name of business:	As provided.
Postal address:	(•) Indicates the dealer's preference for indexing.
Prop:	Name of proprietor(s).
Tel:	Telephone number(s), followed by fax and/or telex number.
Est:	Date at which business was established.
E-Mail:	Electronic mail numbers. Users should ignore the full point at the end of the entry.
Type of premises occupied:	Shop, private, market stand or storeroom.
Opening times:	Of shop, or if premises are private, whether appointments to view stock may be made, or if postal business only.
Normal level of total stock:	Very small (less than 2,000), small (2,000–5,000), medium (5,000–10,000), large (10,000–20,000) or very large (more than 20,000).
Spec:	Subjects in which dealer specialises.
PR:	Price range of stock, shown in sterling, US Dollars, or national currency. This is intended as a guideline only.
CC:	Credit Cards eg. A – Access, AE – American Express, DC – Diners Club, EC – Eurocard, MC – Mastercard, V – Visa.
Important lines of business:	Other than secondhand antiquarian books.
Cata:	Frequency and subject of catalogues, if issued.
Corresp:	Languages, other than English, in which correspondence may be conducted.
Mem:	Membership of book trade organisations, eg. C.L.A.M. – Chambre Professionelle Belge de la Librairie Ancienne et Moderne S.L.A.M. – Syndicat National de la Librairie Ancienne et Moderne I.L.A.B. – International League of Antiquarian Booksellers

The next section is an alphabetical *Index of Businesses*, listing the business name, country and the page on which their full entry is to be found.

There is a new section, the *Index of E-Mail Numbers*, which lists dealers alphabetically with their page reference and E-Mail number.

This is followed by an alphabetical *Index of Proprietors*, giving their name and trading name, country and page number of entry.

The fourth section is the *Speciality Index*. This is presented in alphabetical order by subject heading, listing dealers, country and page number on which their details may be found.

UTILISATION DU REGISTRE

Ce registre est divisé en quatre parties. La première concerne le *Registre géographique des agents*, dans lequel tous les détails qui sont fournis sont donnés à chaque commerce ou agent particulier. Les noms sont par liste alphabétique par ville dans laquelle se trouve soit le commerce ou le magasin. Les détails fournis sont présentés de la manière suivante:

Nom du commerce.

Adresse postale.

Prop:	Nom du/des propriétaire(s).
Tel:	Numéro(s) de téléphone suivi par le/les numéro(s) de télécopie et/ou de télex.
E-Mail:	Numéro de E-Mail.
Est:	Date où le commerce fut établi. Type de locaux occupés.
Heures d'ouverture:	Ou si les locaux sont privés, s'il est possible de prendre rendez-vous ou si on peut contacter par poste uniquement.
Niveau normal du total des stocks:	Trés faible (moins de 2 000), faible (2 000 à 5 000), moyen (5 000 à10 000), large (10 000 à 20 000), ou très large (plus de 20 000).
Spec:	Sujets dans lesquels l'agent se spécialise.
PR:	Gamme de prix des stocks, montrée dans livres sterling, US Dollar ou devise national. Ce sont des grandes lignes.
CC:	Cartes Crédit eg. A – Access, AE – American Express, DC – Diners Club, EC – Eurocard, MC – Mastercard, V – Visa.
Les grandes lignes descriptives des commerces:	En dehors des livres anciens d'occasion.
Cata:	Fréquence et sujets des catalogues, si publieés.
Corresp:	Langues dans lesquelles la correspondance peut étre effectuée.
Mem:	Statut de membre des organisations de commerce des livres, par exemple:

        C.L.A.M. – Chambre Professionelle Belge de la
                Librairie Ancienne et Moderne
        S.L.A.M. – Syndicat National de la Librairie Ancienne
                et Moderne
        I.L.A.B. – International League of Antiquarian Booksellers

La deuxième partie concerne le *Registre des commerces* par ordre alphabétique, dans lequel se trouvent le nom del commerce, le pays et le numéro de page où sont inscrits les renseignements.

Ensuite, la troisième partie concerne le *Registre de propriétaires,* par ordre alphabétique, dans lequel se trouvent le nom des commerces, le pays et le numéro de page.

La quatrième partie concerne le *Registre des spécialités*. Il est présenté par ordre alphabétique par titres de sujets, en donnant une liste des agents, le pays et la page où sont inscrits les renseignements.

BENUTZUNG DES ADRESSBUCHES

Das Adressbuch ist in vier Abschnitte untergliedert. Das erste ist das *Geographische Adressbuch der Händler,* in dem volle Einzelheiten, soweit vorhanden, für jedes Geschäft oder privaten Händler aufgeführt werden. Diese sind in alphabetischer Reihenfolge angegeben, je nach Stadt, in der Geschäft oder Geschäftsräume sich befinden. Die Einzelheiten, den Angaben der Händler zufolge, werden in der folgenden Weise präsentiert:

Name des Geschäfts.	
Postanschrift.	
Prop:	Name des Eigentümers bzw. der Eigentümer.
Tel:	Telefonnummer(n), gefolgt von Fax– und/oder Telexnummer.
Est:	Datum, zu welchem das Geschäft gegründet wurde. Art der Räumlichkeiten, die benutzt werden.
E-Mail:	E-Mail nummer.
Öffnungszeiten des Geschäfts:	Oder, wenn es sich um private Räumlichkeiten handelt, ob Verabredungen zum Zweck der Bestandsbesichtigung gemacht werden können, oder ob es sich ausschließlich um eine Versandhandlung handelt.
Normaler Umfang des gesamten Bestands:	Sehr klein (weniger als 2 000), klein (2 000-5 000), mittelgroß (5 000-10 000), groß (10 000-20 000) oder sehr groß (mehr als 20 000).
Spec:	Bereiche, auf die sich der Händler spezialisiert.
PR:	Preisband des Bestands, in PFund Sterling, US Dollar, oder örtlicher Währung. Dies soll nur eine Richtschnur sein.
CC:	Kreditkarte eg. A – Access, AE – American Express, DC – Diners Club, EC – Eurocard, MC – Mastercard, V – Visa.
Bedeutende Geschäftsbereiche:	Abgesehen von antiquarischen Büchern aus zweiter Hand.
Cata:	Häufigkeit und Themen von Katalogen, sofern herausgegeben.
Corresp:	Sprachen, in denen korrespondiert werden kann.
Mem:	Mitgliedschaft von Vereinigungen des Buchhandels, z.B. C.L.A.M. – Chambre Professionelle Belge de la Librairie Ancienne et Moderne S.L.A.M. – Syndicat National de la Librairie Ancienne et Moderne I.L.A.B. – International League of Antiquarian Booksellers

Der nächste Abschnitt enthält einen alphabetischen *Index der Geschäfte,* wobei den name des Geschäfts, das Land, und die Seite, auf der deren Eintragung gefunden werden kann, angegeben sind.

Dann folgt ein alphabetischer *Index der Eigentümer,* wobei der Name des Geschäfts, das Land und die Seite, auf der dessen Eintragung gefunden werden kann, angegeben sind.

Im vierten Abschnitt befindet sich der *Spezialbereich-Index.* Dieser wird in alphabetischer Ordnung geführt, wobei zunächst der Spezialbereich angegeben wird, gefolgt vom Namen des Händlers, Land und seite, auf der Einzelheiten zu finden sind.

USO DELLA GUIDA

Questo Direttorio è suddiviso in quattro sezioni. La prima sezione è *La Guida Geografica dei venditori*, dove completi dettagli, quando sono provvisti, sono dati per ogni ditta o venditore privato. Questi sono elencati alfabeticamente secondo la città in cui risiedono. I dettagli provvisti vengono presentati nella seguente maniera:

Nome della Ditta.

Indirizzo Postale.

Prop:	Nome del proprietario o titolare/i.
Tel:	Numero di telefono/i, seguito del numero del Fax./o Telex.
E-Mail:	Numero di E-Mail.
Est:	Data d'inizio d'operazione di questa ditta. Tipo di locale in cui la ditta risiede.
Orario operativo della libreria:	Se in residenza privata, conferma dell'opportunità di prendere appuntamento per esaminare la mercanzia, o se operativo unicamente per via postale.
Livello normale di capacità d'assortimento:	Piccolissimo (meno de 2.000), piccolo (2.000-5.000), medio (5.000-10.000), grande (10.000-20.000), grandissimo (più di 20.000).
Spec:	Soggetto in cui il Libraio specializza.
PR:	Prezzo base della merce, presentato in sterline, dollari (Americanï), o valuta locale. Questo inteso unicamente come guida.
CC:	Carte de Credito eg. A – Access, AE – American Express, DC – Diners Club, EC – Eurocard, MC – Mastercard, V – Visa.
Importante linea di affari:	Escluso l'usato e l'antiquariato.
Cata:	Frequenza e argomento dei cataloghi, se publicati.
Corresp:	Lingua in cui la corrispondenza può essere condotta.
Mem:	Se si è soci di un organizzazione di Librai, es. C.L.A.M. – Chambre Professionelle Belge de la Librairie Ancienne et Moderne S.L.A.M. – Syndicat National de la Librairie Ancienne et Moderne I.L.A.B. – International League of Antiquarian Booksellers

La sezione seguente è un *Indice Alfabetico delle Ditte*, con il nome della ditta, il paese, e pagina in cui tutti i dettagli corrispondenti sono elencati.

Questo è seguito poi da un *Indice Alfabetico dei Titolari*, con il nome della ditta, il paese, e il numero di pagina relativa.

La quarta sezione è un *Indice di Specializzazione*. Questo è presentato nell'ordine alfabetico della specializzazione, elen cati il Titolare o Ditta, il paese, e la pagina in cui tutti i dettagli possono essere trovati.

14

PARA USAR EL ANUARIO

Este anuario se divide en cuatro secciones. La primera es el *Anuario Geográfico de Libreros,* en el cual se incluyen detalles completos, si se han proporcionado, de cada empresario comercial o librero particular. Estos son alistados alfabéticamente por orden de las localidades donde están ubicadas las tiendas o los locales comerciales. Los detalles suministrados por los libreros se presentan en el formato siguiente:

Razón social.

Dirección postal.

Prop:	Nombre del propietario (o propietarios).
Tel:	Número(s) de teléfono, seguido del número de fax y/o telex.
E-Mail:	Número de E-Mail.
Est:	Fecha en la cual se estableció la empresa. Tipo de local ocupado.

Horario de apertura y cierre de la tienda o: Si el local es particular, si es posible concertar visitas para inspeccionar las existencias, o si se trata de ventas postales solamente.

Nivel normal de existencias totales: Muy pequeño (menos de 2.000), pequeño (2.000-5.000), medio (5.000-10.000), grande (10.000-20.000) o muy grande (más de 20.000).

Spec:	Temática en la cual se especializa el librero.
PR:	Gama de precios de las existencias, indicados en libras esterlinas, dólares US, o la moneda del país. Estos precios se incluyen a modo de guía solamente.
CC:	Tarjeta de Crédito eg. A – Access, AE – American Express, DC – Diners Club, EC – Eurocard, MC – Mastercard, V – Visa.

Artículos importantes de venta: Aparte de libros antiguos de segunda mano.

Cata:	Frecuencia y temática de los catálogos, si se publican.
Corresp:	Idiomas en los cuales se puede corresponder.
Mem:	Asociación a organizaciones gremiales de librería, e.g. C.L.A.M. – Chambre Professionelle Belge de la Librairie Ancienne et Moderne S.L.A.M. – Syndicat National de la Librairie Ancienne et Moderne I.L.A.B. – International League of Antiquarian Booksellers

La sección siguiente comprende un *Indice alfabético de Empresas,* el nombre de emperesa, il país, y página que incluye la información completa.

Esta sección va seguida de un *Indice Alfabético de Propietarios,* con el nombre de empresa, el país, y número de página de inserción.

La cuarta sección comprende el *Indice de Especialidades.* Este índice está dispuesto en orden alfabético por títulos temáticos, con una lista de los libreros, el país, y número de página en que se incluyen los detalles del mismo.

INTERNATIONAL DIALLING

With the ever increasing use of facsimile machines, we show below the international telephone codes for countries listed in the current, and future, editions of the Sheppard's Directories.

To dial direct: first dial the international access code from the country you are in, then the code of the country you wish to contact, followed by the local area code (omitting the preceding zero), and finally the subscriber's telephone number.

COUNTRY	CAPITAL	GMT +/-	FROM	TO
Australia	Canberra	+10	0011	61
Austria	Vienna	+1	00	43
Belgium	Brussels	+1	00	32
Canada	Ottawa	−5	011	1
Cyprus	Nicosia	+2	00	357
Czechoslovakia	Prague	+2	00	42
Denmark	Copenhagen	+1	009	45
Finland	Helsinki	+2	990	358
France	Paris	+1	19	33
Germany	Berlin	+1	06	49
Greece	Athens	+2	00	30
Hungary	Budapest	+1	00	36
Iceland	Reykjavik	GMT	90	354
India	New Delhi	+5$\frac{1}{2}$	900	91
Ireland (Rep)	Dublin	GMT	16	353
Israel	Tel Aviv	+2	00	972
Italy	Rome	+1	00	39
Japan	Tokyo	+9	001	81
Liechtenstein	Vaduz	+1	00	4175
Luxembourg	Luxembourg	+1	00	352
Malta	Valletta	+1	0	356
Netherlands	Amsterdam	+1	09	31
New Zealand	Wellington	+12	00	64
Norway	Oslo	+1	095	47
Pakistan	Islamabad	+5	00	92
Poland	Warsaw	+1	00	48
Portugal	Lisbon	+1	07	351
Spain	Madrid	+1	07	34
Sri Lanka	Columbo	+5$\frac{1}{2}$	00	94
Sweden	Stockholm	+1	009	46
Switzerland	Berne	+1	00	41
Turkey	Istanbul	+2	99	90
U.K.	London	GMT	00	44
U.S.A.	Washington D.C.	−5	011	1
Yugoslavia	Belgrade	+1	99	381

ABBREVIATIONS
USED IN DESCRIBING BOOKS

Some booksellers and buyers, use highly individualistic systems of abbreviations. The following are sufficiently well known to be generally used, but all other words should be written in full, and the whole typed if possible.

A.D.	Autograph document	Lea.	Leather
A.D.s.	Autograph document, signed	Ll.	Levant morocco
A.D.*	Autograph document with seal	Ll.	Leaves
A.e.g.	All edges gilt	L.P.	Large paper
A.L.s.	Autograph letter, signed	M.	Mint
a.v.	Authorized version	Mco., mor	Morocco
B.A.R.	Book Auction Records	M.e.	Marbled edges
Bd.	Bound	M.S.(S.)	Manuscripts
Bdg.	Binding	N.d.	No date
Bds.	Boards	n.ed.	new edition
B.L.	Black letter	n.p.	no place (of publication)
C., ca.	Circa (approximately)	Ob., obl.	Oblong
C. & p.	Collated and perfect	Oct.	Octavo
Cat.	Catalogue	O.p.	Out of print
Cent.	Century	P.	Page
Cf.	Calf	P.f.	Post free
C.I.F.	Cost, insurance and freight	P.f.	Post free
Cl.	Cloth	Pict.	Pictorial
Col(d).	Colour(ed)	Pl(s).	Plate(s)
C.O.D.	Cash on delivery	Port.	Portrait
Cont.	Contemporary	P.P.	Printed privately
C.O.R.	Cash on receipt	Pp.	Pages
Cr. 8vo.	Crown octavo	Prelims.	Preliminary pages
d.e.	Deckle edges	Pseud.	Pseudonym(ous)
Dec.	Decorated	Ptd.	Printed
D-j., d-w.	Dust jacket, dust wrapper	q.v.	Quod Vide (which see)
E.D.L.	Edition de luxe	Qto.	Quarto
Edn.	Edition	Rev.	Revised
Endp., e.p.	Endpaper(s)	Rom.	Roman letter
Eng., engr.	Engraved, engraving	S.L.	Sine loco (without place of publication)
Ex-lib.	Ex-library		
Facs.	Facsimilie	Sgd.	Signed
Fcp.	Foolscap	Sig.	Signature
F.	Fine	S.N.	Sine nomine (without name of printer)
F.,ff.	Folio, folios		
Fo., fol.	Folio (book size)	Spr.	Sprinkled
F.O.B.	Free on board	T.e.g.	Top edge gilt
Fp., front.	Frontispiece	Thk.	Thick
Free	Post Free	T.L.s.	Typed letter, signed
G.	Good	T.p.	Title page
G., gt.	Gilt edges	T.S.	Typescript
G.L.	Gothic letter	Unbd.	Unbound
Hf. bd.	Half bound	Uncut	Uncut (pages not trimmed)
Illum.	Illuminated	Und.	Undated
Ill(s).	Illustrated, illustrations	V.d.	Various dates
Imp.	Imperial	V.g..	Very good
Impft.	Imperfect	Vol	Volume
Inscr.	Inscribed, inscription	W.a.f.	With all faults
Ital.	Italic letter	Wraps.	Wrappers

Condition is described by the following scale. – Mint – Fine – Very good – Good – Fair – Poor.

SIZES OF BOOKS

These are only approximate, as trimming varies and all sizes ignore the overlap of a book case.

	Octavo (8vo)		Quarto (4to)	
	Inches	*Centimetres*	*Inches*	*Centimetres*
FOOLSCAP	$6^3/_4$ x $4^1/_4$	17.1 x 10.8	$8^1/_2$ x $6^3/_4$	21.5 x 17.1
CROWN	$7^1/_2$ x 5	19.0 x 12.7	10 x $7^1/_2$	25.4 x 19.0
LARGE POST	$8^1/_4$ x $5^1/_4$	20.9 x 13.3	$10^1/_2$ x $8^1/_4$	26.6 x 20.9
DEMY	$8^3/_8$ x $5^5/_8$	22.3 x 14.2	$11^1/_4$ x $8^3/_4$	28.5 x 22.2
MEDIUM	9 x $5^3/_4$	22.8 x 14.6	$11^1/_2$ x 9	29.2 x 22.8
ROYAL	10 x $6^1/_4$	25.4 x 15.8	$12^1/_2$ x 10	31.7 x 25.4
SUPER ROYAL	$10^1/_4$ x $6^3/_4$	26.0 x 17.5	$13^3/_4$ x $10^1/_4$	34.9 x 26.0
IMPERIAL	11 x $7^1/_2$	27.9 x 19.0	15 x 11	38.0 x 27.9
FOOLSCAP FOLIO			$13^1/_2$ x $8^1/_2$	34.2 x 21.5
METRIC A5	$8^1/_4$ x $5^1/_4$	21.0 x 14.8		
A4	$11^3/_4$ x $8^1/_4$	29.7 x 21.0		

BRITISH PAPER SIZES (untrimmed)

Sizes of Printing Papers

	Inches	*Centimetres*
Foolscap	17 x $13^1/_2$	43.2 x 34.3
Double Foolscap	27 x 17	68.6 x 43.2
Crown	20 x 15	50.8 x 38.1
Double Crown	30 x 20	76.2 x 50.8
Quad Crown	40 x 30	101.6 x 76.2
Double Quad Crown	60 x 40	152.4 x 101.6
Post	$19^1/_4$ x $15^1/_2$	48.9 x 39.4
Double Post	$31^1/_2$ x $19^1/_2$	80.0 x 49.5
Double Large Post	33 x 21	83.8 x 53.3
Sheet and $^1/_2$ Post	$23^1/_2$ x $19^1/_2$	59.7 x 49.5
Demy	$22^1/_2$ x $17^1/_2$	57.2 x 44.5
Double Demy	35 x $22^1/_2$	88.9 x 57.2
Quad Demy	45 x 35	114.3 x 88.9
Music Demy	20 x $15^1/_2$	50.8 x 39.4
Medium	23 x 18	58.4 x 45.7
Royal	25 x 20	63.5 x 50.8
Super Royal	$27^1/_2$ x $20^1/_2$	69.9 x 52.1
Elephant	28 x 23	71.1 x 58.4
Imperial	30 x 22	76.2 x 55.9

METRIC CONVERSIONS

SIZES

inches	m.m.	inches	m.m.
$1/4$	6	$7^3/_4$	197
$1/2$	13	8	203
$3/4$	19	$8^1/_4$	210
1	25	$8^1/_2$	216
$1^1/_4$	32	$8^3/_4$	222
$1^1/_2$	38	9	229
$1^3/_4$	44	$9^1/_4$	235
2	51	$9^1/_2$	241
$2^1/_4$	57	$9^3/_4$	248
$2^1/_2$	64	10	254
$2^3/_4$	70	$10^1/_4$	260
3	76	$10^1/_2$	267
$3^1/_4$	83	$10^3/_4$	273
$3^1/_2$	89	11	279
$3^3/_4$	95	$11^1/_4$	286
4	102	$11^1/_2$	292
$4^1/_4$	108	$11^3/_4$	298
$4^1/_2$	114	12	305
$4^3/_4$	121	$12^1/_4$	311
5	127	$12^1/_2$	318
$5^1/_4$	133	$12^3/_4$	324
$5^1/_2$	140	13	330
$5^3/_4$	146	$13^1/_4$	337
6	152	$13^1/_2$	343
$6^1/_4$	159	$13^3/_4$	349
$6^1/_2$	165	14	356
$6^3/_4$	171	$14^1/_4$	362
7	178	$14^1/_2$	368
$7^1/_4$	184	$14^3/_4$	375
$7^1/_2$	191	15	381

To convert inches to millimetres multiply by 25.4. Millimetres to inches may be found by multiplying by .0394.

WEIGHTS

lbs.	kgs.
1	0.45
2	0.91
3	1.36
4	1.81
5	2.27
6	2.72
7	3.18
8	3.63
9	4.08
10	4.54
11	4.99
12	5.44
13	5.90
14	6.35
15	6.80
16	7.26
17	7.71
18	8.16
19	8.62
20	9.07
21	9.53
22	9.98
23	10.43
24	10.89
25	11.34
26	11.79
27	12.25
28	12.70
56	25.40
112	50.80

To convert pounds to kilogrammes multiply by .4536. Kilogrammes to pounds may be found by multiplying by 2.205.

ANTIQUARIAN BOOKSELLERS' ASSOCIATIONS

Australia and New Zealand

AUSTRALIAN AND NEW ZEALAND ASSOCIATION OF ANTIQUARIAN BOOKSELLERS, 24 Glenmore Road, Paddington, N.S.W. 2021, Australia. Est 1977. President: Susan Tompkins. Vice-Presidents: Sally Burdon, Michael Treloar. Secretary: John Fisher. Treasurer: Paul Feain. 41 members.

Austria

VERBAND DER ANTIQUARE ÖSTERREICHS, Gruënangergasse 4, 1010 Wien, Austria. Tel: (+43 1) 512 1535. Fax: +43 1 512 8482.

Belgium

CHAMBRE PROFESSIONELLE BELGE DE LA LIBRAIRIE ANCIENNE ET MODERNE/BELGISCHE BEROEPSKAMER VAN ANTIQUAREN (C.L.A.M.), 53 Boulevard Saint-Michel, 1040 Bruxelles, Belgium. Est: 1946. President: Eric Speeckaert. Vice President: Johan Devroe. Treasurer: Wim De Goeij. Secretary: Evelyn Morel. 45 members.

Brazil

ASSOCIAÇÃO BRASILEIRA DE LIVREIROS ANTIQUÁRIOS, Rua Visconde de Caravelas 17, 22.271-030 Rio de Janeiro, RJ, Brazil. Tel: (55 21) 226-3590. Fax: (55 21) 246-6940. Est: 1961. President: Patrick Levy. 3 members.

Canada

ANTIQUARIAN BOOKSELLERS' ASSOCIATION OF CANADA, c/o Alphabet Bookshop, 145 Main Street West, Port Colborne, Ontario, Canada L3K 3V3. President: Richard D. Shuh.

Denmark

DEN DANSKE ANTIKVARBOGHANDLER-FORENING, Fiolstraede 34, P.O. Box 2028, DK-1017 Copenhagen K, Denmark. Fax: 33.125494. Est: 1920. President: Poul Jan Poulsen. 29 members.

Finland
SUOMEN ANTIKVARIAATTIYDISTYS RY. (Finska antikvariatföreningen rf.), Fredrikinkatu 35, PL 364, 00120 Helsinki, Finland. Tel: (90) 649291. Est: 1941.

France
SYNDICAT NATIONAL DE LA LIBRAIRIE ANCIENNE ET MODERNE, 4 rue Gît-le-Coeur, 75006 Paris, France. Tel: 43 29 46 38. Est: 1913. President: Jean Etienne Huret. 250 members.

S L A M

Germany
VERBAND DEUTSCHER ANTIQUARE E.V., Die Vereinigung von Buchantiquaren, Autographen-und Graphikhändlern, P.O. Box 18 01 80, D-50504 Köln, Kreuzgasse 2-4, D-50667, Köln. Tel: (0221) 92 54 82 62. Fax: (0221) 92 54 82 82. Est: 1949. President: Dr. Christine Grahamer. Vice-President: Edmund Brumme. Chairman: Jochen Gramíer and Michael Steinbach. Treasurer: Gundel Gelbert. 275 members.

Italy
ASSOCIAZIONE LIBRAI ANTIQUARI D'ITALIA, via Jacopo Nardi 6, 50132 Firenze, Italy. Tel: (055) 243253. Fax: (055) 243253. Est: 1947. President: Dr. Vittorio Soave. Secretary: Dr. Francesco Scala. Treasurer: Francesco Chellini. 88 members.

Japan
THE ANTIQUARIAN BOOKSELLERS' ASSOCIATION OF JAPAN, 29 San-ei-cho, Shinjuku-ku, Tokyo 160, Japan. Tel: (03) 3357-1411. Fax: (03) 3351-5855. Est: 1963. President: Takehiko Sakai. Secretary: Ichiro Kitazawa. Treasurer: Kazuhiro Tomaru. 29 members.

Netherlands
NEDERLANDSCHE VEREENIGING VAN ANTIQUAREN, Prinsengracht 445, 1016 HN Amsterdam, Netherlands. Tel: (020) 6272285. Fax: (020) 6258970. Est: 1935. President: Drs. F.W. Kuyper. Secretary: A. Gerits. 68 members.

ANTIQUARIAN BOOKSELLERS' ASSOCIATIONS

Norway

NORSK ANTIKVARBOKHANDLERFORENING, Universitetsgaten 20, 0162 Oslo, Norway. Tel: (47) 2242 1570. President: Idar Nilstad. 21 members.

Sweden

SVENSKA ANTIKVARIATFÖRENINGEN, Box 22549, 104 22 Stockholm, Sweden. Tel: (08) 6548086. Fax: (08) 6548006.

Switzerland

SLACES (Syndicat de la librairie ancienne et du commerce de l'estampe en Suisse) or VERBUKU (Verband der Buchantiquare und Kupferstichändler der Schweiz) Bäumleingasse 18, 4051 Basel, Switzerland. Tel: (061) 233088. President: Brigitta Laube, Trittligasse 19, CH-8001 Zürich. Tel: (01) 251 85 50. Secretary: Karl Ruetz. Treasurer: Gerhard Zähringer. 88 members.

United Kingdom

THE ANTIQUARIAN BOOKSELLERS' ASSOCIATION, Suite 2, 26 Charing Cross Road, London WC2H 0DG, England. Tel: (071) 379-3041. Fax: (071) 497 2114. Est: 1906. President: Margaret Eaton. Secretary: Jacqueline White.

PRIVATE LIBRARIES ASSOCIATION, Ravelston, South View Road, Pinner, Middlesex HA5 3YD. Est: 1956. The Private Libraries Association is an international society of book collectors with about 650 private members (about one third of them in America) and about 150 library members.

PROVINCIAL BOOKSELLERS' FAIRS ASSOCIATION, The Old Coach House, 16 Melbourn Street, Royston, Hertfordshire SG8 7BZ. Tel: (01763) 248400. Fax: (01763) 248921. Fairs information line: (01763) 249212. E-Mail: PBFA@antiquarian.com URL http://www.antiquarian.com/pbfa. Est: 1974. Chairman: Tony Lambert. Vice-Chairman: Jean Hedger. Honorary Secretary: Sarah Key. Honorary Treasurer: Ann Young. Membership Secretary: Mrs Gabby Besley. Administrator: Gina Dolan. Over 670 members.

PROVINCIAL BY NAME

For over 20 years the Provincial Booksellers Fairs Association has been organising book fairs - large fairs, small fairs, in the North and in the South. But large or small and wherever located a PBFA book fair stands out by its quality - quality of presentation, quality of organisation and quality of stock offered.

All PBFA members are established bookdealers who abide by a code of practice and trading details are readily available in the Directory of Members available at £2.00 (p + p extra).

Nor is our membership restricted to UK dealers. We have a number of North American members and have been encouraged by the number of European booksellers who have joined us and regularly exhibit at our fairs. All are very welcome.

Our fairs in the Hotel Russell have a well-deserved reputation as **the** place to buy books in London (see our separate page for details) and in the past few years we have added more events for the specialist dealer and collector. Our Natural History & Gardening Book Fair at the Royal Botanic Gardens Kew attracts buyers from all over the world and the latest venture, the Travel Book Fair at the Royal Geographical Society is fast becoming similarly well-established. We also work in conjunction with the Royal Academy to stage a Fine Arts Book Fair during the Academy's own Summer Exhibition.

Further details of all our book fairs or membership of the Provincial Booksellers Fairs Association is available on request from:

PBFA, The Old Coach House, 16 Melbourn Street, Royston, Herts, England, SG8 7BZ. Tel: +44 1763 248400; Fax: +1763 248921.
e-mail: pbfa@antiquarian.com
Web site: http://www.antiquarian.com/pbfa

WORLDWIDE BY REPUTATION

ANTIQUARIAN BOOKSELLERS' ASSOCIATIONS

WELSH BOOKSELLERS' ASSOCIATION, c/o Hay Castle, Hay-on-Wye, Powys, via. Hereford, Wales HR3 5DL. Tel. (0497) 820238. Est. 1987. Chairman: Richard Booth. Secretary and Treasurer: Jennifer Preston. 50 members.

United States of America

ANTIQUARIAN BOOKSELLERS' ASSOCIATION OF AMERICA, 50 Rockefeller Plaza, New York, N.Y. 10020, U.S.A. Tel: (212) 757 9395. Est: 1949. President: Robert D. Fleck. Secretary: Thomas E. Congalton. Treasurer: Donald A. Heald. Over 450 members.

The badge of the

INTERNATIONAL LEAGUE OF ANTIQUARIAN BOOKSELLERS (I.L.A.B.) to which most national associations belong. President: Anton Gerits, 5 Delilaan, 1217 HJ Hilversum, The Netherlands. Secretary: Helen R. Kahn, P.O. Box 323, Victoria Station, Montreal Quebec H3Z 2V8, Canada. Treasurer: Poul Jan Poulsen, P.O. Box 2028, DK-1012 Kobenhavn K, Denmark.

PERIODICALS

Literary Magazines and Book Trade Papers

Please note that magazine prices and subscriptions are given as a guide only, and are liable to change.

AB BOOKMAN'S WEEKLY: ANTIQUARIAN BOOKMAN. Est: 1948. Weekly, and AB Bookman's Yearbooks. Subscription: $80.00 a year (U.S.A., bulk mail), $80.00 (other countries, bulk mail), $125.00 (U.S.A., Canada and Mexico, first-class mail), foreign air mail, enquire. Editor and Publisher: Jacob L. Chernofsky, AB Weekly, P.O. Box AB, Clifton, NJ 07015, U.S.A. Tel: (201) 772-0020. Fax: 772-9281.

ABM (ANTIQUARIAN BOOK MONTHLY). Magazine containing articles, book reviews, auction reports and catalogue news. Est: 1974. Subscription: £28.00 a year (U.K.), £36.00 (Europe), £44.00 (Rest of the World). ANTIQUARIAN BOOK MONTHLY, 1 Park Parade, Park Road, Farnham Royal, Bucks SL2 3AU. Tel: (0753) 645999. Fax: 645255.

THE AFRICAN BOOK PUBLISHING RECORD. Covers new and forthcoming African publications. Est: 1975. Quarterly. Subscription: £110.00 a year. Editor: Hans M. Zell. Published by: Hans Zell Publishers (an imprint of Bowker-Saur Ltd.), P.O. Box 56, Oxford OX1 2SJ. Tel: (01865) 511428. Fax: 311534.

ALMANACCO DEL BIBLIOFILCO. Yearly. Published at: Edizioni Rovello di Mario Scognamiglio, P.za Castello, 11, 20121 Milano, Italy. Tel: (02) 86464661 or 866532. Fax: 72022884.

ANTIQUES BULLETIN. Weekly, Fortnightly, Three Weekly or Monthly Subscription. £39.50 all four (U.K.), £50.00 (Europe). Any Fortnightly £21.00 (U.K.), £27.50 (Europe); any Three Weekly £31.00 (U.K.), £39.00 (Europe); any Monthly £14.00 (U.K.), £18.00 (Europe). Published by: H.P. Publishing, 2, Hampton Court Road, Harborne, Birmingham B17 9AE. Tel: (0121) 681-8001/2/3/4/7. Fax: 681-8005.

ANTIQUES FAIRS GUIDE. Six monthly. £1.50 per copy plus 50p p&p. (5 year subscription only £16.00 - as 4 year subscription). Published by: H.P. Publishing, 2, Hampton Court Road, Harborne, Birmingham B17 9AE. Tel: (0121) 681-8001/2/3/4/7. Fax: 681-8005.

ANTIQUES TRADE GAZETTE. Contains comprehensive weekly reports on antiquarian book sales world-wide plus auction and fairs calendars. Est: 1971. Weekly. Subscription: £52.00 ($210.00) a year. Editor: Mark Bridge; Books Editor: Ian McKay. Published by: Metropress Ltd., 17 Whitcomb Street, London WC2H 7PL. Tel: (0171) 930-4957. Fax: 930-6391.

AUS DEM ANTIQUARIAT. Monthly. Editor: Dr. Karl H. Pressler. Published at: Münchener Freiheit 16, D-80802 München, Germany. Tel: (089) 34 13 31 + 39 84 30.

AUSTRALIAN BOOK COLLECTOR. Est: 1989. Monthly. News, features, books wanted and for sale. Subscription: (Australia) $48.00, (New Zealand) $61.00, (U.S.A.) $68.00, (Britain and Europe) $75.00 or £38.00 by airmail. Published by: ABC, Ross Burnet, P.O. Box 2, Uralla, N.S.W. 2358, Australia. Tel: (067) 784-682. Fax: 784-516. Email: austbook@anzaab.com.au. USA advertising and subscriptions: BookQuote, 2319C West Rohmann Avenue, Peoria, IL 61604. Tel: (309) 672 2665. Fax: 672 7853.

BIBLIO. Est: 1996. The first global magazine for book lovers and collectors covering all types of printed collectables from Antiquarian to Modern First Editions and Ephemera. Subscription: £48 (Europe). Published by: Richard E. Lawson, Aster Publishing, Suite B31, Grosvenor House, Central Park, Telford, Shropshire TF2 9TU. Tel: (01952) 200207. Fax: 200277.

PERIODICALS

THE BIBLIOTHECK. Bibliographical articles, notes and reviews of Scottish interest; annual supplement lists books, reviews, essays and articles on Scottish literature published in the preceding year. Est: 1956. 1 volume a year. Subscription: for institutions and individuals, £15.00 ($31.50) a year 10% discount for supplies. Edited by W.A. Kelly, Dept. of Printed Books, National Library of Scotland, George IV Bridge, Edinburgh EH1 1EW. Tel: (031) 226-4531 ext. 2304. Fax: 220-6662. Published by the Scottish Group of the University, College and Research Section of the Library Association, from The National Library of Scotland.

BOEKBLAD. Magazine for the Dutch book trade. Est: 1834. 50 issues a year. Subscription: 599 guilders a year. Edited at: Frederiksplein 1, 1017 XK Amsterdam, Netherlands. Tel: (020) 6253131. Fax: 6220908.

BOOK AND MAGAZINE COLLECTOR. Biographies and bibliographies of collectable 19th- and 20th-century authors and illustrators, plus lists of books for sale and wanted. Est: 1984. Monthly. Subscription: £30.00 a year (U.K.), £38.00 (Europe, Airmail), £33.00 (Europe, Surface), £52.00 (USA/Canada), £54.00 (Australia). Editor: Crispin Jackson. Publisher: John Dean. Published by: Diamond Publishing Group Ltd., 43–45 St. Mary's Road, Ealing, London W5 5RQ. Tel: (081) 579-1082. Fax: 566-2024.

THE BOOK COLLECTOR. Est: 1952. Quarterly. Subscription: £34.00 (overseas £36, US $60.00) a year. Editor: Nicolas Barker. Published by: The Collector Ltd., 43 Gordon Square, London WC1H 0PD. Tel: (0171) 388-0846. Fax: 388-0854.

BOOK WORLD. Articles, reviews, advertisements and news of the book world in general. Monthly. Subscription: £25 (U.K.), $50.00 (surface mail U.S.), $75.00 (air mail U.S.). Published by: Christchurch Publishers Ltd., 2 Caversham Street, Chelsea, London SW3 4BR. Tel: and Fax: (0171) 351-4995.

THE BOOKDEALER. Trade weekly for secondhand and antiquarian books for sale and wanted. £47.00 (within UK) a year (incl. p. & p.). Editor: Barry Shaw. Published by: Werner Shaw Ltd., Suite 34, 26 Charing Cross Road, London WC2H 0DH. Tel: (0171) 240-5890. Fax: 379-5770.

BOOKS FROM FINLAND. English-language journal presenting Finnish literature and writers. Est: 1976. Editor-in-chief: Jyrki Kiiskinen. Quarterly. Subscription: FIM 120 a year (Finland and Scandinavia), FIM 150 (all other countries). Editors: Soila Lehtonen & Hildi Hawkins. Published by: Helsinki University Library, P.O. Box 15 (Unioninkatu 36) SF-00014 University of Helsinki, Finland. Tel. and Fax: 358+0+1357942. E-Mail: bff@kaapeli.fi

BOOKQUOTE. Trade fortnightly for secondhand and antiquarian books for sale and wanted. Est: 1990. Subscription: $32.00 (North America) by first-class mail; £35.00 (Britain and Europe) by airmail. Published by: BookQuote, 2319-C West Rohmann, Peoria, IL 61604-5072, U.S.A. Tel: (309) 672-2665. Fax: 672-7853.

THE BOOKSELLER. Journal of the book trade in Great Britain. Weekly. Subscription: £115.00 a year (U.K.), £138.00 (overseas). Editor: Louis Baum. Published by: J. Whitaker & Sons Ltd., 12 Dyott Street, London WC1A 1DF. Tel: (0171) 420-600. Fax: 420-6103.

BOOTH'S ASSOCIATION OF INTERNATIONAL SECONDHAND BOOKSELLERS. Publisher of Booth's Gazette des Villages de Livres. This Gazette provides all essential information on Hay-on-Wye (1961), Redu (1984), Becherel (1988), Montolieu (1989), St. Pierre de Clages (1993), Bredevoort (1993), Stillwater (1993) and Fjaerland (1995). It seeks to encourage international secondhand bookselling via container shipping, the increasing move towards specialisation, and the winter economy which is essential for rural prosperity. Any articles and advertising welcomed from secondhand booksellers/ dealers anywhere in the world. Please contact the editorial offices. Booth's Gazette of International Booktowns, Editorial Office, 44 Lion Street, Hay on Wye, Herefordshire HR3 5AA. Tel: (01497) 820322. Fax: 821150.

PERIODICALS

BÖRSENBLATT FÜR DEN DEUTSCHEN BUCHHANDEL. Angebotene und gesuchte Bücher. Est: 1834. Weekly. Published by: Buchhändler-Vereinigung GmbH., Großer Hirschgraben 17/21, 60311 Frankfurt am Main, Postfach 10 04 42, 60004 Frankfurt am Main, Germany. Tel: (069) 1306-353. Telex: 413573, Fax: 1306-394.

THE BRITISH LIBRARY JOURNAL. A scholarly journal devoted to the study of the library's collections. Est: 1975. Published in 2 parts each year, in May and November. Annual subscription for 2 parts: £35.00 (U.K.), $60.00 (U.S.A.), £40.00 (other countries). Editor: Christopher Wright. Tel: (0171) 412-7516. Fax: 412-7745. Available from: Turpin Distribution Services Ltd., Blackhorse Road, Letchworth, Hertfordshire SG6 1HN. Tel: (01462) 672555. Fax: (01462) 480947.

BULLETIN DU BIBLIOPHILE. Est: 1834. 2 issues a year. Subscription: Fr 475 a year. Published at: 35 rue Grégoire-de-Tours, 75006 Paris, France. Tel: 44-41-28-00.

CLASSICAL QUARTERLY. Graeco-Roman antiquity in the English-speaking world. Includes research papers and short notes in the fields of language, literature, history and philosophy, usually in English. Est: 1906 (new series 1951). 2 issues a year. Subscription: £26.00 a year (U.K. and Europe), U.S. $54.00 (rest of the world). Editor: P.C. Millett and S.J. Heyworth. Published by: Oxford Journals, Oxford University Press, Pinkhill House, Southfield Road, Eynsham, Oxfordshire OX8 1JJ. Tel: (01865) 882283. Telex: 837330 OXPRESS G. Fax: 882890.

CLASSICAL REVIEW. Critical reviews by experts of new publications in the fields of Graeco-Roman antiquity from all countries. Est: 1886 (new series 1951). 2 issues a year. Subscription: £42.00 a year (U.K. and Europe), U.S. $76.00 (rest of the world). Editors: C. Carey and R.G. Mayer. Published by: Oxford Journals, Oxford University Press, Walton Street, Oxfordshire OX2 6DP. Tel: (01865) 56767. Telex: 837330 OXPRESS G. Fax: 267773.

CONTEMPORARY REVIEW. On politics, current affairs, theology, social questions, literature and the arts. Monthly. Subscription: £40.00 a year (U.K. surface mail), $160.00 (U.S.A. and Canada, airfreight), others on application. Editor: Dr. Richard Mullen. Published by: Contemporary Review Co. Ltd., Cheam Business Centre, 14 Upper Mulgrave Road, Cheam, Surrey SM2 7AZ. Tel: (0181) 643-4546. Fax: 241-7507.

CRITICAL QUARTERLY. On literature and the arts. Quarterly. Subscription: £31.00/ $58.00 (personal), £57.00/$99.00 (institutional); add £3.00 per issue for airmail postage. Editors: Brian Cox, Colin MacCabe, Kate Pahl. Published by: Blackwell Publishers, 108 Cowley Road, Oxford OX4 1JF. Tel: (01865) 791100. Fax: 791347.

L'ESOPO. Bibliophile magazine. Quarterly. Published at: Edizioni Rovello di Mario Scognamiglio, P.za Castello, 11, 20121 Milano, Italy. Tel: (02) 86464661 or 866532. Fax: 72022884.

FINE PRINT. The review for the Design of Literature. Est: 1975. Quarterly. $57.00 a year. With membership in Pro Arte Libri, a non-profit, educational organisation for the heritage of the graphic and book arts, special introductory offer, $36.00 plus $4.00 postage, surface. Editor: Sandra Kirshenbaum. Published by: Pro Arte Libri, P.O. Box 193394, San Francisco, CA 94119, U.S.A. Tel: (415) 543-4455.

FOLIO. Quarterly, to members only. Editor: Sue Bradbury. Published by: The Folio Society Ltd., 44 Eagle Street, London WC1R 4FS. Tel: (0171) 400-4200.

GAZZETTINO LIBRARIO. Requests and offers antiquarian and secondhand books. Est: 1958. 6 issues a year. Subscription: L. 65,000 a year. Editor: Dr. Francesco Scala. Published by: Gazzettino Librario, via Jacopo Nardi 6, 50132 Firenze, Italy. Tel: (055) 243024.

PERIODICALS

GREECE AND ROME. Literary evaluation of the major Greek and Roman authors, and articles on ancient history, art, archaeology, philosophy and religion, the classical tradition, and on the teachings of classics at the tertiary level. Est: 1931. 2 issues a year. Subscription: £35.00 a year (U.K. and Europe), U.S. $66.00 (rest of the world). Editors: Ian McAuslan and P. Walcot. Published by: Oxford Journals, Oxford University Press, Walton Street, Oxfordshire OX2 6DP. Tel: (01865) 56767. Telex: 837330 OXPRES G. Fax: 267773.

INDEX ON CENSORSHIP. Concerned with writers and journalists who are silenced for political reasons. 10 issues a year. Subscription: £36.00 a year (U.K.), U.S.$50.00 (U.S.A.), £42.00 (other countries), £25.00/U.S.$35.00 (students). Editor: Ursula Owen. Published by: Writers & Scholars (International) Ltd., 33 Islington High Street, London N1 9LH. Tel: (0171) 278-2313. Fax: 278-1878.

JOURNAL OF THE HISTORY OF COLLECTIONS. Dedicated to the study of collections, ranging from the contents of palaces and accumulations in more modest households, to the most systematic collections of academic institutions. Est: 1989. 2 issues a year. Subscription prices 1996: Institutions £60.00 / $110.00; Individuals £30.00 (U.K. and Europe), $52.00 (rest of the world). Editors: Oliver Impey, Arthur MacGregor. Published by: Oxford Journals, Oxford University Press, Walton Street, Oxford OX2 6DP. Tel: (01865) 56767. Telex: 837330 OXPRESS G. Fax: 267773.

THE LITERARY REVIEW. Covers books, arts, poetry and theatre. Est: 1978. Monthly. Subscription: £22.00 a year (U.K.), £28.00 (Europe), £32.00 (USA & Canada Airspeed), £44.00 (rest of the world Air Mail). Editor: Auberon Waugh. Published by: The Namara Group, 44 Lexington Street, London W1R 3Lh. Tel: (0171) 437-9392. Fax: 734-1844.

LONDON MAGAZINE. On arts, literature, memoirs and travel. Est: 1954. 6 issues a year. Subscription: £28.50/$67.00 a year (world-wide). Editor: Alan Ross. Published at: 30 Thurloe Place, London SW7. Tel: (071) 589-0618.

LONDON REVIEW OF BOOKS. Reviews of books on the humanities. Est: 1979. 24 issues a year. Subscription: £51.60 a year (U.K.), £63.00 (Europe). Editors: Mary-Kay Wilmers. Published by: LRB Ltd., 28-30 Little Russell Street, London WC1A 2HN. Tel: (0171) 404 3338. Fax: 404 3339.

MINIATURE BOOK NEWS. Est: 1965. Quarterly. Subscription: $13.00 a year (overseas). Editor: Julian I. Edison. Published at: 16 Dromara Road, St. Louis, Missouri 63124, U.S.A.

PHILOBIBLON. For book and print collectors. Quarterly. Est: 1957. Subscription: DM148.00 a year plus approximately DM10.00 postage. Editor: Reimar W. Fuchs. Published by: Dr. Ernst Hauswedell & Co., Verlag, Postfach 140155, D-70071 Stuttgart (Rosenbergstr. 113, D-70193 Stuttgart), Germany. Tel: (0711) 638265. Fax: 6369010.

THE PRIVATE LIBRARY. Established 1957. Quarterly. Distributed free to members of the Private Libraries Association, annual subscription £25.00 ($40.00). Editor: David Chambers. Sample copy free on request. Published by: The Private Libraries Association, Ravelston, South View Road, Pinner, Middlesex HA5 3YD.

PRIVATE PRESS BOOKS. An annual bibliography of books printed by private presses in the English speaking world. 1991 edition: 78 pp, £20.00 or $40.00 (£13.50 or $27.00 to PLA members). Editor: David Chambers. Published by: The Private Libraries Association, Ravelston, South View Road, Pinner, Middlesex HA5 3YD.

QUAERENDO. A quarterly journal from the Low Countries devoted to manuscripts and printed books. Est: 1970. Individuals - NLG 98.00/US$ 63.00, Institutions - NLG 160.00/US$ 97.00, Postage & packing - NLG 25.00/US$ 15.00. Editor: A.R.A. Croiset van Uchelen. Published by: E.J. Brill, P.O. Box 9000, 2300 PA Leiden, Netherlands. Tel: (071) 5312624. Fax: 5317532. TA: Brill, Leiden.

PERIODICALS

QUILL AND QUIRE. Canada's magazine of Book News and Reviews. Est: 1935. Monthly. Subscription: $75.00 a year (includes $30.00 postage outside Canada and two issues of the Canadian Publishers' Directory). Editor: Ted Mumford. Published by: Key Publishers, 70 The Esplanade (2nd Floor), Toronto, Ontario M5E 1R2, Canada. Tel: (416) 360-0044. Fax: 955-0794.

RARE BOOKS NEWSLETTER. Est: 1974. 3 issues a year. Subscription: £16.00 (U.K. & Europe), £22.00 (outside Europe). Editor: Richard Ovenden, Department of Printed Books, National Library of Scotland, George IV Bridge, Edinburgh, EH1 1EW. Subscriptions to: Dr. M.C. Simpson, Department of Special Collections, Edinburgh University Library, George Square, Edinburgh EH8 9LJ. Published by: The Library Association Rare Books Group.

SCOTTISH BOOK COLLECTOR. Est: 1987. 6 issues a year. Subscription: £11.00 a year (U.K.), £13.50 (Europe, airmail), £15.00 or $30.00 (U.S.A. and Canada, airmail), £16.00 (Australia and Japan, airmail). Editor: Jennie Renton. Published at: c/o 36 Lauriston Place, Edinburgh EH3 9EZ. Tel: (0131) 228-4837. Fax: 228-3904.

THE TIMES LITERARY SUPPLEMENT. Est: 1902. Weekly. Subscription: £69.50 (U.K.), £90.00 (Europe), U.S. $110.00 (U.S.A. and Canada). Editor: Ferdinand Mount. Published by: Admiral House, 66-68 East Smithfield, London E1 9XY. Tel: (0171) 782 3000. Telex: 24460 TTSUPP. Fax: 782 3333.

TRIBUNE. Books/Arts Editor: Caroline Rees. Published by: Tribune Publications Ltd., 308 Grays Inn Road, London WC1X 8DY. Tel: (0171) 278-0911.

WORLD BOOK INDUSTRY. In English. Est: 1975. Quarterly. Subscription: U.S. $10.00 a year. Editor: Kunnuparambil P. Punnoose. Published by: Jaffe Publishing Management Service, Kunnuparambil Buildings, Kurichy, Kottayam 686549, India. Tel: (04826) 470. Fax: 0091-481-561190. Telex: 888220 Mark In.

AUCTIONEERS

J.L. BEIJERS B.V., Achter Sint Pieter 140, 3512 Ht. Utrecht, Netherlands. Tel: (030) 310958. Fax: 312061. Sales of books and prints two or three times a year. Catalogue on request.

TON BOLLAND, Prinsengracht 493, 1016 HR, Amsterdam, Netherlands. Tel: (020) 6221921. Fax: 6257912. Sales of old and rare books: Theology-Church-History-Judaica.

LIBRAIRIE DES ELÉPHANTS, Place van Meenen 19, 1060 Bruxelles, Belgium. Tel: (32) 2-5390601. Fax: 2-5344447. *Enquiries to:* Antoine Jacobs.

GRANIER, Auktionshaus, Otto-Brenner-Str., 186, 33604 Bielefeld; P.O. Box 10 12 87, D-33512, Bielefeld, Germany. Tel: (521) 285005. Fax: 285015. Sales of valuable and fine books, manuscripts, old paintings and prints, modern art paintings and prints. Sales in March and September. Catalogue on request.

HAUSWEDELL UND NOLTE, Poeseldorfer Weg 1, 20148 Hamburg, Germany. Tel: (040) 4132100. Fax: 41321010. E-Mail: info@hauswedell-nolte.de. Sales of rare books, autograph letters, manuscripts, prints and works of art. Catalogue on request.

AUKTIONSHAUS THOMAS LEON HECK, Kaiserstrasse 64, 72764 Reutlingen, Germany. Tel: (7121) 370911. Fax: (7071) 87408.

JESCHKE, MEINKE & HAUFF, Habsburgerstrasse 14, 10781 Berlin, Germany. Tel: (030) 2161584 or 2170874. Fax: 2169594. Sales of valuable books, manuscripts and prints in Spring & Autumn. Catalogue on request.

BUBB KUYPER, 2011 KM Haarlem, Netherlands. Tel: (31) 235323986. Fax: 235323893. Sales of valuable books, manuscripts & prints in Spring & Autumn. Catalogue on request.

ANTYKWARIAT NAUKOWY, ul. Piotrkowska 85, 90-420 Lòdż, Poland. Tel: 331891. Two book auctions a year. *Enquiries to:* J. Plòciennik, M. Sobczak.

VAN STOCKUM'S VEILINGEN, 15 Prinsegracht, 2512 EW den Haag, Netherlands. Tel: (31) 0-70 3649840/41. Fax: 3643340. Book & print sales - 3 a year, antique sales - 4 a year. *Enquiries to:* Drs. P.A.G.W.E. Pruimers.

VENATOR & HANSTEIN, Cäcilienstrasse 48, 50667 Köln, Germany. Tel: (0221) 2575419. Fax: 2575526. One or two auctions per year with books, prints, drawings, autographs and manuscripts. Catalogue on request.

F. ZISSKA & R. KISTNER, Unterer Anger 15, 80331 München, Germany. Tel: (089) 263855. Fax: 269088.

INDEX OF CITIES AND TOWNS

Dealer locations listed alphabetically by country, city, town and village, as shown in the Geographical section.

INDEX OF CITIES AND TOWNS

INDEX OF CITIES AND TOWNS

AUSTRIA

Country dialling code: 43   *Currency:* Schilling (A$)

FELDKIRCH

Antiquariat Montfort, Neustadt 36, Postfach 570, 6800 Feldkirch. Prop: Traugott Schneidtinger. Tel: & Fax: (05522) 71783 or (0663) 053497 (mobile). Est: 1981. Shop; open Monday to Friday 2–6 and Saturday 9–12. Medium stock. Spec: Austriaca; alpinism; skiing. Cata: on specific subjects, infrequently. Mem: V.A.Ö.

GRAZ

Münzhandlung Lanz, Hauptplatz 14/I, 8010 Graz. Prop: Dr. Hubert Lanz. Tel: (0316) 829345. Est: 1947. Shop; appointment necessary. Very small stock. Spec: numismatics. *Also at:* Numismatik Lanz München, Maximilianspl. 10, 80333 München, Germany.

Antiquariat der Buchhandlung Moser, Hans–Sachs–Gasse 14/I, 8010 Graz. Booksearch service.

Matthäus Truppe, Stubenberggasse 7, P.O.B 402, 8011 Graz. Prop: Peter Truppe. Tel: & Fax: (0316) 829552. Est: 1921. Shop; open 9–12.30 & 3–6. Medium stock. Spec: art; literature; science; economics; law; fine & rare. Cata: 1 a year on specialities. Corresp: German. VAT No: ATU 276 164 07.

INNSBRUCK

Antiquariat Gallus, 6020 Anichstrasse 25, Innsbruck.

Innsbrucker Antiquariat Dieter Tausch, Adolf-Pichler-Platz 12, 6020 Innsbruck. Tel: (0512) 562769. Fax: 582132. Est: 1978. Shop; open Tuesday to Friday 3–7, and at other times by appointment. Small stock. Spec: old and rare. PR: A$1,000–5,000. Corresp: French, Italian. Mem: I.L.A.B.; V.A.Ö.

Buchhandlung und Antiquariat Herwig Widmoser, Maria–Theresien–Str. 8, 6020 Innsbruck. Tel: & Fax: (0512) 584848. Est: 1978. Shop; open Monday to Friday 10–7, Saturday 10–1. Medium general stock. CC: AE; DC; EC; MC; V. Corresp: German, French, Italian. VAT No: ATU 317 080 06.

KLAGENFURT

Wilfried Magnet, Kärntner Antiquariat, Arthur-Lemisch-Platz 2, 1st Floor, 9020 Klagenfurt. Prop: Wilfried Magnet. Tel: & Fax: (0463) 516785. Est: 1988. Storeroom; open Monday to Friday 9–12.30 & 3–6.30 and Saturday 9–12.30. Very small stock. Spec: old and rare; literature; local history (southern Austria, northern Yugoslavia, northern Italy). Cata: on history and literature, 2 or 3 a year. Also, paintings. Corresp: Italian. Mem: V.A.Ö.

SALZBURG

Michael Menzel, Burgerspitalpplatz 5, 5020 Salzburg.

Kunsthandlung Johannes Müller, Hildmannplatz 1A, 5020 Salzburg.

Antiquariat Weinek, Steingasse 14 & 21, 5020 Salzburg. Prop: Dr. Elisabeth & Dr. Christian Weinek. Tel: (0662) 882949. Fax: 627214. Est: 1986. Shop; open Tuesday to Friday 2–6 and Saturday 10–12. Very large stock. Spec: alpinism/ mountaineering; architecture; art history; avant–garde; bindings; earth sciences; literature; literature in translation; maritime/nautical; mathematics; motoring; music; natural health; philosophy; photography; railways; science; signed editions; theatre; travel; war. Cata: 1 a year. Also, graphics, paintings and a booksearch service. Corresp: French. VAT No: ATU 340 432 00.

VIENNA (WIEN)

Aichinger, Bernhard & Co. GmbH, Weihburggasse 16, 1010 Wien. Prop: Veronika Aichinger. Tel: (01) 512-88-53. Est: 1975. Shop; open Monday to Friday 9.30–6, Saturday 10–1, first Saturday in month 10–5. Medium stock. Spec: literature; illustrated; children's; art and craft; photography; Viennesia curiosities; old journals. PR: A$100–5,000. CC: V; AE; EC. Also, new books on literature, interiors, gardening, art and craft, photography and children's. Corresp: French, Italian. VAT No: ATU 148 938 00.

Georg Bartsch, Lerchenfelderstrasse 138, 1081 Wien. Prop: Hannelore Strauch. Tel: (01) 406-12-75. Telex: 75310636 ba a. Fax: 406-12-84. Est: 1934. Shop; open Monday to Friday 8–12.30 & 2.30–6. Very small stock. Spec: astronomy; mineralogy. Corresp: German. Mem: Hauptverband des Österreichischen Buchandels.

Bourcy und Paulusch, Wipplingerstrasse 5, 1010 Wien. Prop: Hans Paulusch & Jörg Treytl. Tel: (01) 533-71-49. Est: 1917. Shop; open Monday to Friday 8.30–6. Very large stock. Spec: alpine; Austriaca; genealogy; history. Cata: periodically. Mem: V.A.Ö.

Der Buchfreund (Walter R. Schaden), Sonnenfelsgasse 4, 1010 Wien. Prop: Rainer Schaden. Tel: (01) 512-48-56 or 513-82-89. Fax: 512-60-28. Est: 1955. Shop; open Monday to Friday 9–6, Saturday 9–12.30. Very large stock. Spec: literature; art; natural sciences; travel. PR: £1–100. Cata: 2 a year. Also, importers of scientific literature for institutions and universities. Corresp: German, French, Italian. Mem: V.A.Ö; I.L.A.B. VAT No: ATU 102 414 06.

Antiquariat Franz Deuticke, Helferstorferstrasse 4, Postfach 761, 1011 Wien. Tel: (01) 533-64-29. Fax: 533-23-47. Est: 1878. Storeroom; open Monday to Friday 9–6, Saturday 9–12. Very large general stock. PR: DM1–100,000. CC: All. Cata: 4 to 6 a year. Mem: V.D.A.; V.A.Ö.; I.L.A.B. VAT No: ATU 368 615 07.

Georg Fritsch, Antiquariat, Schönlaterngasse 7, Postfach 883, 1011 Wien. Tel: (01) 512-62-94. Fax: 513-88-14. Shop; appointment necessary. Very large stock. Spec: German literature; children's; psychoanalysis. Cata: 1 a year. Also, a booksearch service. Corresp: German, Dutch. Mem: I.L.A.B. VAT No: ATU 128 847 07.

Antiquariat Helmut Fröhlich, Florianigasse 36, 1080 Wien. Tel: & Fax: (01) 402-39-06. Est: 1989. Shop; open Tuesday to Friday 3–6, Saturday 10–12. Small stock. Spec: applied art; architecture; art; artists; the arts; autographs; avant–garde; cinema/films; economics; fine art; first editions; foreign texts; Holocaust; humanism; international affairs; limited editions; literature; philosophy; photography; politics; psychoanalysis; psychology/psychiatry; radical issues; Jewish religion; Judaism; signed editions; social history; social sciences; socialism. PR: DM30–1,500. Cata: 4 lists a year. Corresp: German. VAT No: ATU 123 966 00.

Gerold & Co., Bestellabteilung, Weihurgg. 26, 1011 Wien.

A. Hartleben – Dr. Rob, Schwarzenbergstrasse 6, 1015 Wien. Prop: Dr. Walter Rob. Tel: (01) 512-62-41. Fax: 513-94-98. Est: 1803. Shop and storeroom; open Monday to Friday 9–6, Saturday 9–12.30. Medium stock. Spec: travel guides; antiquarian; multi–media. CC: V; MC; AE; DC. Cata: 3 a year. Also, over 1,400 special interest magazines (subscriptions). Corresp: German. Mem: Austrian Trade Organisation. VAT No: ATU 102 371 08.

A.L. Hasbach - Buchhandlung & Antiquariat, Wollzeile 9, 1010 Wien.

Wiener Graphik-Kabinett und Buchhandlung Karl Hölzl K.G., Seilergasse 3, 1010 Wien. Tel: & Fax: (01) 512-28-96. Est: 1852. Shop. Medium stock. Spec: bibliophily. Cata: 1 a year. Mem: V.A.Ö. VAT No: ATU 102 435 01.

Antiquariat Informatio, Seilergasse 19, 1010 Wien. Prop: Hans Lugmair. Tel: & Fax: (01) 512-82-68. Open Monday to Friday 10–1 and 4–6. Small stock. Spec: advertising; antiquarian; natural history; natural sciences; periodicals/magazines; photography; history of science. Corresp: French. VAT No: ATU 102 456 07.

Antiquariat Inlibris Hugo Wetscherek & Co. KEG, Schreyvogelgasse 12, 1010 Wien. Tel: & Fax: (01) 535-41-78. Est: 1993. Shop; open Monday to Friday 10–6 or by appointment. Medium stock. Spec: autographs; fine & rare; opera. Cata: 1 a year. Also, a booksearch service. Corresp: German, French. Mem: I.L.A.B. VAT No: ATU 102 465 08.

Antiquariatsbuchhandlung Hans Jauker, Sampogasse 4, Postfach 240, 1142 Wien. Tel: & Fax: (01) 985-97-77. Est: 1982. Shop; open Tuesday to Friday 9.30–6. Large stock. Spec: antiquarian; art; ecclesiastical history & architecture; general, local and national history; Holocaust; journals; middle ages; monographs; philosophy; politics; general, Christian and Jewish religion; science; history of science; social history; social sciences; socialism; theology; university texts. Cata: 6 to 8 a year. Also, a booksearch service and reprints. Corresp: German. Mem: H.O.B. VAT No: ATU 134 970 09.

Walter Klügel, Gumpendorferstrasse 33, 1060 Wien. Tel: (01) 581-84-28. Est: 1921. Storeroom; open Monday to Friday 9–6, Saturday 9–1. Very large stock. Spec: war; politics; geography; literature; art; bibliography; Austriaca; history of customs; Kubiniana. Cata: periodically. Mem: V.A.Ö.

Cottage Antiquariat R. Knessl, Gymnasiumstrasse 17, 1180 Wien. Prop: Renate Knessl. Tel: (01) 470-70-22. Fax: 470-70-23. Est: 1947. Shop; open Monday to Friday 8.30–12.30 & 2–6. Large general stock. Also, new books. Mem: V.A.Ö.

Akademische Buchhandlung Kuppitsch, Schottengasse 4, 1010 Wien.

Antiquariat Löcker & Wögenstein, Annagasse 5, 1015 Wien. Prop: Erhard Löcker. Tel: (01) 512-73-44. Fax: 512-87-42. Est: 1970. Shop; open Monday to Friday 9.30–6, Saturday 9–1. Very large stock. Spec: German literature; art; Judaica; music - opera; comtemporary history; old and valuable books from 15th to 18th century; architecture; children's; early imprints; first editions; Freemasonry; Holocaust; illustrated; incunabula; philosophy; psychoanalysis; Jewish religion; socialism; travel. CC: AE; DC; MC; V. Cata: 4 a year. Also, run a shop for opera lovers in the State Opera House. VAT No: ATU 102 410 04.

Malota, Wiedner Hauptstrasse 22, 1040 Wien. Prop: Franz Stern. Tel: & Fax: (01) 587-92-75. Est: 1901. Shop; open Monday to Friday 8–12.30 & 1–6, Saturday 9–12. Medium stock. Spec: history; Austria. CC: All. Mem: V.A.Ö. VAT No: ATU 113 497 08.

Wilhelm Maudrich, Spitalgasse 21a, 1096 Wien. Prop: Dr. Heinz Pinker. Tel: (01) 402-47-12. Fax: 408-50-80. Est: 1909. Shop; open Monday to Friday 8.30–6, Saturday 9–12. Large stock. Spec: medicine; homeopathy; natural health; natural sciences; psychoanalysis; psychology/psychiatry. Corresp: French, German. Mem: O.B.V.

Buchhandlung Octopus, Fleischmarkt 16, 1010 Wien. Prop: Erich Skrleta. Tel: (01) 512-71-46. Telex: 75312017 Ocps A. Est: 1972. Shop; open Monday to Friday 1–6 and Saturday 10–1. Medium stock. Spec: Buddhism and Oriental books. Cata: 2 a year. Mem: Hauptverband des Österreichischen Buchandels.

Dr. A. Schendl GmbH & Co. K.G., Karlsgasse 15, Postfach 29, 1041 Wien.

Buchhandlung Rupert Schoefegger, Schaumburgergasse 5/3, 1040 Wien. Tel: (01) 504-26-60. Est: 1978. Shop; open Monday to Friday 12–6. Very small general stock. Also, new books and translations. Corresp: Italian, French, German.

Schottenfeld & Partner Antiquariat, Kaiserstrasse 32/1/2, 1070 Wien. Prop: Sabine Haase and Manfred Lamping. Tel: (01) 526-15-09. Fax: 526-39-39. Est: 1990. Office; appointment necessary, also postal business. Small stock. Spec: architecture; art; children's; first editions; literature; photography; travel - Africa, Americas, Asia, Australasia/Australia, Europe, General, Middle East, Polar. Cata: 4 a year.

Bookshop Josef Otto Slezak, Wiedner Haupstrasse 42, 1040 Wien 4. Tel: (01) 587-02-59. Est: 1960. Shop; open daily 9–12 and 3–6 (closed on Saturday). Small stock. Spec: railways and tramways. PR: £5–200. Cata: 6 to 8 a year on specialities. Corresp: German, French. Mem: Austrian Bookseller Society.

Buchhandlung Stöhr, Lerchenfelderstrasse 78-80, 1080 Wien. Prop: Heide Stöhr. Tel: (01) 406-13-49. Fax: 403-04-10. Est: 1976. Shop; open Monday to Friday 9–6, Sunday 9–12. Large general stock. Spec: military; politics; antiquarian. Cata: 2 a year in general and 2 a year on military. Also, publishers for Austrian military, new books and videos on World War II. Mem: O.B.V. VAT No: ATU 123 883 07.

Wiener Antiquariat, Seilergasse 16, 1014 Wien. Tel: (01) 512-54-66. Fax: 512-546-69. Est: 1963. Shop; open 9–1 and 2–6, Saturday 9–12. Very large stock. Spec: autographs; fine & rare. PR: DM50–50,000. CC: V; EC; MC. Cata: 4 a year (1 each on books, autographs, prints & a special). Corresp: German, French. Mem: I.L.A.B.; L.I.A.B. VAT No: ATU 149 060 02.

Buchhandlung Wolfrum, Augustinerstrasse 10, 1010 Wien.

BELGIUM

Country dialling code: 32 *Currency:* Belgian franc (Bfr)

ANTWERP (ANTWERPEN)

Jan Ceuleers, BVBA, Schildersstraat 2, 2000 Antwerpen. Tel: (03) 216-41-90. Fax: 238-94-08. Est: 1989. Private premises; appointment necessary. Small stock. Spec: archives; art; art reference; autographs; avant–garde; illustrated; periodicals/magazines; surrealism. Cata: 1 a year on books and autographs related to modern art and literature. Corresp: French, German, Dutch. Mem: C.L.A.M.; B.B.A.; I.L.A.B. VAT No: BE 456 086 377.

Cosy Corner, 4 Leeuw van Vlaanderen Straat, 2000 Antwerpen. Prop: N. van Hoofstadt. Manager: G. de Roo. Tel: (03) 232-05-00. Est: 1976. Shop; open Tuesday to Friday 1–5, or by appointment. Medium stock. Spec: antiquarian; antiques; applied art; art; artists; avant–garde; books about books; children's; collecting; comics; decorative art; ex–libris; graphic art; illustrated; surrealism; typography. PR: Bfr.100–5,000. Corresp: French, Dutch. VAT No: BE 685 015 582.

Antiquariaat W. de Goeij, Tolstraat 11, 2000 Antwerpen. Prop: Wim De Goeij. Tel: & Fax: (03) 238-21-15. Est: 1983. Private premises; appointment necessary. Large stock. Spec: almanacs; antiquarian; archaeology; architecture; art; art history; art reference; the arts; avant–garde; bibliography; bindings; books about books; Catalogues Raisonées; ceramics; documents; illustrated; periodicals/magazines; travel. Cata: 2 a year. Corresp: Dutch, French, German. Mem: I.L.A.B.; B.B.A.; C.L.A.M. VAT No: BE 501 238 293.

Antikwariaat & Boekhandel Jennes, Lange Nieuwstraat 91, 2000 Antwerpen. Prop: Michel Jennes. Tel: & Fax: (03) 231-90-23. Est: 1982. Shop; open Tuesday to Thursday 2–6, Saturday 10–1. Large stock. Spec: Flemish art and history. Also, a booksearch service and exhibition catalogues. Mem: C.L.A.M.

Joyce-Royce, Lge. Leemstraat 144b, 2018 Antwerpen. Est: 1986. Shop; open weekdays 1–6.30. Medium stock. Spec: literature; literature in translation; the arts; transport. PR: £2 up. Also, a booksearch service. Corresp: Dutch, French.

Boekhandel J. de Slegte b.v., Wapper 5, 2000 Antwerpen. Prop: J. de Slegte. Tel: (03) 231-66-27. Fax: 226-40-14. Shop; open Monday to Saturday 9.30–6. Very large stock. Spec: scholarly; rare antiquarian. CC: all major. Corresp: German. Mem: L.I.L.A. VAT No: BE 455 023 238. *Also shops at:* Amsterdam, Rotterdam, The Hague, Eindhoven, Utrecht, Arnhem, Groningen, Haarlem, Leiden, Enschede, Zwolle, Maastricht, Nijmegen, Gent, Leuven, Brussels, Bruges, Hasselt (q.v.).

BELGIUM

Antiquariaat Leon Sternberg, Sint Jorispoort 35, 2018 Antwerpen. Tel: (03) 232-34-89. Est: 1964. Shop; open Monday, Wednesday & Friday 2–5.30. Very small general stock. Spec: autographs; fine & rare. Corresp: Dutch, French, Spanish. Mem: I.L.A.B.; C.L.A.M. VAT No: BE 535 225 610.

BEYNE-HEUSAY

Aquacom S.A., Rue de Magnee 110, 4610 Beyne-Heusay.

BORSBEEK

Antiquariaat De Hertogh, 47 Corluylei, 2150 Borsbeek, Antwerp. Prop: Chr. Leon De Hertogh. Tel: (03) 321-81-32. Est: 1945. Private premises; postal business only. Very large general stock. Spec: Belgicana; Flemish literature; culture; history; folklore; science; history of science. Cata: 4 a year. Also, a booksearch service and large print books. Corresp: Dutch, German, Italian, Spanish.

BRASSCHAAT

De Tweede Lezer v.z.w., Bredabaan 501, 2930 Brasschaat. Prop: Mrs. Lutgart Sturm. Tel: (03) 652-13-62. Est: 1987. Shop; open Monday, Wednesday, Friday and Saturday 9.30–6. Medium general stock. PR: Bfr.50–10,000. Cata: 4 a year on Dutch and international literature, arts, history. Corresp: French, Dutch, German. VAT No: BE 431 418 881.

BRUGES (BRUGGE)

Antikwariaat–Boekhandel Degheldere, Leemputstraat 2-4, (Smedenstraat), 8000 Brugge. Prop: Willy Degheldere. Tel: (050) 33-88-58. Est: 1938. Shop; open Monday to Saturday 9–12.30 & 1.30–6.30. Books are shown by subject on request, but there is no public access to the general stock. Very large general Flemish and French language stock. Spec: lace; music; religion; philosophy; topography; medicine; World Wars I and II; Belgian history; art; literature; architecture; Flemish Movement; politics. Cata: 3 a week. Also, a booksearch service, old newspapers & periodicals, new books about World War II, and provide new Belgian books or periodicals to Institutions or Libraries. Corresp: French, German.

In den Eenhoorn, Ezelstraat 84, 8000 Brugge. Prop: Titia Vandevelde. Tel: (050) 33-42-46. Est: 1954. Shop and market stand; open 9–12 and 2–7. Very large general stock. Spec: children's; cookery/gastronomy; Romans; religion. PR: 50p–£10. Also, records. Corresp: French, German, Russian, Italian.

Boekhandel J. de Slegte b.v., Vlamingstraat 37–39, 8000 Brugge. Tel: (050) 34-04-38. Shop. General stock. *Also shops at:* Amsterdam, Rotterdam, The Hague, Eindhoven, Utrecht, Arnhem, Groningen, Haarlem, Leiden, Enschede, Zwolle, Maastricht, Nijmegen, Antwerpen, Gent, Leuven, Brussels, Bruges, Hasselt (q.v.).

A.W. Vandevelde, Dweersstraat 6, 8000 Brugge. Tel: (050) 33-61-05. Est: 1967. Shop; open Monday to Saturday 10–12 & 2–6.30. Medium stock. Spec: Dutch literature; Flanders; the Far East. Cata: 1 or 2 a year on the Far East. Corresp: French, German. VAT No: BE 518 363 446.

Antiquariaat Marc van de Wiele, St. Salvatorkerkhof 7, 8000 Brugge. Tel: (050) 33-63-17; 33-38-05. Fax: 34-64-57. Est: 1976. Shop and private premises; open Monday to Friday 2.30–6, Saturday 10–12 & 2.30–6 (closed Wednesday). Medium general stock. CC: AE; V; MC. Cata: 2 or 3 a year. Also, a booksearch service. Corresp: French. Mem: C.L.A.M. *Also at:* Zeewindstraat 4, 8300 Knokke–Zoute (q.v.).

BRUSSELS (BRUXELLES)

Arnoldi Anticailles, S.p.r.l., 46 Boulevard de l'Empereur, 1000 Bruxelles. Prop: H.P. & M. Arnoldi & L. Lebrun. Tel: (02) 502-07-70 or home 672-69-96. Est: 1986. Shop; open Tuesday, Thursday, Friday and Saturday 11–5, and at other times by appointment. Very small stock. Spec: arts. Also, large print books. Corresp: German. VAT No: BE 429 599 835.

Librairie de l'Astronomie, 68 Chaussée d'Alsemberg, 1060 Bruxelles.

Le Bateau–Livre, 14 rue des Eperonniers, 1000 Bruxelles. Prop: Françoise de Paepe. Tel: (02) 511-98-08. Est: 1982. Shop; open Monday to Saturday (except Wednesday) 12–6. Small stock. Spec: cinema. Also, cinema related items.

J.S. van Berchem, 68 rue de la Fauvette, 1180 Bruxelles. Tel: (02) 374-47-81. Est: 1977. Private premises; appointment necessary, also postal business. Small stock. Mainly books in the French language. PR: Bfr.500. Cata: in French, 4 a year. Corresp: German.

Book Market, 47 rue de la Madeleine, 1000 Bruxelles. Prop: Gilbert A. Toussaint. Tel: (02) 512-92-53. Est: 1963. Shop; open Monday to Saturday 12–7. Very large stock. Spec: children's; travel; illustrated; history; fine arts; religion; novels in French, English, Dutch and German. Corresp: French.

Bouquinerie des Grands Carmes, rue des Grands Carmes, 15, 1000 Bruxelles.

Librairie des Éléphants, Place van Meenen 19, 1060 Bruxelles. Prop: Antoine Jacobs. Tel: (02) 539-06-01. Est: 1976. Private premises; appointment necessary. Spec: first editions; illustrated. Cata: 10 a year. Also, auctioneers and large print books. Corresp: French, German, Spanish. Mem: L.I.L.A.; C.L.A.M; Plaisir du Livre; Bibliophilies. VAT No: BE 556 235 909.

Le Libraire Alain Ferraton, 162 Chaussée de Charleroi, 1060 Bruxelles. Tel: (02) 538-69-17. Est: 1975. Shop; open Tuesday to Saturday 10–6.30. Large stock. Spec: the Middle Ages; history; philosophy; fine arts; literature; scholarly. Cata: monthly. Also, a booksearch service & public auctions. Corresp: Italian. Mem: C.L.A.M. VAT No: BE 535 256 292.

Yves Gevaert S.p.r.l., 160 rue du Pinson, 1170 Bruxelles.

Hanotiau Bruyns & Associates, Avenue Louise 391 Bte 11, 1050 Bruxelles.

Librairie des Galeries, 2 Galerie du Roi, 1000 Bruxelles. Prop: J. Boloukhère. Tel: & Fax: (02) 511-24-12. Est: 1941. Shop. Small stock. Spec: art; architecture; antiquarian. Also, new books. VAT No: BE 406 028 340.

Librairie Claude van Loock, 51-53 rue Saint Jean, 1000 Bruxelles. Tel: (02) 512-74-65. Fax: 502-15-92. Shop; open Tuesday to Friday 9–12 and 2–6. Medium stock. Spec: atlases/cartography; bindings; book of hours; countries & continents; early imprints; fine & rare; graphic art; iconography; illustrated. Also, large print books. Corresp: French. Mem: I.L.A.B.; L.I.L.A. VAT No: BE 536 098 214.

"Ma Maison De Papier", Galerie de la rue de Ruysbroeck, 6, 1000 Bruxelles. Prop: Marie Laurence Bernard. Tel: (02) 512-22-49. Fax: 652-08-20. Est: 1990. Shop; open Monday to Friday 1–7, Saturday 11–7. Medium stock. Spec: advertising; aeronautics; archives; aviation; caricature; children's; cinema/films; circus; decorative art; documents; fashion & costume; graphic art; travel guides; industry; maritime/nautical; motoring; periodicals/magazines; pubs; railways; vintage cars. Corresp: French, Flemish. Mem: C.L.A.M.; L.I.L.A. VAT No: BE 535 429 805.

Bouquinerie le Meridien, 15 rue de la Vierge Noire, 1000 Bruxelles.

Librairie Ancienne Minet Frères, 60–62 rue des Éperonniers, 1000 Bruxelles. Prop: Dirk Minet. Tel: (02) 513-45-42. Fax: 513-86-75. E-Mail: dkmt@glo.be. Est: 1984. Shop; open Tuesday to Saturday 2.30–6.30. Small stock. Spec: the Ancient Regime; law; medicine; sciences; natural history; travel. PR: Bfr.2,000–100,000. CC: V; MC; AE. Cata: 3 a year. Corresp: French, Dutch. Mem: L.I.L.A.; C.L.A.M. VAT No: BE 437 562 446.

Louis Moorthamers, Avenue Louise 230, Box 6, 1050 Bruxelles. Tel: (02) 647-85-48. Fax: 640-73-32. Shop; open Tuesday to Friday 10–12 and 2–6. Very large general stock. Cata: approximately 4 a year. Also, auctions. Corresp: French, German. Mem: L.I.L.A.; I.L.A.B. (International); C.L.A.M./B.B.A. (Belgium). VAT No: BE 553 046 488.

Librairie E. & A. Morel de Westgaver, 24 Rue Henri Marichal, 1050 Bruxelles. Prop: Mr. A. Morel de Westgaver & Mss. E. Fitch–Boribon. Tel: (02) 511-63-88. Fax: 644-27-81. Est: 1982. Shop at: 5A Boulevard de l'Empereur, 1000 Brussels; open Monday to Friday 11.30–6.30, Saturday 2–6. General stock. Mem: I.L.A.B. VAT No: BE 554 303 728.

Au Paradis de la Bande Dessinée, Chaussée de Charleroi 245, 1060 Bruxelles. Prop: Charles Losson. Tel: (02) 538-52-35. Shop; open Monday to Saturday afternoons. Medium stock. Spec: cartoons and comic strips; military; newspapers. Mem: Chambre Belge des Experts en Bandes-Dessinée.

Au Paradis des Chercheurs, 245 Chaussée de Charleroi, 1060 Bruxelles.

Passé-Present, 40 rue Baron de Laveleye, 1090 Bruxelles.

Francine van der Perre, rue de la Madeleine, 23, 1000 Bruxelles. Tel: (02) 511-75-59. Est: 1954. Shop. Medium stock. Spec: genealogy; heraldry; topography. Also, new books. Mem: C.L.A.M.

Librairie van der Perre, rue Van Moer 6 & 8, 1000 Bruxelles. Tel: (02) 512-14-33. Est: 1960. Shop; open 11–7. Large stock. Spec: almanacs; Catalogues Raisonées; children's; cookery/gastronomy; first editions. Also, large print books. VAT No: BE 535 063 975.

Pique-Puces, 204 Chaussée de Wavre, 1050 Bruxelles.

Polar & Co., Chaussée d'Ixelles 257, 1050 Bruxelles. Prop: Alain Devalck. Tel: (02) 648-01-94. Shop; open Tuesday to Saturday 11–6.30. Medium stock. Spec: cinema/film; true crime; detective, spy, thrillers; fantasy, horror; science fiction. PR: £1–200. CC: V; EC; MC. Cata: 4 a year. Corresp: French. VAT No: BE 553 369 360.

Posada Art Books S.p.r.l., 29 rue de la Madeleine, 1000 Bruxelles.

Librairie Yves De Prins, 36 rue Saint Lambert, 1200 Bruxelles.

Rainbow Grafics International, 63 rue Charles Legrelle, 1040 Bruxelles.

Librairie Hervé Renard, 71 rue des Éperonniers, 1000 Bruxelles. Tel: (02) 512-97-44. Fax: 513-96-85. Est: 1978. Shop; open Monday to Saturday 12–6. Very large stock. Spec: books in German; Austria-Hungary and the Balkans and all languages. Cata: monthly. Corresp: French, German.

Pascal de Sadeleer, rue des Drapiers, 62, 1050 Bruxelles.

Librairie Schwilden, 5 Galerie Bortier, 1000 Bruxelles.

Librairie Simonson S.A., 227 Chaussée de Charleroi, 1060 Bruxelles.

Boekhandel J. de Slegte b.v., Lievevrouwbroersstraat 17, Rue des Grands Carmes 17, 1000 Bruxelles. Tel: (02) 511-61-40. Shop. General stock. *Also shops at:* Amsterdam, Rotterdam, The Hague, Eindhoven, Utrecht, Arnhem, Groningen, Haarlem, Leiden, Enschede, Zwolle, Maastricht, Nijmegen, Antwerp, Gent, Leuven, Brussels, Bruges, Hasselt (q.v.).

Eric Speeckaert, 53 Boulevard Saint-Michel, 1040 Bruxelles. Tel: (02) 736-43-29. Fax: 732-10-52. Est: 1978. Private premises; appointment necessary. Small stock. Spec: fine antiquarian; bindings. Cata: 1 or 2 a year. Also, manuscripts and autographs. Mem: C.L.A.M. VAT No: BE 557 463 750.

Librairie Michel Stiernet, 8 rue des Moissonneurs, 1040 Bruxelles.

Librairie-Editions Thanh-Long, 34 rue Dekens, 1040 Bruxelles.

Librairie Fl. Tulkens, 21, rue du Chêne, 1000 Bruxelles. Prop: Jacques Van der Heyde. Tel: (02) 513-05-25. Fax: 513-67-46. Est: 1848. Shop; open Monday to Friday 9–12 and 2.30–6. Medium general stock. Spec: antiquarian; archaeology; architecture; art; bibliography; bindings; botany; caricature; cookery/gastronomy; fashion & costume; first editions; gardening; history; history of ideas; illuminated manuscripts; illustrated; incunabula; music; natural sciences; travel. Cata: very occasionally. Corresp: French. Mem: I.L.A.B.; C.L.A.M. VAT No: BE 535 475 236.

Émile Van Balberghe Libraire, 4 rue Vautier, 1050 Bruxelles. Tel: (02) 649-46-08. Est: 1976. Private premises; appointment necessary. Very small stock. Spec: rare antiquarian. Also, manuscripts. VAT No: BE 556 211 757.

Ch. de Wyngaert, 127a rue R. Vandevelde, 1030 Bruxelles. Tel: (02) 242-80-76. Est: 1949. Shop; open Monday to Friday 2–6. Large stock. Spec: natural history (including zoology, entomology and botany); geology. PR: £1–100. Cata: irregularly. Corresp: French. VAT No: BE 557 468 502.

DEINZE

Centrum Voor Scriptophilie p.v.b.a., Kouter 126, 9800 Deinze.

DEURNE

Vilain, 287 Ten Eekhovelei, Deurne. Tel: (03) 324-21-28. Est: 1970. Shop and market stand; appointment necessary. Medium general stock. PR: £5. Also, a booksearch service. Corresp: French, German, Dutch. Mem: V.B.V.B. VAT No: BE 506 292 884.

GHENT (GENT)

Librairie A. Rombaut, Lievestraat 14, 9000 Gent. Prop: Charles Lammens. Tel: (09) 223-56-46. Est: 1923. Shop; open Tuesday to Friday 10–12.15 & 2–6.30, Saturday 10–12.15. Medium stock. Spec: fine arts, music; genealogy; topography. Also new books. Corresp: German. VAT No: BE 587 101 012.

Sanderus Antiquariaat, Nederkouter, 32, 9000 Gent. Prop: Filip Devroe. Tel: (09) 223-35-90. Fax: 223-39-71. Est: 1979. Shop; open Monday to Saturday 10–12 and 2–6. Medium stock. Spec: atlases/cartography; botany; early imprints; local history; national history; illuminated manuscripts; illustrated. Cata: 1 a year. Corresp: Dutch, French, German. Mem: C.L.A.M. VAT No: BE 525 351 208.

Boekhandel J. de Slegte b.v., Voldersstraat 7, 9000 Gent. Tel: (09) 225-59-18. Shop. General stock. *Also shops at:* Amsterdam, Rotterdam, The Hague, Eindhoven, Utrecht, Arnhem, Groningen, Haarlem, Leiden, Enschede, Zwolle, Maastricht, Nijmegen, Antwerp, Leuven, Brussels, Bruges, Hasselt (q.v.).

GOUVY

Christian F. Verbeke - Antiquarian Law Booksellers, rue du Centre 10, 6670 Gouvy. VAT No: BE 673 140 804.

HASSELT

De Oude Librije, Schrijnwerkersstraat 16, 3500 Hasselt. Prop: Antoine Doppegieter. Tel: (011) 22-55-99. Est: 1981. Shop and market stand; open Tuesday to Saturday 12–6. Medium general stock. Corresp: German, French, Dutch. VAT No: BE 647 204 091.

Boekhandel J. de Slegte b.v., Havermarkt 14, 3500 Hasselt. Tel: (011) 22-74-00. Shop. General stock. *Also shops at:* Amsterdam, Rotterdam, The Hague, Eindhoven, Utrecht, Arnhem, Groningen, Haarlem, Leiden, Enschede, Zwolle, Maastricht, Nijmegen, Antwerp, Gent, Leuven, Brussels, Bruges (q.v.).

KNOKKE-ZOUTE

Antiquariaat Marc van de Wiele, Zeewindstraat 4, 8300 Knokke–Zoute. Tel: (050) 62-04-27. Fax: 34-64-57. Est: 1996. Shop; open Sunday 10–12 and 2.30–6, plus Holy days. Small stock. Spec: antiquarian; applied art; art; the arts; atlases/ cartography; botany. PR: £10–500. CC: AE; V; MC. Cata: 2 or 3 a year. Corresp: French. Mem: C.L.A.M. VAT No: BE 518 525 079. *Also at:* St. Salvatorkerkhof 7, Brugge (q.v.).

LEUVEN (LOUVAIN)

Boekhandel J. de Slegte b.v., Bondgenotenlaan 47, 3000 Louvain. Tel: (016) 22-68-81. Fax: 20-56-91. Shop; open Monday to Saturday 9.30–6. General stock. CC: V; EC; MC; EDC; Maestro; Electron; AE. VAT No: BE 455 023 238. *Also shops at:* Amsterdam, Rotterdam, The Hague, Eindhoven, Utrecht, Arnhem, Groningen, Haarlem, Leiden, Enschede, Zwolle, Maastricht, Nijmegen, Antwerp, Gent, Brussels, Bruges, Hasselt.

LIÈGE (LUIK)

Le Cadre d'Art, 5 rue Bonne Fortune, 4000 Luik.

La Bouquinerie des Carmes, 35b rue St. Paul, 4000 Luik.

Michel Grommen, Libraire, 159a rue St. Gilles, 4000 Luik. Tel: & Fax: (04) 222-24-48. Est: 1971. Shop; open Thursday and Friday 1–6, Saturday 10–1. Medium stock. Spec: local & general history; genealogy; sciences. Cata: 2 or 3 auctions a year plus lists. Corresp: Italian. Mem: C.L.A.M. VAT No: BE 600 310 036.

Michel LHomme – Librairie, 9 rue des Carmes, 4000 Luik.

NAMUR

Au Vieux Quartier, Rue de la Croix 30, 5000 Namur. Prop: Adrienne Goffin. Tel: & Fax: (081) 22-19-94. Est: 1976. Shop; open Monday to Saturday (except Tuesday) 10–12.30 & 1.30–6. Medium stock. Spec: antiquarian; books about books; general & local history; literature; religion; general & local topography. Cata: 2 a year. Corresp: French, Dutch. Mem: C.L.A.M.; L.I.L.A.

Rita De Maere, rue Saint Luc, 46, 5004 Namur.

Bruno Matossian, Rue du Longeau, 50, 5100 Dave. (•) Fax: (081) 40-27-95. Est: 1984. Market stand at: Marché Livres et Antiquités du Sablon, Ville de Bruxelles; open Saturday and Sunday 9–2. Very small stock. Spec: books from 16th to 18th century. Corresp: Flemish, French. Mem: C.L.A.M.; L.I.L.A. VAT No: BE 549 587 647.

NIVELLES

Bouquinerie Préfaces, 16 rue des Vieilles Prisons, 1400 Nivelles.

REDU

Librairie Ancienne Noël Anselot, 18 rue de Transinne, 6890 Redu. Tel: & Fax: (061) 65-60-91. Est: 1980. Shop; open Tuesday pm to Sunday 10.30–1 and 2–6.30. Very large stock. Spec: history; Belgicana; history of ideas; antiquarian; medicine; sciences; travel; gastronomy; oenology; esoterism; fine & rare; ancient & modern. PR: £10–20,000. CC: MC; V; AE (with charge). Cata: 2 a year plus lists issued on various subjects. Corresp: French, German. Mem: L.I.L.A.; C.L.A.M. VAT No: BE 694 089 240.

La Librairie Ardennaise, rue de St. Hubert 14, Redu.

ArTchives - Pierre Dailly, Rue Neuve, 73, 6890 Redu. Tel: (061) 65-61-84. Fax: 65-65-84. Est: 1984. Shop; open Sunday or by appointment. Medium stock. Spec: architecture; avant–garde; calligraphy; caricature; decorative art; fine art; first editions illustrated; French literature; photography; science; surrealism; travel; typography. PR: 50p–£100. CC: V; EC. Cata: 3 a year. Corresp: French. VAT No: BE 613 951 503.

De Boekenwurm & Crazy Castle, Voie d'Hurleau 51, 6890 Redu. Prop: Miep Van Duin. Tel: (061) 65-66-15. Est: 1992. Shop; open Friday to Sunday 10–6 and every day in summer holidays. Medium stock. Spec: children's; general history; history of civilisation; humanities; foreign languages; literary criticism; literature; literature in translation. Books mainly Dutch and English. PR: Bfr.100–10,000. CC: V; EC; MC; Corresp: Dutch, German, French, Italian. VAT No: BE 694 299 076.

"La Boite aux Lettres", rue de St. Hubert 14, Redu.

Book Inn, place de l'Esro 58, 6890 Redu-Libin. Prop: Michel De Selys Longchamps. Est: 1996. Private premises; open Friday mid-day–Sunday 8pm. Small stock. Spec: literature, art & sciences in French, English, Russian, German, Dutch, Italian, Korean and Japanese. PR: £1–15. Cata: on request. Also, a booksearch service and import–export and shipping information. Corresp: French, Italian, Dutch, German.

La Bouteille a' Ancre, rue de la Prairie 38, 6890 Redu.

Le Clip/La Beguine, rue de Hamaide 53C, Redu.

Au Feuillet Jauni, place de l'Esro 64, Redu.

Au Feuillet Jauni II, rue de St. Hubert 17D, Redu.

Librairie La Forge, rue Neuve 72, 6890 Redu. Prop: Mrs. Renée Fuks. Tel: (061) 65-61-46. Fax: 65-61-70. Est: 1984. Open Saturday & Sunday - all year, vacations, every day 10–6. Medium stock. Spec: children's; fables; fairy tales; feminism; folklore; 19/20th century illustrated; juvenile; literature; puppets & marionettes; scouting; theatre; women. PR: Bfr.450–4,500. CC: V; EC; MC. Also, a booksearch service. Corresp: French, Dutch, Spanish, German, Hebrew. Mem: "Redu - Le Village du Livre". VAT No: BE 694 228 010.

De Griffel II, rue de Transinne 34, 6890 Redu.

La Memoire Ni l'Oubli, 19 rue de Transinne, Redu.

Bouquinerie Préfaces, 64 place de l'Esro, 6914 Redu.

Librairie Yves De Prins, rue de St. Hubert 14, Redu.

"Le Rat des Champs", rue de Hamaide 53B, Redu.

ST. NIKLAAS (SINT NIKLAAS)

Standaard Boekhandel NV, Industriepark - Noord 28A, 9100 Sint Niklaas.

VERVIERS

Librairie la Dérive S.p.r.l., 2 place du Martyr, 4800 Verviers. Prop: Jacques Thonnart. Tel: (087) 31-03-60. Est: 1977. Shop; open Monday 2–6, Tuesday to Saturday 10–12.30 & 2–6. Small stock. Spec: literature in French; Belgicana; antiquarian. Cata: 4 a year on specialities. Also, an editor. Corresp: French.

CYPRUS

Country dialling code: 357 *Currency:* Cyprian pound (C£)

M A M, P.O. Box 1722, Nicosia.

A.G. Pitsillides, Collectors' Centre, P.O. Box 1019, 1500 Nicosia. Tel: (02) 336241 & 474780. Fax: 337879. Est: 1965. Shop at: 10, Pythonas Street, 1011 Nicosia; open Monday to Friday 9–5, and by appointment. Small stock. Spec: Cyprus, Greece, Greek Islands; antiquarian; decorative art; documents; fine art; genealogy; heraldry; local history; history of civilization; illustrated; limited editions; manuscripts; numismatics; periodicals/magazines; sigillography; travel - Europe, Middle East; voyages & discovery. Cata: occasionally. Corresp: Greek, French.

CZECH REPUBLIC

Country dialling code: 42 *Currency:* Koruna

LOUNY

Fabio-Antikvariát, Beneše z Loun 137, 440 01 Louny.

NÁCHOD

Antikvariát Náchod, Náměstí TGM 1, 547 01 Náchod. Prop: Jiri Hora. Tel: (441) 21694. Shop; open Monday to Friday 9–6, Saturday 9–12. Medium general stock.

DENMARK

Country dialling code: 45 *Currency:* Danish krone (DKr)

ÅLBORG

Antikvariat J. Pilegaard, Algade 65, 9000 Ålborg. Prop: Jens Pilegaard. Tel: 98-13-90-00. Fax: 98-13-92-21. Est: 1963. Shop; open Monday to Friday 9–5.30 and Saturday 10–1. Very large general stock. Cata: 2 a year. Corresp: Dutch. Mem: A.B.F. VAT No: DK 161 573 76.

ÅRHUS

Åbenhus Århus Antikvariat/Boøckmann's Antikvariat, Åboulevarden 39, 8000 Århus C. Prop: H. Åbenhus. Tel: 86-12-02-78. Est: 1942. Shop; open Monday to Friday 11–5.30, Saturday 11–1 (first Saturday of each month 11–3). Very large general stock. PR: £5–5,000. Corresp: German.

BRONDBY

O.K. Kenvig A/S, Vibeholms alle 20, Brondby.

COPENHAGEN (KØBENHAVN)

Antikvariatet, Amagerbrogade 22, 2300 København S. Prop: Uffe Sand. Tel: 31-57-41-72. Est: 1979. Shop; open Monday to Thursday 11–5.30, Friday 11–6.30 and Saturday 10–2. Large general stock. Also, old and secondhand Danish, English and American comics.

Antikvariatet, Gammel Jernbanevej 39, 2500 Valby (København).

The Booktrader, Skindergade 23, 1159 København K. Prop: Lars Rasmussen. Tel: 33-12-06-69. Fax: 33-12-04-98. Est: 1982. Shop; open Monday to Thursday 11–5.30, Friday 11–6 and Saturday 10–1. Large stock. Spec: art; architecture; literature; history; seafaring. Cata: 4 or 6 a year. Also, book publishing. Corresp: German.

Arnold Busck Antikvariat, Fiolstræde 24, 1171 København K.

Dansk Bog Service, Amager Fælledvej 9, 2300 København S.

Fantask A/S, Skt. Pedersstraede 18, 1453 København. Tel: 33-11-85-38. Fax: 33-13-85-01. Est: 1971. Shop; open Monday to Thursday 11–6, Friday 11–7, Saturday 11–3. Very small stock. Spec: science fiction and fantasy. VAT No: DK 12 62 21 39.

DENMARK

Dan Fog Musikantikvariat, Graabroedretorv 7, 1154 København K. Tel: 33-11-40-40. Fax: 33-11-40-60. Est: 1906. Shop; open Tuesday to Friday 10–4. Very large stock. Spec: music. Cata: 8 a year. Also, sheet music. Corresp: German, French. Mem: A.B.F.

Peter Grosell's Antikvariat, Læderstræde 15, 1201 København K. Tel: 33-93-45-05. Fax: 33-93-53-72. Est: 1986. Shop; open Monday to Friday 9.30–5.30, Saturday 10–1. Small stock. Spec: art; antiques; crafts; architecture; culture; history; old and rare. Cata: 5 to 8 a year on specialities. Also, graphics and drawings. Corresp: German, Norwegian, Swedish. Mem: A.B.F.; I.L.A.B.; L.I.L.A.

Einar Harcks Antikvariat, G.E.C. Gad, Nørreport A/S, Fiolstræde 34, 1171 København K. Tel: 33-12-13-44. Fax: 33-12-54-94. Mem: A.B.F.

Kaabers Antikvariat, Skindergade 34, 1159 København K.

Lynge & Søn, A/S, Internationalt Antikvariat, Silkegade 11, P.O. Box 2041, 1113 København K. Prop: K.A.M. Girsel. Tel: 33-15-53-35. Fax: 33-91-53-35. Est: 1821. Shop; open Monday to Friday 10–5. Large stock. Spec: Arctic (Greenland); linguistics; natural science. Cata: 4 a year on science, old books, linguistics, history and law. Also, periodicals. Mem: I.L.A.B.; A.B.F. VAT No: DK 168 950 16.

Nansensgade Antikvariat, Nansensgade 70, 1366 København K.

Antikvariat Østerbro, Strandboulevarden 166, 2100 København.

Dr. Octopus, Åhusgade 2, 2100 København Ø. Tel: 35-26-28-48. E-Mail: ailen@dk-online.dk. Est: 1973. Shop; open Monday to Friday 12–6 and Saturday 10–2. Medium stock. Spec: comic strips. Also, secondhand records, C.D.s and video tapes.

Tegneserieparadiset Pegasus, Nansensgade 60, 1366 København K. Tel: 33-32-56-50. Est: 1972. Shop; open Monday, Wednesday and Friday 1–6. Very large stock. Spec: American and Danish comic books.

Politikens Antikvariat, Rådhuspladsen 37, 1785 København V. Tel: 33-47-23-97; 33-47-27-63. Fax: 33-11-14-10. Est: 1919. Shop; open Monday to Friday 9.30–5.30, Saturday 9–1. Large stock. Spec: fine and antiquarian; finely bound English sets; art; Freemasonry. Cata: 5 a year. Also, manuscripts. Corresp: German. Mem: A.B.F. No: VAT No: DK 515 954 16.

Puks Butik, Hans Egedesg. 13, København.

Skakhuset (The Chess House), Studiesstraede 24, 1455 København K. Prop: Stellan Persson. Tel: 33-14-62-91. Est: 1947. Shop; open Tuesday to Friday 10–5.30, Saturday (except from mid-May to mid-September) 10–2. Small stock. Spec: chess. Cata: every 18 months. Also, new chess books. Corresp: German, Swedish.

HORSENS

C.N. Borma A/S, Chr Nielsensjej 3, DK-8700 Horsens.

MARIBO

Lollands Antikvariat, Suhrsgade 4 C, 4930 Maribo.

NYKOBING FALSTER

K.E. Skafte, 4800 Nykobing Falster. Fax: 54-85-15-06. Est: 1962. Postal business only. Spec: arms and armour from Europe, Near East, Indonesia and Japan. Also, time measuring instruments, Netsuke and Inro, fans and portrait miniatures. Corresp: German.

SKJERN

Ornis Bookshop, Holstebrovej 16, 6900 Skjern. Prop: Sigurd Rosendahl. Tel: & Fax: 97-35-16-61. Est: 1974. Shop; open Monday to Friday 10–5. Medium stock. Spec: nature; angling; hunting; birds. PR: DKr.20–18,000. Cata: 1 or 2 a year. Also, new foreign books and publishers. Corresp: German, Swedish. VAT No: DK 140 904 36.

STEGE

Læsehesten – Møns Antikvariat, Lendemark Hovedgade 7, 4780 Stege. Prop: Per R. Johnsen. Est: 1983. Shop; open Monday to Friday 9–6 and Saturday 9–3. Medium stock. Cata: 1 or 2 a year. Also, secondhand records, music and musical instruments. Corresp: German.

FINLAND

Country dialling code: 358   Currency: Markka (M)

Kauppamakasiini T:MI, Vvorimiehenkatu 10, 00140 Helsinki. Prop: Mrs. Jaana Wikgren. Tel: (0) 628004. Est: 1972. Shop; open Monday to Friday 11–6, Saturday 10–2. Large stock. Corresp: German.

Kampintorin Antikvaarinen Kirjakauppa, Fredrinkinkatu 63, 00100 Helsinki. Prop: Timo Surojegin & Raimo Saastamoinen. Tel: (0) 6943306. Fax: 6943650. Est: 1931. Shop; open Monday to Friday 10–6, Saturday 10–2. Very large stock. Spec: biography; genealogy; local & national history; literature in translation; philosophy; local topography; war. PR: M20–200. CC: V; MC. Cata: 4 a year on general subjects. Mem: I.L.A.B. VAT No: FI 061 927 6-0.

Lauttasaari Press, Polando Pieracchini, Helsinki.

Nordiska Antikvariska Bokhandeln, Norra Magasinsgatan 6, 00130 Helsinki. Prop: Mrs. Tove Olsoni-Nilsson. Tel: (0) 626352. TA: Antiqva, Helsinki. Est: 1918. Shop; open 10–4. Large stock. Spec: rare; travels, Russia, Scandinavia. Cata: occasionally. Corresp: German, French, Russian.

Runebergin Antikvariaatti, Runeberginkatu 37 B, 00100 Helsinki. Prop: Andrew Eriksson. Tel: & Fax: (0) 499930. Shop; open 11–6. Spec: academic/scholarly; art; folklore; genealogy; natural sciences. CC: V; MC; EC. Also, a booksearch service. Mem: I.L.A.B. VAT No: FI 099 107 48.

Antikvariaatti Syvä Uni Oy, Fredrikinkatu 55, 00100 Helsinki.

Kukunor, Rautatienkatu 18, P.O. Box 185, Tampere 33101.

Komisario Palmu, Itsenaisuudenkatu 18, 33500 Tampere. Prop: Hannu Peltonen. Tel: (03) 2230115. Est: 1988. Shop; open Monday to Friday 9–5, Saturday 9–2. Medium general stock. Spec: detective fiction; Finnish literature; Lappland; history of war (Finland). PR: £1–100. Also, a booksearch service. Mem: Finnish Mystery Club.

ABC-Kirja, Linnankatu 33, 20100 Turku. Prop: Antero Merilä. Tel: (02) 2517252. Est: 1983. Shop; open Monday to Friday 11–5, Saturday 10–2. Large general stock. Mem: Suomen Antikvariaattiyhdistys - Finska Antikvariatföreningen.

FRANCE

Country dialling code: 33 *Currency:* French franc (Ffr)

AGEN

Librairie Gauzy, 1 rue Courteline, 47000 Agen. Prop: Jean-Louis Gauzy. Tel: 05-53-66-38-89. Fax: 05-53-66-03-28. Est: 1984. Shop; (on corner of boulevard Sylvain Dumon, between The Place du 14 Juillet and the train station); open Tuesday 2–7, Wednesday to Saturday 9.30–12 and 2–7, (except July & August afternoons 4–7). Medium stock. Spec: antiquarian; dictionaries; general and local history; illustrated; medicine; religion; travel. PR: £2–2,000. Cata: 3 or 4 a year on medicine and history (depending on our acquisitions). Also, a booksearch service and sale of products for care and restoration of antiquarian books. Corresp: French.

AIX EN PROVENCE

Laurent Borreani, 11, cours Saint–Louis, 33100 Aix en Provence.

K Livres, 8, rue Cardinale, 13100 Aix en Provence. Prop: Pierre Dedet. Tel: 04-42-26-35-11. Shop. Medium stock. Spec: first editions; art; antiquarian. Cata: occasionally. Mem: S.L.A.M.

ALBA-LA-ROMAINE

Librairie Le Capricorne, Rue de la Tour, 07400 Alba-la-Romaine, Prop: Daniel Santais. Tel: 04-75-52-43-40. Est: 1979. Shop; open Monday to Sunday 10–7. Small stock. Spec: history - French regionalism. PR: Ffr.50–500. Cata: 4 a year. Corresp: French, German, Italian. VAT No: FR 34 316 254 895.

AMIENS

L'Or du Temps, 7 Place du Don, 80000 Amiens. Prop: Guy Gavois. Tel: 03-22-92-39-49. Est: 1981. Shop; open Tuesday to Friday 2–7, Saturday 10–12 & 3–7, Sunday 3–7. General stock. Cata: 2 a year.

ANGERS

Gillard Bertrand, Librairie, 13 Rue Toussaint, 49100 Angers.

Josse-Rosière Bouquinistes, Charcé St. Ellier, 49320 Brissac-Quincé. (•) Prop: Pierre Josse and Gilles Rosière. Tel: 02-41-54-22-79. Fax: 02-41-54-21-92. Est: 1985. Market stand and storeroom; postal business only. Very large stock. Spec: literature; history; regional interest; science; agriculture; alpinism/ mountaineering; education; travel - Africa. Cata: lists issued on request.

ANGOULÊME

Livres d'Autrefois, 23 rue de Beaulieu, 16000 Angoulême. Prop: Nicole Perray. Tel: & Fax: 05-45-95-77-75. Shop; open Thursday to Saturday 10–12 & 3–7. Small general stock. Cata: 4 to 6 a year. Corresp: Spanish.

ANNECY

Librairie Chaminade, 2, rue Jean-Jacques Rousseau, 74000 Annecy. Prop: Jacques Chaminade. Tel: 04-50-51-57-31. Est: 1972. Shop; open Tuesday, Wednesday, Friday and Saturday 2–7. Medium stock. Spec: regional interest; antiquarian; history. Also, engravings. Cata: 6 a year. Mem: S.L.A.M. *Also at:* Librairie Chaminade, Lyons (q.v.).

ANTIBES

Brigitte Maurel, Les Bleuets, Pavillon 31, 594 chemin des Combes, 06600 Antibes.

AUXERRE

Depardieu Bouquiniste, 38–40 rue Joubert, 89000 Auxerre. Prop: Gilles Depardieu. Tel: 03-86-52-17-50. Est: 1982. Shop; open Tuesday to Saturday 10–12 & 2–7. Medium stock. Spec: religion; politics and nationalism; children's; Scouting. Cata: 4 a year on specialities. Corresp: French, Latin.

AVIGNON

G. de Lucenay Livres Anciens, 15 rue Petite Fusterie, 84000 Avignon. Tel: 04-90-82-15-69. Fax: 04-90-86-59-99. Est: 1970. Shop; open 10–12.15 & 2.30–7 daily except Monday morning. Medium stock. Spec: antiquarian music; history; literature; science; technology; travel. Cata: 3 a year. Also, a booksearch service. Corresp: French, Spanish, Italian. Mem: S.L.A.M. VAT No: FR 19 702 612 292.

Philippe Serignan, 15, rue Joseph Vernet, 84000 Avignon.

BAIXAS

Librairie Haffner, 11 Avenue Maréchal Joffre, 66390 Baixas. Prop: Hervé Haffner. Tel: 04-68-64-00-54. Private premises. Medium stock. Spec: history; religion; memoirs; literature; medicine. Cata: 1 a year. Mem: S.L.A.M.

BAVAY

Maison du Hainaut, 5, rue des Soupirs, 59570 Bavay.

BEAUNE

Mille et Une Feuilles, 20 rue Maufoux, 21200 Beaune. Prop: M. Chavroche. Tel: 03-80-24-67-71. Est: 1987. Shop; open Tuesday to Saturday 10–12 & 3–7. Small stock. Spec: Burgundy; vines; wine. Cata: 1 a year.

BECHEREL-RENNES

Librairie Saphir, 7 Faubourg Bertault, 35190 Becherel-Rennes. Prop: Mrs. F. Szapiro. Tel: 02-99-66-83-60. Fax: 01-43-80-23-49. Est: 1992. Shop; open Sunday to Friday 10.30–6.30. Small stock. Spec: autographs; general history; local history; literature; manuscripts; photography; Christian religion; Jewish religion. PR: £10–500. Cata: 1 a year on general subjects. Corresp: Spanish, Hewbrew. Mem: S.L.A.M. *Shops also in:* Dinard and Paris.

BERGERAC CEDEX

Arcane, 33, rue des Fontaines, B.P. 424, 24104 Bergerac Cedex.

BESANÇON

Bouquinerie Comtoise S.a.r.l., 9 rue Morand, 25000 Besançon. Prop: Jean-Paul Chenu. Tel: 03-81-81-02-93. Shop; open 10–12 & 2–7. Medium stock. Spec: France–Comté; regionalism; 17th- to 18th-century books; technical. Also, new books. Mem: S.L.A.M.

Alain Guyon, 22 rue Pasteur, 25000 Besançon.

FRANCE

BIHOREL-ROUEN

Jean Morel, 33 rue du Dr. Caron, 76420 Bihorel-Rouen. Tel: 02-35-59-77-33; 01-45-44-43-26. Fax: 02-35-59-73-41. Est: 1978. Private premises; appointment necessary. Medium general stock. Cata: 4 a year on auctions. Corresp: French. Mem: C.N.E. *Also at:* 19 rue du vieux-Columbier, 75006 Paris (q.v.).

BLÉRÉ

Jean Louis Mathis, Librairie, 12, rue Madame, 37150 Bléré. Tel: 02-47-30-31-82. Private premises; appointment necessary. Medium stock. Spec: French seas; history; regionalism. Cata: 4 a year. Also, large print books and shows. Corresp: French.

BLOIS

Librairie Xavier Charmoy, 11 Rue Cobaudière, 41000 Blois. Tel: 02-54-74-45-29. Shop and private premises. Small general stock. CC: V. Also, bookbinding.

BOIS COLOMBES

Librairie Marges, 27 rue Mertens, 92270 Bois Colombes. Prop: François-Jérôme Benedetti. Tel: & Fax: 01-42-42-78-30. Premises at: Marché Georges Brassens (7 minutes from Paris from St. Lazare Station, alighting at Bois Colombes Station); open Monday to Friday 4–6.45. Very small stock. Cata: 4 a year.

Librairie Rouam, 1, rue des Bourguignons, 92270 Bois Colombes. Prop: Mme. Rouam. Tel: 01-41-19-62-00. Fax: 01-47-60-17-32. Shop; open Tuesday to Friday (afternoon), Saturday (morning and afternoon). Medium general stock. PR: Ffr.100–5,000. CC: V. Cata: 4 a year plus numerous specialised catalogues. Also, a booksearch service. Corresp: French. Mem: S.L.A.M. VAT No: FR 65 401 149 661.

BORDEAUX

Librairie Montaut, 87 rue de la Course, 33000 Bordeaux. Prop: Denis Montaut. Tel: 05-56-81-96-38. Fax: 05-56-44-81-03. Shop; open 9.30–12 and 2–6.30. Small stock. Spec: cookery/gastronomy; wine. Cata: 1 a year on specialities. Mem: S.L.A.M.

BOURG LA REINE

Librairie Henri Vignes, 64, avenue du Général Leclerc, 92340 Bourg La Reine. Tel: 01-41-13-68-68. Shop. Spec: Antiquarian. *Also at:* 57, rue Saint–Jacques, 75005 Paris (q.v).

BOURGES

Livres Anciens Rousseau, 8 Place Mirpied, 18000 Bourges. Prop: Nadine Rousseau. Tel: 02-48-20-15-45. Est: 1984. Private premises; appointment necessary. Medium general stock. Spec: illustrated. Cata: 2 a year. Mem: S.L.A.M. VAT No: FR 71 330 371 188.

BRIVE

Librairie Lemarie, 14 bis, rue Elie Breuil, 19100 Brive. Tel: 05-55-24-56-49. Fax: 05-55-17-04-95. Est: 1985. Shop, market stand and storeroom; open Tuesday to Saturday 10–12.30 and 2–7. Medium stock. Spec: antiquarian; the arts; caricature; cartoons; children's; comic books and annuals; comics; general fiction; history; illustrated; literature; history of civilisation; religion; travel. PR: Ffr.5–10,000. CC: V. Cata: 2 a year. Also, a booksearch service. Corresp: French. VAT No: FR 24 329 862 569.

CACHAN CEDEX

Lavoisier, 14 rue de Provigny, 94236 Cachan Cedex.

CAEN

Librairie Aux Collectionneurs, 30 rue Froide, 14000 Caen.

Librairie la Rose des Vents, Esplanade du Théâtre, 51–63 rue de l'Oratoire, 14000 Caen. Prop: Jean–Claude Guillon. Tel: 02-31-86-05-86. Fax: 02-31-86-59-92. Shop; open daily 9–12 and 2–7, except Monday morning. Small stock. Spec: Normandy.

CALVISSON

J. Gandini - Librairie et Edition, 11, Grand–Rue, 30420 Calvisson. Prop: Jacques Gandini. Tel: 04-66-01-40-42. Fax: 04-66-01-43-39. Private premises; postal business only. Spec: Sahara (small stock) and Algeria (medium stock), including Mauritania, Algeria, Mali, Niger, Tunisia, Libya and Chad. Cata: 4 a year. Also, new books and an editor. VAT No: FR 17 322 851 536.

FRANCE

CAMPS-LA-SOURCE

Bernard Mamy, Grande–Rue, 83170 Camps–La–Source. Tel: 04-94-80-89-89. Fax: 04-94-33-25-40. Mobile: 06-07-04-80-84. Est: 1976. Storeroom; appointment necessary. Large stock. Spec: art history; travel guides; general history; philosophy; tobacco; general travel; Regionalism - Provence. PR: Ffr.300–2,000 and up. Also, selling by lots to other librarians only. Mem: U.F.E.

CANNES

La Livrairie, 1 rue Alliéis, 06400 Cannes.

Librairie Rossignol, 1 rue Jean Daumas, 06400 Cannes. Prop: Louis Daniel Rossignol. Tel: 04-93-39-70-55. Fax: 04-94-47-43-79. Est: 1928. Shop. Medium stock. Spec: Africana. Cata: 4 a year. Also, large print books. Mem: S.L.A.M. *Also at:* Librairie Rossignol, Les Arcs sur Argens (q.v.).

CHAMBÉRY

Bouquinerie Croix D'Or, 109, rue Croix-d'Or, 73000 Chambéry.

CHAMONIX

Library Gendrault, 232 La Mollard, 74400 Chamonix. Prop: Jacques Gendrault. Tel: & Fax: 04-50-53-67-47. Private premises; open Monday to Friday 8.30–4. Very small stock. Spec: Pyrennées; Alps; mountains; mineralogy; sciences. Cata: 1 a year. Corresp: French.

CHARLEVILLE-MÉZIÈRES

Le Temps des Cerises, 3 rue d'Aubilly, 08000 Charleville–Mézières. Prop: Philippe Majewski. Tel: 03-24-33-56-22. Fax: 03-24-59-95-67. Est: 1983. Shop; open Tuesday to Saturday 10–12 & 2.30–7. Very large stock. Spec: local history; literature; poetry; politics; war. PR: £1–100. Cata: 6 a year on Arthur Rimbaud, Verlaine, local history, wars (recent history). Also, a booksearch service. Corresp: French.

CHARTRES

Patrick & Elisabeth Sourget, 28 bis, rue du Docteur Maunoury, 28000 Chartres.

CLERMONT-FERRAND

Librairie Duclos La Chine, 4 place des Gras, B.P. 416, 63011 Clermont-Ferrand Cedex.

Librairie Abbe Girard, 17, rue des Petis–Gras, 63000 Clermont–Ferrand. Prop: Alan Bayssat. Tel: 04-73-91-16-13; 04-73-31-06-06. Fax: 04-73-36-42-96. Shop; open Monday to Saturday. Large print books.

CLICHY

Jean Mallet, 65, rue de Neuilly, 92110 Clichy. Tel: 04-42-70-28-72. Est: 1981. Shop; open Tuesday to Saturday 11–6.30. Medium stock. Cata: 6 a year. Corresp: French.

COLMAR

Lire et Chiner (S.a.r.l.), 36, rue des Marchands, 68000 Colmar. Prop: Schnell Fabrice. Tel: 03-89-24-16-78. Est: 1988. Shop; open every day 9.30–7. Very large stock. Spec: alpinism/mountaineering; art; bibles; comics; cookery/gastronomy; dictionaries; geography; local and national history; illustrated; literature; medicine; military; parapsychology; psychology/psychiatry. Jewish religion; sport; travel - Africa, Polar; voyages & discovery; war; wine. PR: Ffr.10–1,000. CC: EC; MC; V; CB. Cata: 1 a year. Corresp: French, German. VAT No: FR 13 343 998 787 (88B86).

DIJON

Bouquiniste Le Capricorne, 16 Rue Vauban, 21000 Dijon. Tel: 03-80-30-88-12. Shop; open Monday to Saturday 9.30–12 and 2–7. Medium general stock. PR: £5–200. Also, a booksearch service. VAT No: FR 01 332 229 038.

Librairie Le Meur, 12, place du Théâtre, 21000 Dijon. Prop: Christian Le Meur. Tel: 03-80-67-13-03. Fax: 03-80-63-75-13. Est: 1900. Shop; open Monday to Saturday 10–12 and 3–7. Very large general stock. Cata: 2 a year. Corresp: French. Mem: Compagnie Nationale des Experts.

Available from Richard Joseph Publishers Ltd
Sheppard's International Directory of
PRINT AND MAP SELLERS

3rd Edition 1995   £24.00 352pp

FRANCE

DINAN

Livres en Liberté - Librairie Serge Davy, 4 place Saint-Sauveur, 22100 Dinan. Prop: Serge Davy. Tel: 02-96-39-63-00. Fax: 02-96-87-06-47. Est: 1980. Shop; open Thursday, Friday and Saturday 2–7. Medium stock. Spec: ancient sciences; medicine; maritime/nautical; voyages & discovery; cartography. Cata: 1 a year. Corresp: Spanish. Mem: S.L.A.M.; C.N.E.S.

DINARD

Galerie Saphir, 38 rue du Marechal Leclerc, 35800 Dinard. Prop: Mrs. F. Szapiro. Est: 1991. Shop; open March to November, Sunday to Friday 10.30–12.30 and 2.30–7.30. Very small stock. Spec: antiquarian; autographs; bindings; first editions; general and local history; illustrated; literature; manuscripts; maritime/ nautical; medicine; navigation; photography; Christian and Jewish religion. PR: Ffr.500–20,000. CC: V; AE; JCB. Cata: 2 a year. Corresp: French, Spanish. Mem: S.L.A.M. VAT No: FR 77 316 418 904. *Also at:* Paris and Becherel (q.v.).

DOUAI

Librairie Ancienne Bouquinerie - Irène Garcia - Leclercq, 29, rue du Clocher St-Pierre, 59500 Douai. Prop: Irène Garcia - Leclercq. Tel: 03-27-96-96-47. Shop and market stand. Medium general stock. Corresp: French, Spanish.

ÉPERNAY

Le Cosmographe, 58, rue Saint–Thibault, 51200 Épernay. Prop: Pierre-Yves Erbland. Tel: 03-26-51-60-40. Est: 1989. Shop and market stand; open Monday to Friday 2.30–7 and Saturday 10–12 and 2.30–7. Medium stock. Spec: voyages; history; oenology and vineyards; travel; wine. PR: Ffr.1–100. Cata: 3 a year. Also, large print books.

ÉVREUX

Librairie Floréal, 41 rue de la Harpe, B.P. 872, 27008 Évreux Cedex. Prop: Mr. Pelletier. Tel: 02-32-33-22-33. Est: 1984. Shop; open Tuesday to Saturday 9–12 & 2–7. Large stock. Spec: history; French regional interest.

GARDOUCH

Librairie de Latude, B.P.2, 31290 Gardouch. Prop: Hugues de Latude. Tel: 05-61-81-51-21. Fax: 05-61-81-51-44. Private premises; appointment necessary. Very small stock. Spec: economics; fine and rare; illustrated; incunabula; medicine; natural history; science; voyages & discovery. PR: £100 and up. Cata: 1 a year. Mem: S.L.A.M.; I.L.A.B. VAT No: FR 47 332 612 365.

GINESTAS

Le Trouve Tout du Livre, Le Somail, 11120 Ginestas. Prop: Raymond Gourgues. Tel: 04-68-46-21-64. Fax: 04-68-46-39-16. Shop; open seven days a week. Large general stock of over 30,000 books. Also, a booksearch service (French books only).

GRENOBLE

La Bouquinerie, 9 boulevard Agutte Sembat, 38000 Grenoble. Prop: François Gaspari. Tel: & Fax: 04-76-46-15-32. Shop; open Monday to Saturday 9–12 and 1.30–7. Medium stock. Spec: academic/scholarly; alpinism/ mountaineering; art; books about books; local topography and history (Dauphiné); general history; literature; philosophy; university texts. PR: Ffr.7–2,000

Le Bouquiniste, 18, rue La-kanal, 38000 Grenoble.

Librairie des Hautebises, 8 rue Dominique Villars, 38000 Grenoble. CC: C.B. Cata: 1 a year.

La Nouvelle Saison, 2, rue Voltaire, 38000 Grenoble. Prop: Geneviève Souquet. Tel: 04-76-51-23-73. Est: 1993. Shop; open 10–12.15 and 2–7.15. Medium stock. Spec: modern literature; philosophy; social history. VAT No: FR 86 391 460 920 000 13.

Librairie Stendhal, 4 rue de Sault, 38000 Grenoble.

L'ISLE-SUR-LA-SORGUE

La Marge, Quai de la Gare, Village des Antiquaires, 84800 L'Isle-sur-la-Sorgue.

FRANCE

LA BAULE

E. Seguineau, 24 boulevard Hennecart, (B.P. 158), 44500 La Baule. Tel: 02-40-24-04-62. Est: 1978. Shop; open every day 9.30–1 & 3–8 in summer, and Monday to Saturday 9.30–12 & 2–7 in winter. Medium stock. Spec: literature; first editions; illustrated. Cata: 2 a year. Also, a booksearch service. Corresp: Japanese.

LA RICHE CEDEX

Librairie Nizet, BP 103, 37521 La Riche Cedex. Tel: 02-47-45-50-41. Est: 1922. Storeroom; open Monday to Friday 9–1 and 2.30–7. Very large stock. Spec: scholarly; belles-lettres; first editions. Cata: 2 a year. VAT No: FR 89 572 095 388.

LA ROCHELLE

Quartier Latin S.a.r.l., 21 rue Albert 1er, 17000 La Rochelle. Prop: Franck-Noël Mornet. Tel: 05-46-41-28-05. Est: 1950. Shop. Small stock. Spec: education; regional interest. Also, new books. Mem: S.L.A.M.; Syndicat des Libraires Classiques de France. VAT No: FR 88 393 650 825.

LANDERNEAU

Librairie de Rohan, 9, rue St-Thomas, 29800 Landerneau. Tel: & Fax: 02-98-21-38-88.

LE CHANGE

P.G. Chautru's, Chateau du Roc-Chautru, Le Roc, 24640 Le Change.

LE HAVRE

L'Écho du Passé, 62, rue Maréchal– Gallieni, 76600 Le Havre. Prop: Jean Cadiou. Tel: 02-35-21-42-71. Est: 1989. Shop and market stand; open Wednesday and Thursday 2–7, Saturday 10–12 and 2–7. Medium stock. Spec: general history - 19th century; history of ideas; maritime/nautical; memoirs; military; social history; socialism; general travel; voyages & discovery; war. PR: Ffr.30–3,000. Cata: 2 a year plus thematic lists. Also, a booksearch service. Corresp: French, Spanish. Mem: A.L.I.N.E.A. VAT No: FR 94 349 324 464 0.

LE MANS

Brocéliande, 21 rue de la Reine Bérengère, 72000 Le Mans. Prop: Bernard Rebeyrol. Tel: 02-43-24-18-27. Est: 1969. Shop; appointment necessary. Medium general stock. Cata: 4 a year. Also, valuations. Corresp: French.

LE MESNIL LE ROI

Rogers Turner Books, 24 rue du Buisson Richard, 78600 Le Mesnil le Roi. Tel: 01-39-12-11-91. Fax: 01-39-62-07-22. Private premises; appointment necessary. Spec: horology; history of science; history; German studies; linguistics. Cata: 6 to 8 a year. Also, a booksearch service. Corresp: German, Spanish. Mem: A.B.A. (U.K.); P.B.F.A. (U.K.). *Also at:* Rogers Turner Books Ltd., 22 Nelson Road, London SE10.

LE POËT-LAVAL

Bouquinerie Dit Elle, Maison des Remparts, 26160 Le Poët–Laval. Prop: Mireille Morin. Tel: 04-75-46-23-05. Est: 1986. Shop; open every day 11–7 1st April to 30th September or by appointment. Medium stock. Spec: literature; periodicals/magazines; art. Cata: irregularly. Also, a tearoom.

LECTOURE

Vielle Maison Vieux Papiers, Marsolan, 32700 Lectoure. Prop: Alain Collier. Tel: 05-62-68-85-16. Est: 1983. Shop; open Saturday and Sunday 3–7. Very large general stock. Cata: on fiction, 5 or 6 a year.

LES ARCS SUR ARGENS

Librairie Rossignol, "Saint Pierre", RD 555 B.P. 36, 83460 Les Arcs Sur Argens. Prop: L. Daniel Rossignol. Tel: 04-94-73-30-17. Est: 1928. Shop. Medium stock. Cata: 4 a year. Mem: S.L.A.M. *Also at:* Librairie Rossignol, Cannes (q.v.). VAT No: FR 60 742 840 663.

LILLE

Librairie L'Éclipse, 10, rue de la Barre, 59800 Lille. Prop: S. & J. Godon. Tel: 03-20-31-56-19. Fax: 03-20-13-19-87. Shop; open Tuesday to Saturday 2–9. Small general stock. CC: V; MC; EC. Cata: 6 a year. VAT No: FR 93 315 902 643.

Librairie Favereaux, 19 ter rue de l'Hôpital Militaire, 59800 Lille.

FRANCE

Librairie Fr. Giard, Le Maître Mot, 188, rue Jules–Delcenserie, BP 1014, 59701 Marcq-en-Baroeul. (•) Tel: 03-20-45-83-71. Fax: 03-20-89-79-11. Private premises. Very large stock. VAT No: FR 64 349 762 294.

LIMOGES

Jean–Claude Laucournet, 45, bd Carnot, 87000 Limoges.

Librairie Livresse, 12, rue de la Boucherie, 87000 Limoges. Prop: Frèdéric Bazin. Tel: 05-55-34-23-32. Fax: 05-55-32-73-62. Est: 1987. Shop; open Tuesday to Saturday 2.30–7. Small stock. Spec: art (enamels, porcelain); ceramics; illustrated. PR: Ffr.10–10,000. CC: V; EC. Cata: 1 a year. Corresp: French. Mem: S.L.A.M. VAT No: FR 34 399 520 568 000 11.

LUZARCHES

Daniel Morcrette, 4 avenue Joffre, B.P. 26, 95270 Luzarches.

LYON

Ajasse, 62, rue Tramassac, 69005 Lyon.

Alcade, 1 quai Fulchiron, 69005 Lyon.

L'Ancre Aldine, 62 rue Auguste Comte, 69002 Lyon. Prop: D. Martin. Tel: 04-78-42-07-60. Shop; open 10–12 and 3–7. Large general stock. Cata: 2 a year on general subjects. Corresp: French. Mem: S.L.A.M. VAT No: FR 66 347 907 008.

Librairie du Bât d'Argent et du Chariot d'Or, 38 rue des Remparts d'Ainay, 69002 Lyon. Manager: Pascal Chartier. Tel: 04-78-37-41-53. Fax: 04-78-42-49-47. E-Mail: bat@serveur.dtr.fr. Est: 1936. Shop; open every day. Very large general stock. Spec: antiquarian; history; literature; regional interest. Cata: periodically. Also, information available on http://www.dtr.fr/bat. Corresp: German. Mem: S.L.A.M.

Librairie Chaminade, 35 rue Auguste Comte, 69002 Lyon. Prop: Jacques Chaminade. Tel: 04-78-92-87-40. Est: 1972. Shop; open Thursday, Friday and Saturday 10–12 & 2–7. Small general stock. Cata: 2 or 3 a year. Mem: S.L.A.M. *Also at:* Librairie Chaminade, Annecy (q.v.).

Henri Lardanchet, 5, rue Servient, 69003 Lyon. Tel: 04-78-71-00-70. Fax: 04-78-95-22-28. Est: 1899. Private premises; open Mondays 2–6 or by appointment. Very small general stock. Spec: fine & rare. Cata: occasionally. Also, valuations. Corresp: French.

Galerie Laurencin, 17 rue August Comte, 69002 Lyon. Prop: Alain Cano & Gérard Chevé. Tel: 04-78-37-86-19. Fax: 04-78-42-91-85. Est: 1977. Shop; open Monday to Saturday 10–12 & 2–7. Medium stock. Spec: illustrated (natural history, art, etc.); books with original etchings. PR: Ffr.500–15,000. Also, large print books. Corresp: Spanish. Mem: S.L.A.M; Syndicat de l'Estampe.

Lucas et Vermorel, 9 Quai de la Pecherie, 69001 Lyon. Prop: Philippe Lucas & Bernard Vermorel. Tel: & Fax: 04-78-30-94-84. Est: 1982. Shop; open Tuesday to Saturday 10–6.30. Medium stock. Spec: alpinism/mountaineering; antiquarian; art reference; atlases/cartography; children's; cookery/gastronomy; Italy; games; natural sciences; science. CC: V. Cata: 2 to 4 a year on specialities. Also, large print books. Corresp: French. Mem: Cercle Lyonnais du Livre Ancien (CLLA). VAT No: FR 42 398 746 834.

Librairie Méridies, 36 Rue Sainte-Hélène, 69002 Lyon.

La Parchemine, 6 rue du Palais de Justice, 69005 Lyon. Prop: Roseline Tardy. Tel: 04-78-42-23-14. Est: 1981. Shop; open Tuesday to Saturday 10–12 & 2.30–7. Medium stock. Spec: children's. Cata: irregularly. CC: V; MC; EC; DC; JCB. Also, a booksearch service.

MÂCON

Librairie Norbert Darreau, 9, place St-Pierre, BP 47, 71002 Mâcon Cedex. Tel: 03-85-39-28-00. Est: 1984. Shop; open Tuesday to Saturday 10.30–12 and 3–7. Small stock. Spec: South Burgundy; first editions; illustrated; literature; poetry; surrealism; general travel; voyages & discovery; wine. PR: Ffr.50–10,000. Cata: 1 or 2 a year. Corresp: French.

MARIEL-MARLY

Luc Bitoun, 3 rue de la Foret, 78750 Mariel-Marly.

MARIGNY

Librairie Jean-Paul Delon, Saint Marcel, 74150 Marigny. Tel: 04-50-01-46-05. Fax: 04-50-01-45-66. Est: 1973. Private premises; postal business only. Small stock. Spec: bibliography. Cata: 2 a year plus small lists. VAT No: FR 44 788 020 865.

FRANCE

MARSEILLE

Accents Toniques Librairie, 52, Rue Grignan, 13001 Marseille. Prop: Alain Bouze. Tel: 04-91-33-56-18. Fax: 04-91-54-92-75. Shop; open Monday to Saturday 10–12 and 2–7. Medium general stock. Mem: S.L.A.M.; L.I.L.A.

Au Carrosse D'Or, 254 chem Armée d'Afrique, 13010 Marseille.

Librairie Jeanne Laffitte, Les Arcenaulx, 25 cours d'Estienne d'Orves, 13001 Marseille. Tel: 04-91-54-39-37. Est: 1972. Shop; open Monday to Saturday 10–7. Medium stock. Spec: French folklore; French history; illustrated. Cata: 2 or 3 a year. Also, restaurant facilities. Mem: S.L.A.M.

La Légende, 58 rue d'Aubagne, 13001 Marseille.

Henri Martin–Brès, 60, rue Grignan, 13001 Marseille.

MAUSSANE LES ALPILLES

L'Antiquarie de Maussane (sarl), Bastide Saint Bastien, 99 Avenue de la Vallée des Baux, 13520 Maussane-les-Alpilles. Tel: 04-90-54-37-64. Fax: 04-90-54-49-30. Shop; closed on Mondays. CC: V; AE. Mem: S.N.C.A.O.

METZ

Libraire Mnemosyne, 18, rue Sainte Marie, 57000 Metz. Prop: Giovanni Di Biase. Tel: & Fax: 03-87-36-49-79. Est: 1988. Shop; open Monday to Saturday 2.30–7. Small stock. Spec: antiquarian; architecture; cookery/gastronomy; decorative art; erotica; esoteric; ethnology; local & national history; horology; illustrated; limited editions; linguistics; mathematics; medicine; memoirs; natural history; natural sciences; religion; travel; voyages & discovery. PR: Ffr.100–15,000. CC: EC; MC; V. Cata: 1 a year. Corresp: French, Italian. VAT No: FR 67 345 118 517.

MILLAU

Librairie Alauzet, 25, boulevard de l'Ayrolle, 12100 Millau. Prop: Yvon Alauzet. Tel: 05-65-60-10-39 or 05-65-60-13-12. Est: 1963. Shop; appointment necessary. Large general stock. Spec: antiquarian; regional interest. Also, antiquities. Corresp: Spanish.

MOISSAC

Librairie J.L. Sainte-Marie, 6, rue Guileran, B.P. 24, 82201 Moissac. Prop: Jean-Louis Sainte-Marie. Tel: 05-63-04-00-93. Est: 1929. Postal business only. Medium stock. Spec: history; antiquarian. Cata: 6 a year. Mem: S.L.A.M.

MONTAUBAN

Roselyne Layan, 28, Faubourg Lacapelle, 82000 Montauban. Tel: 05-63-63-72-68. Shop; open Tuesday to Friday 2–7. Medium stock. Spec: modern literature - first editions, limited editions; literary criticism; gastronomy; wine. Also, a booksearch service and attend book fairs.

MONTIGNY-SUR-CANNE

Manoir de Pron, 58340 Montigny-sur-Canne. Prop: Gerard Oberle. Tel: 03-86-50-05-22. Fax: 03-86-50-06-16. Est: 1971. Private premises; appointment necessary. Large stock. Spec: first editions; literature; gastronomy; humanism; neo latin; early printing; manuscripts; erotica; illustrated(16th to 20th); emblemata. Cata: 1 or 2 a year. Corresp: German, Italian, Latin. VAT No: FR 66 379 307 945.

MONTOLIEU

La Chouette, 11170 Montolieu. Prop: Laurens van Baardewijk. Tel: 04-68-24-80-63. Shop; open Monday to Sunday 10–7 (closed Monday afternoon). Large general stock. Spec: geography; topography. Corresp: Dutch, French, German.

Colophon - Second Hand Books in English, 11170 Montolieu. Prop: Heather Chan & John Sime. Tel: 04-68-24-87-43. Fax: 04-68-60-68-28. Est: 1996. Shop; open Monday to Sunday 11–6. Medium stock. Spec: archaeology; art; artists; Egyptology; general fiction; detective, spy, thrillers; fine art; performing arts; photography; Christian religion; travel - general, Africa, Americas, Asia, Australasia/Australia, Europe, Middle East, Polar. PR: Ffr.5–10,000. Corresp: French.

Au Bibliotaphe Converti, rue de la Tour, 11170 Montolieu.

Le Dilettante, Montolieu 11170. Open Saturday and Sunday 4–7 and every day during summer. Spec: 20th century literature. *Also at:* 11 rue Barrault, 75013 Paris *and* le hall du Lucernaire, 53 rue Notre–Dames–des–Champs, 75006 Paris (q.v.).

Galerie des Bouquinistes, Manufacture Royale, 11170 Montolieu. Prop: Laurens van Baardewijk. Tel: & Fax: 04-68-24-85-30. Est: 1993. 10 shops in one; open daily 10–7. Very large general stock. PR: Ffr.10–5,000. CC: Yes. Corresp: German, French, Dutch.

L'Ile Lettrée, Village du Livre, 11170 Montolieu.

MONTPELLIER

Librairie Pierre Clerc, 13 rue Alexandre Cabanel, 34000 Montpellier.

Librairie Rouchaleou Jean, 4–6, boulevard du Jeu de Paume, 34000 Montpellier. Prop: Jean Rouchaleou. Tel: 04-67-58-38-60. Fax: 04-67-92-47-26. Very large stock. Spec: antiquarian; architecture; archives; art; bibliography; ecclesiastical history & architecture; first editions; general, local and national history; illustrated; literary criticism; literature; medicine; music; social history; theatre; general travel. CC: CB; MC; EC; V. Cata: 2 a year. Also, a booksearch service. Corresp: French, Spanish. VAT No: FR 327 427 464.

MOULINS

Librairie Devaux, 26 rue F. Péron, 03000 Moulins.

MULHOUSE

Alsaticarta, 31, avenue Clemenceau, 68100 Mulhouse. Prop: Lisa Coral. Tel: 03-89-46-13-57. Tel: & Fax: 03-89-56-37-77 (Home). Est: 1984. Shop; open Thursday and Friday 2–6.30, Saturday 9–12 and 2–6. Small stock. Spec: Alsace; children's; art; illustrated; travel; botany; technical; zoology; gastronomy. PR: Ffr.30–30,000. CC: V; MC. Also, a booksearch service, paintings and bronze. Corresp: French, German. VAT No: FR 40 368 828 000 25.

NANCY

La Nancéide, 19 Grand Rue, 54000 Nancy. Prop: Vedrenne Didier. Tel: & Fax: 03-83-37-25-52. Est: 1981. Shop; open Monday to Saturday 3–7. Medium general stock. Spec: sciences; historic voyages of the 16th to 20th centuries; technology.

Librairie A. Rémy, 25 rue Stanislas, 54000 Nancy. Tel: 03-83-35-64-23. Est: 1910. Shop; open Tuesday to Saturday 10–12 & 2.10–7. Large stock. Spec: literature; history; regional interest. Mem: S.L.A.M.

NANTES

Brocante du Palais, 28, rue Jean–Jaurès, 44000 Nantes.

Librairie du Casoar, 10, rue de Ploërmel, 44300 Nantes. Prop: Olivier Luczkiewicz. Tel: & Fax: 02-40-52-29-29. Est: 1977. Private premises; appointment necessary. Small stock. Spec: French literature and translations; literary criticism; general history in French; Christian religion; French autographs. PR: Ffr.20–5,000. Cata: 6 a year. Corresp: French. Also, a booksearch service. VAT No: FR 61 310 961 420.

Librairie Bellanger, 4 Passage Pommeraye, 44000 Nantes. Prop: Marie-France Marambaud. Tel: 02-40-69-51-70. Fax: 02-40-71-92-74. Est: 1942. Shop; open Monday 2–7, Tuesday to Saturday 10–7, closed on Mondays during holidays. Medium stock. Spec: literature; regional interest; travel; marine; history; medicine. Cata: 2 or 3 a year on fine & rare books; fine printing; illustrated books; literature; science; regional interest. CC: MC; V. Also, large print books. Mem: S.L.A.M. VAT No: FR 39 33 183 671 800 014.

NEUILLY-SUR-SEINE

Charles Blackburn, F.R.G.S., 27 rue Pierret, 92200 Neuilly-sur-Seine. Tel: 01-47-22-82-30. Fax: 01-40-88-35-13. Est: 1990. Private premises; appointment necessary. Very small stock. Spec: Far East, especially Japan; Travel; Oriental mission presses. PR: Ffr.1,000 plus. Cata: 4 lists a year on Japanology and general Orientalia. Corresp: Japanese (spoken only), French. Mem: S.L.A.M.; I.L.A.B. VAT No: FR 66 353 257 140.

NEVERS

Librairie Ancienne Sarl Le Ver–Vert, 32, rue St-Étienne, 58000 Nevers.

FRANCE

NICE

Bouquinerie Bonaparte, 10, rue Gioffredo, 06000 Nice. Prop: Roberte Boilet. Tel: 04-93-13-80-70. Est: 1989. Shop; open Monday to Saturday 10–12.30 and 2.15–7.15. Very large general stock. Spec: alpinism/mountaineering; animals; antiquarian; art; autobiography; cartoons; chess; cinema/films; cookery/gastronomy; esoteric; general fiction; history; maritime/nautical; music; philosophy; photography; poetry; religion; theatre; travel - Polar. CC: CB.

Librairie de l'Escurial, 29 rue Alphonse Karr, 06000 Nice. Prop: Jean-Michel Belle. Tel: 04-93-88-42-44. Fax: 04-93-87-43-37. Est: 1934. Shop; open Monday to Saturday 10–12 & 2–6.30. Medium stock. Spec: fine antiquarian and modern illustrated. Cata: 3 a year. Also, a booksearch service. Expert près les Dounes and Expert près la Cour d'Appel. Mem: S.L.A.M. VAT No: FR 83 316 229 368.

Gentile Antonio Livres Anciens, 9 bis rue Defly, 06000 Nice.

Librairie Hirlam, 8 avenue Auber, B.P. 315, 06006 Nice Cedex 1. Prop: R. & G. Hirlam. Tel: 04-93-88-93-51. Fax: 04-93-88-97-01. Est: 1974. Shop at: 8 Avenue Auber, Nice; open Monday to Friday 9–12 & 2–6.30. Medium stock. Spec: history; illustrated. Cata: 6 a year. Mem: S.L.A.M.

Librairie-Galerie Jacques Matarasso, 2 rue Longchamp, 06000 Nice. Prop: Laure Matarasso. Tel: 04-93-87-74-55. Fax: 04-93-82-53-73. Est: 1950. Shop. Medium stock. Spec: fine arts; illustrated; first editions. Mem: S.L.A.M.; Chambre Syndicale de l'Estampe.

Michel Meyer, 3 rue Defly, 06000 Nice .

NIMES

Thierry Gauville Livres Anciens, Mas La Valette, 30350 Cardet. (•) Tel: & Fax: 04-66-83-85-61. Est: 1980. Private premises; appointment necessary. Small stock. Spec: Islam; curiosities; antiquarian; books about books; cookery/gastronomy; economics; social history; travel - general, Africa, Middle East; linguistics. Cata: 5 a year. Corresp: French. Mem: S.L.A.M.; L.I.L.A. VAT No: FR 79 320 272 941.

NOGENT LE ROI

Librairie des Arts et Métiers, 20 rue de Verdun, Lormaye, 28210 Nogent le Roi. Prop: Jacques Laget. Tel: 02-37-51-44-29. Fax: 02-37-51-48-51. E-Mail: lame@pel.remcomp.fr. Est: 1973. Storeroom; open Monday to Friday 8–6. Very large stock. Spec: art; religion - general. CC: V; EC; MC; CB. Cata: 12 a year. Corresp: Spanish, Italian. VAT No: FR 38 780 060 752.

OLLIOULES

Bouquinerie de la Reppe, 114, avenue Dagnan, B.P. 63, 83190 Ollioules. Prop: V. Komar. Shop. Small stock. Spec: illustrated; travel; children; history; medicine; science; art. PR: Ffr.10–1,000. Cata: 2 a year. Also, a booksearch service. Corresp: French, Italian.

ORLÉANS

Eurl. F. Comellas, Domaine du Lumina, 45560 Saint-Denis-en-Val, Orléans.

Librairie Eric Lefebvre, 1 rue Lucien, Pean, 45750 St. Pryvé-St. Mesmin, Orléans. Tel: 02-38-66-63-24. Fax: 02-38-56-28-31. Est: 1984. Shop; open Monday to Friday 2.30–7. Medium stock. Spec: national authors; early imprints; first editions; local history; illustrated; limited editions; miniature books; signed editions; hunting. Cata: 3 a year on first editions, rare books and illustrated contemporary books. Also, Bibliographer (Hermine David, Albert Paraz).

La Malle du Martroi, 14 rue Adolphe Crespin, 45000 Orléans. Prop: Michel P. Glucksmann. Tel: 02-38-53-50-36. Fax: 02-38-54-03-98. Est: 1960. Shop; open Monday to Saturday 9–7. Very large general stock. Cata: 6 a year. Corresp: Spanish.

PACY SUR EURE

Roger Pelletier, 15 rue du Bout de Bas, Jouy sur Eure, 27120 Pacy sur Eure.

PARIS

La 42ᵉ Ligne, 83 avenue de Ségur, 75015 Paris.

Librairie Abencerage, 159 bis Boulevard du Montparnasse, 75006 Paris. Prop: Abdelaziz Ghozzi. Tel: 01-40-46-99-70. Fax: 01-43-26-91-20. Est: 1983. Shop; open 9–12.30 and 2.30–6.30. Medium stock. Spec: colonial; photography; Oriental religion; travel - Africa, Asia. PR: Ffr.100–1,000. Cata: 3 a year. Corresp: Arabic. Mem: S.L.A.M. VAT No: FR 27 331 316 406.

FRANCE

"**AH, Les Beaux Livres**", Village Suisse, 78, Ave. de Suffren, Boutique No. 4, 75015 Paris. Prop: Bernard Pettit. Tel: 01-44-49-91-66. Fax: 01-45-54-77-70. Est: 1996. Shop; open every day except Tuesday & Wednesday 3–7. Small general stock. Corresp: Spanish. VAT No: FR 18 301 341 269.

L'Albertine, 9 rue Maître Albert, 75005 Paris. Prop: C. Mafart. Tel: 01-43-29-39-20. Fax: 01-42-74-17-46. Est: 1982. Shop; open Tuesday to Saturday 2.30–7. Large stock. Spec: literature; iconography. PR: Ffr 250–1,000. CC: V; MC.

Jean–Christophe Alexandridis, 12, rue Frochot, 75009 Paris.

Librairie des Alpes, 6 rue de Seine, 75006 Paris. Prop: Elise Vibert-Guigue. Tel: 01-43-26-90-11. Fax: 01-44-01-03-66. Est: 1932. Shop. Medium stock. Spec: skiing; alpinism; speleology; mountaineering; Jules Verne first editions. CC: V; MC; AE. Mem: S.L.A.M.

Librairie Alphée, 22, boulevard Beaumarchais, 75011 Paris.

Les Amazones, 4, rue des Grands–Degrés, 75005 Paris. Prop: Chantal Bigot. Tel: & Fax: 01-46-34-25-67. Est: 1993. Private premises; appointment necessary. Small stock. Spec: women; feminism; homosexuality. Cata: 3 a year plus speciality lists. Corresp: French. VAT No: FR 85 390 785 541.

Librairie d'Amérique et d'Orient, 11 rue St. Sulpice, 75006 Paris. Prop: Jean Maisonneuve. Tel: & Fax: 01-43-26-86-35. Est: 1926. Shop at: 3 bis Place de la Sorbonne; open Monday to Friday 9–12 and 1.30–6.30. Very large stock. Spec: history; geography; archaeology; religion; philosophy; the Orient. Cata: 1 a year. Also, publishers of Orientalism. VAT No: FR 11721 015 485.

Arenthon S.A., 3 quai Malaquais, 75006 Paris. Prop: L. Desalmand. Tel: 01-43-26-86-06. Fax: 01-43-26-62-08. Est: 1972. Shop; open Monday to Friday 8.30–12.30 and 3–7, Saturday 8.30–12.30 and 3–6. Very large stock. Spec: art; artists. Also, books and illustrated books from 20th-century. Corresp: French. Mem: S.L.A.M; L.I.L.A.; I.F.P.D.A.

Les Argonautes, 74 rue de Seine, 75006 Paris. Prop: Jean-Edouard Gautrot. Tel: 01-43-26-70-69; 01-43-37-90-02. Fax: 01-43-26-99-88. Shop; open Monday to Saturday 10–12 & 3–7. Small stock. Spec: modern illustrated; bindings; first editions. Cata: 1 a year. Corresp: French. Mem: S.L.A.M.

Florence Arnaud, 10 rue de Saintonge, 75003 Paris.

Art de la Publicité, 3 rue Dolomieu, 75005 Paris. Prop: Claude Courtet. Tel: 01-47-07-77-71. Est: 1983. Shop; open Monday to Saturday 2–7. Small stock. Spec: books about advertising. Cata: on speciality, 2 a year. Corresp: Italian.

80

Arts Graphiques du Japon, 2 rue de Provence, 75009 Paris. Prop: Bernard Rousseau. Tel: & Fax: 01-45-23-52-65. Est: 1970. Shop; open 2–6 but appointment advised. Medium stock. Spec: illustrated. Mem: S.L.A.M. VAT No: FR 63 701 004 855.

Librairie "Au Vieux Document", 6 bis, rue de Chateaudun, 75009 Paris.

Les Autographes, 45 rue de l'Abbé Grégoire, 75006 Paris.

Librairie Barbéry, 2 rue des Grands Degrés, 75005 Paris. Prop: Annick Barbéry. Tel: 01-43-25-33-76. Est: 1966. Shop; open Tuesday to Saturday 1–7, and in the mornings by appointment. Medium stock. Spec: antiquarian; art; fine & rare; first editions; illustrated; limited editions; literature; textiles. Cata: 2 a year. Corresp: French, Italian. VAT No: FR 20 399 401 512.

Librairie Fabrice Bayarré, 21 rue de Tournon, 75006 Paris.

Guy Bellou, 7 bis r Saints Pères, 75006 Paris.

Librairie Benedetti-Estève, 80 rue de Charonne, 75011 Paris.

Jacques Benelli, 244, rue St. Jacques, 75005 Paris.

Le Bibliophile Russe, 12 rue Lamartine, 75009 Paris. Prop: André Savine. Tel: 01-48-78-91-02. Fax: 01-49-95-08-05. Est: 1978. Shop; appointment necessary. Medium stock. Spec: books in Russian in all subjects. Corresp: Russian, French. Mem: S.L.A.M.; L.I.L.A.

Librairie Auguste Blaizot, 164 rue du Faubourg Saint-Honoré, 75008 Paris. Prop: Claude Blaizot. Tel: 01-43-59-36-58. Fax: 01-42-25-90-27. E-Mail: blaizot@platique.fr. Est: 1940. Shop; open Tuesday to Saturday 9.30–12.30 and 2–6.30. Medium stock. Spec: French literature; illustrated; first editions; bindings. CC: V; MC; EC; AE. Cata: 3 or 4 a year. Corresp: French. Mem: S.L.A.M; S.N.A.; C.N.E. VAT No: FR 82 582 014 056.

Albert Blanchard, 9, rue de Médicis, 75006 Paris.

Librairie Bonaparte, 31 rue Bonaparte, 75006 Paris. Prop: J. Buisson. Tel: 01-43-26-97-56. Fax: 01-43-29-44-65. Est: 1937. Shop; open Monday to Saturday. Medium stock. Spec: theatre; dance; circus; music; opera; music hall; magic and conjuring; puppets. Cata: 1 a year on each of circus, dance and general. Also, a booksearch service and new books. Corresp: Spanish. Mem: S.L.A.M. VAT No: FR 57 652 022 278.

Henri Bonnefoi Livres Anciens, 1 rue de Médicis, 75006 Paris.

Books & Research France, 8 rue Gracieuse, 75005 Paris. Tel: 01-43-36-33-31. Fax: 01-43-36-44-45. Est: 1987. Open 9–6. No stock, booksearch only. Corresp: French.

Bouquins 67, 67, rue Saint Charles, 75015 Paris.

Librairie Bourguignat, 10 bis rue de Châteaudun, 75009 Paris. Prop: Pierre Bourguignat. Tel: 01-48-74-76-80. Fax: 01-40-22-97-63. Shop; open every afternoon except Saturday. Medium stock. Spec: history of locomotion (aviation, railways etc.); science; technical. Cata: 2 a year. VAT No: FR 89 309 783 041.

Boutique de l'Histoire, 24, rue des Ecoles, 75005 Paris. Prop: Pierre Borella. Tel: 01-46-34-03-36. Fax: 01-43-26-83-96. E-Mail: 101725.1110@compuserve.com. Est: 1986. Shop; open Monday 2–7, Tuesday to Saturday 9–7. Large stock. Spec: biography; Egyptology; general, industrial, local and national history; history of civilisation; Holocaust; social history. PR: Ffr.50–1,000. CC: V. Cata: 12 a year. VAT No: FR 05 348 741 802.

Roland Buret Librairie, 6 passage Verdeau, 75009 Paris.

Cabinet Revel, (E. de Broglie), 57 rue de Verneuil, 75007 Paris.

Alain Cambon, 30, rue Monsieur le Prince, 75006 Paris.

Librairie du Camée, 70 rue St. André des Arts, 75006 Paris.

Librairie François et Rodolphe Chamonal, 5, rue Drouot, 75009 Paris.

Charavay, 3, rue de Furstenberg, 75006 Paris.

Librairie Florence de Chastenay, 76, rue Gay-Lussac, 75005 Paris.

Chateaudun, 17, rue de Chateaudun, 75009 Paris.

Les Chevau-Légers, 34 rue Vivienne, 75002 Paris.

Cinémagence, 12 rue Saulnier, 75009 Paris. Prop: Troussier. Tel: 01-42-46-21-21. Fax: 01-42-46-20-20. Est: 1969. Shop; open 2–6 and at other times by appointment, also postal business. Medium stock. Spec: cinema/films; photography; theatre; autographs. Cata: 1 a year. Also, a booksearch service, large print books, and international film books.

Le Conservateur, 98 bis, Boulevard de Latour-Maubourg, 75007 Paris.

Librairie Ancienne Th. Corcelle, 5, rue Isabey, 75016 Paris. Tel: 01-45-25-93-36. Fax: 01-42-15-01-13. Shop; open Tuesday to Friday 10–12.30 or 2.30–7 or by appointment. Spec: children's; circus; education; fables; science-fiction; illustrated. CC: V. Cata: 2 a year on specialities. Corresp: French. Mem: S.L.A.M. VAT No: FR 93 333 705 150.

Paul–Louis Couailhac, 10, allée Riesener (Louvre des Antiquaires), 2, place du Palais-Royal, 75001 Paris. Tel: 01-42-61-56-91. Fax: 01-42-61-10-70. Est: 1982. Shop and storeroom; open 11–7. Small stock. Spec: good texts, fine condition, nice bindings. PR: $100 upwards. CC: V; MC; AE; JCB. Cata: several thematic lists a year. Also, a booksearch service and large print books. Corresp: French, Spanish. Mem: A.E.E. (Alliance Européenne des Experts). VAT No: FR 325 119 154 000 12 5252.

Librairie Coulet et Faure, 1 rue Dauphine, 75006 Paris. Prop: Claude Coulet. Tel: 01-43-26-42-40. Fax: 01-43-25-34-60. Open 9–12 and 2–6.30, closed Monday. Medium stock. Spec: bindings; illustrated; literature (only French). PR: Ffr.1,000–50,000. Cata: 4 a year. Mem: S.L.A.M.; I.L.A.B. VAT No: FR 66 582 131 744.

Librairie Delatte S.a.r.l., 15 rue Gustave Courbet, 75116 Paris.

Solange Delmas, 62, rue Vanneau, 75007 Paris. Tel: 01-45-48-37-81. Est: 1987. Shop; open Monday to Saturday 3–7. Medium stock. Spec: travel - general, Africa, Americas, Asia, Australasia/Australia, Europe, Middle East, Polar; voyages; navigation; history - general, industrial, local, national and history of civilisation; literature. Cata: lists for auction sales (9 a year). Also, large print books. Corresp: French. Mem: U.F.E. (Union Francaise des Experts).

Librairie Les Deux Mondes, 84 rue de Vaugirard, 75006 Paris.

Librairie Dhennequin, 76 rue du Cherche Midi, 75006 Paris. Prop: Michele Dhennequin. Tel: 01-42-22-18-53. Spec: travel (former French colonies); ethnography; ethnology; Orientalism. Also, a booksearch service. Mem: S.L.A.M.

Le Dilettante, 11 rue Barrault, 75013 Paris. Tel: 01-45-80-08-71. Fax: 01-45-65-08-64. Est: 1976. Shop; open Monday to Sunday 10.30–7.30. Medium stock. Spec: 20th-century literature. CC: V. Cata: 6 a year on speciality. VAT No: FR 27 307 013 250. *Also at:* Le Dilettante, dans le hall du Lucernaire, 53, rue Notre-Dame-des-Champs, 75006 Paris *and* Le Dilettante, Montolieu, 11170. (q.v.).

Doc'Auto, 70, rue Laugier, 75017 Paris. Prop: Chantal Pougeux. Tel: & Fax: 01-43-80-84-99. Est: 1984. Shop; open Monday to Friday 2.30–7. Large stock. Spec: automobilia (specialising in French makes). Corresp: French, Spanish, Italian. VAT No: FR 37 334 316 296 00014.

Dudragne, 86 rue de Maubeuge, 75010 Paris. Prop: Patrick Dudragne. Tel: 01-48-78-50-95. Fax: 01-40-05-98-04. Mobile: 06-07-75-80-83. Est: 1979. Shop; open Monday to Friday 9–1 & 3–6.30 but prior telephone call advised, also Saturday and other times by appointment. Medium stock. Spec: antiquarian; architecture; atlases/cartography; books about books; botany; Catalogues Raisoneés; cinema/films; colonial; colour-plate; decorative art; economics; fashion & costume; fine & rare; genealogy; geography; hydrography; iconography; illuminated manuscripts; illustrated; incunabula and many others. Cata: 6 a year on auctions. Corresp: Spanish.

Librairie Dutel, 16 rue Jacques Callot, 75006 Paris. Prop: Jean-Pierre Dutel. Tel: 01-43-54-17-77. Fax: 01-43-25-83-01. Est: 1980. Shop; open Tuesday to Saturday 11–12.30 & 4–7. Very small stock. Spec: modern illustrated and curiosa. Mem: S.L.A.M.

Librairie Elbé, 213 bis, boulevard Saint-Germain, 75007 Paris. Prop: Jean-Louis Bonvallet. Tel: 01-45-48-77-97. Est: 1976. Shop; open Tuesday to Saturday 10–1 & 2–6.30. Very large stock. Spec: horses; hunting. PR: Ffr.300–500. Cata: 1 a year on specialities. Also, large print books. Mem: S.L.A.M.; L.I.L.A.

Les Enluminures, Le Louvre des Antiquaires, 2 Place du Palais Royal, 75001 Paris. Prop: Sandra Hindman. Tel: 01-42-60-15-58. Fax: 01-40-15-00-25. Est: 1991. Shop; open Tuesday to Sunday 11–7. Very small stock. Spec: illuminated manuscripts; manuscripts. PR: £100–1,000,000. Cata: 1 a year. Also, drawings, gouaches, illuminations. Corresp: French, Italian, German, Dutch. Mem: A.B.A.A.; S.L.A.M.; I.L.A.B.

Librairie Entrée des Artistes, 161 rue St. Martin, 75003 Paris.

Librairie Farfouille, 27 passage Verdeau, 75009 Paris. Prop: Michel Siegelbaum. Tel: 01-47-70-21-15. Fax: 01-45-23-28-57. Shop; open Monday to Friday 12–7 & Saturday 1–7. Medium stock. Spec: antiquarian; bibliography. Cata: 1 a year. Corresp: German. Mem: S.L.A.M. VAT No: FR 52 307 550 509.

Librairie Fata Libelli S.a.r.l., 9 rue de Médicis, 75006 Paris. Prop: Danuta Cichocka. Tel: 01-44-07-16-44. Fax: 01-44-07-16-45. Est: 1985. Shop; open 11–7. Small stock. Spec: illustrated; erotica; bindings; fashion and costume; fine art; old and rare. PR: Ffr.1,000–30,000. Cata: 3 a year. Also, a booksearch service. Corresp: French, Polish, Russian. Mem: L.I.L.A.; I.L.A.B.; S.L.A.M. VAT No: FR 38 341 418 119 000 28.

La Fontaine Charlemagne, 5, rue Charlemagne, 75004 Paris. Prop: Pierre Besnault. Tel: 01-42-71-63-55. Est: 1987. Shop; open Wednesday to Monday 3–8 and by telephone. Small stock. Spec: agriculture; animals; botany; dogs; games; gardening; horticulture; literature; veterinary medicine; zoology. PR: Ffr.100–3,000. CC: AE. Corresp: French.

Fougerolle Livres Rares, 67, avenue de Suffren, 75007 Paris. Prop: Cédric & Ithier de Fougerolle. Tel: 01-43-06-96-82. Fax: 01-40-65-91-47. E-Mail: fougerol@club-internet.fr. Est: 1989. Shop; open Monday to Saturday 9–7.30. Medium stock. Spec: science; architecture; fine art; gardening; aeronautics; maritime/nautical; travel - Polar; fine & rare; incunubula; Helvetica. PR: Ffr. 2,000. CC: V; MC; AE. Cata: 4 a year. Corresp: French, Italian. Mem: S.L.A.M.; L.I.L.A. VAT No: FR 40 404 332 934.

Librairie J.F. Fourcade, 3, rue Beautreillis, 75004 Paris. Tel: 01-48-04-82-15. Fax: 01-48-04-75-62. Est: 1995. Shop; open Monday to Saturday 11–1.30 and 4–7. Small stock. Spec: first editions; illustrated; signed editions; autographs; literature; literary criticism; poetry; artists. PR: Ffr.200–10,000. Also, a booksearch service and large print books. Cata: 5 a year.

Fournier, 44, rue Quincampoix, 75004 Paris.

Christian Galantaris, 15 rue des Saints Pères, 75006 Paris. Tel: 01-47-03-49-65. Fax: 01-42-60-42-09. Est: 1974. Shop. Spec: first editions; bindings; illustrated. Also, autographs and auctions.

La Galcante, 52, rue de l'Arbre–Sec, 75001 Paris. Prop: Irma Auclert. Tel: 01-44-77-87-40. Fax: 01-42-96-80-13. Est: 1980. Shop; open Tuesday to Saturday 10–7. Very large stock. Spec: news; history; satirical; fashion; sport; movies; music; countries; war; periodicals. PR: Ffr.100. CC: V; AE. Corresp: French, Spanish.

Galerie D'Autographes, 5, rue du Vieil Abreuvoir, 78100 St.–Germain–En–Laye. Prop: Jean Emmanuel Raux. Tel: 01-34-51-96-12. Fax: 01-34-51-42-29. Shop; open Tuesday to Saturday 10–12.30 and 2.30–7. Very large stock. Spec: history; literature; painting; music; autographs. PR: Ffr.100–200,000. CC: V; MC. Cata: 4 a year. Corresp: French. Mem: S.L.A.M. VAT No: FR 04 302 256 136.

Librairie Galignani, 224 rue de Rivoli, 75041 Paris Cedex 01. Tel: 01-42-60-76-07. Fax: 01-42-86-09-31. Est: 1802. Shop; open 10–7. Very large stock of 50,000 volumes. Spec: French and English Books; International Fine Arts. Mem: S.L.A.M. VAT No: FR 79 552 145 039.

Gérard Ganet, 10 Passage Verdeau, 75009 Paris.

Bernard Gaugain, 13, passage Véro–Dodat, 75001 Paris. Tel: 01-45-08-96-89. Est: 1976. Shop; open 9–12 and 3–7, closed Sunday. Small stock. Spec: illustrated; literature. PR: Ffr.1,000–50,000. Also, a booksearch service and large print books. Corresp: German.

Librairie Orientaliste Paul Geuthner S.A., 12 rue Vavin, 75006 Paris.

Girand, 76, rue de Seine, 75006 Paris.

Librairie Giraud–Badin, 22 rue Guynemer, 75006 Paris. Prop: Mr. D. Courvoisier & E. Lhermitte. Tel: 01-45-48-30-58. Fax: 01-42-84-05-87. Shop; open 9–1 and 2–6. Spec: bibliography; bindings; literature. Also, auctioneers. VAT No: FR 31 784 271 843. *Also at:* 1 rue de Fleurus, Paris (q.v.).

Librairie Giraud–Badin, 1, rue de Fleurus, 75006 Paris. *Also at:* 22 rue Guynemer, Paris (q.v.).

Librairie du Graal, 15 rue Jean Jacques Rousseau, 75001 Paris.

Les Grands Prés, 4, rue Lacepède, 75005 Paris.

Alain de Grolée–Virville, 19, rue de Valois, 75001 Paris. Tel: 01-42-96-01-59. Fax: 01-42-96-18-32. Est: 1761. Medium stock. Spec: heraldry; genealogy; manuscripts.

Librairie Guenegaud, 10 rue de l'Odion, 75006 Paris. Est: 1947. Shop; open Tuesday to Saturday 10–12.45 & 2–6.30. Medium stock. Spec: antiquarian; heraldry; local history. Cata: 3 a year.

Guilbert, 137, boulevard du Montparnasse, 75006 Paris.

Librairie L'Harmattan, 16 rue des Écoles, 75005 Paris. Tel: 01-43-26-04-52. Fax: 01-43-29-86-20. Est: 1975. Shop; open Monday to Saturday 10–12.30 & 1.30–7. Very large general stock. Spec: Africa; Asia; Latin America; reference. CC: V; CB. Corresp: French, Spanish, Portuguese. VAT No: FR 11 318 850 963.

Librairie Hatchuel sarl, 21, rue Saint–Jacques, 75005 Paris. Prop: Patrick Hatchuel. Tel: 01-43-29-41-31. Fax: 01-46-33-25-90. Est: 1975. Shop; open Monday to Friday 10–1 and 2–7 or by appointment. Medium stock. Spec: French colonial; economics; education; erotica; feminism; general, industrial and national history; humanities; law; pacifism; pedagogy; philosophy; politics; psychoanalysis; psychology/psychiatry; social history; social sciences; socialism; sociology. Cata: 4 a year. Also, a booksearch service and specialist in buying and selling subject collections. Corresp: French. VAT No: FR 10 331 604 264.

Société Hebraica–Judaica, 12 rue des Hospitalières Saint Gervais, 75004 Paris. Prop: Bernard Liebermann. Tel: 01-48-87-32-20. Est: 1933. Shop; open 2–6.15, closed Saturdays. Very small stock. Spec: Judaica and Hebraica; books in foreign languages; art. CC: All. Mem: S.L.A.M. VAT No: FR 58 592 068 001.

Librairie Henner, 9 rue Henner, 75009 Paris. Prop: Alain Sinibaldi. Tel: 01-48-74-60-38. Fax: 01-48-74-03-88. E-Mail: ashenner@imaginet.fr. Est: 1976. Shop; open Tuesday to Friday 10–12 and 3–5, Saturday 10–12. Small stock. Spec: bindings; fine & rare; first editions. PR: £100–10,000. Cata: 4 a year on antiquarian, fine & rare and first editions (French). Mem: S.L.A.M. VAT No: FR 47 309 026 524.

Librairie Jacques Herbinet, 39 rue de Constantinople, 75008 Paris.

Les Images de Marc, 69, boulevard Beaumarchais, 75003 Paris. Prop: Marc LeFebvre. Tel: 01-42-71-36-69. Fax: 01-42-71-54-94. Est: 1981. Shop; open Tuesday to Saturday 2–7. Very large stock. Also, large print books. Corresp: Spanish, Italian. Mem: Chambre Nationale des Experts (C.N.E.).

L'Intersigne, 66 rue du Cherche Midi, 75006 Paris. Prop: Alain Marchiset. Tel: 01-45-44-24-54. Fax: 01-45-44-50-55. E-Mail: tersign@worldnet.fr. Est: 1985. Shop; open Monday to Friday 11–7 and Saturday 11–2. Small stock. Spec: esoteric; alchemy; science; medicine; homeopathy; magic & conjuring; philosophy; early imprints. PR: Ffr.500–50,000. CC: V; MC. Corresp: French, German, Arabic. Mem: S.L.A.M.; Compagnie Nationale des Experts.

Jadis et Naguère, 166 Faubourg St. Honoré, 75008 Paris. Prop: P. & O. Ract-Madoux. Tel: 01-43-59-40-52. Fax: 01-45-62-93-54. Est: 1975. Shop; open Monday to Friday 11–7, Saturday 2–7. Spec: rare and valuable; bindings; illustrated (art nouveau and art deco). Cata: 1 a year.

Librairie Paul Jammes, 3, rue Gozlin, 75006 Paris.

Katz, 40, rue des Saints Pères, 75007 Paris.

Librairie–Galerie René Kieffer, 46, rue St-André-des-Arts, 75006 Paris.

Librairie Léonce Laget, 76 rue de Seine, 75006 Paris. Tel: 01-43-29-90-04. Fax: 01-43-26-89-68. Spec: antiquarian; applied art; architecture; art; art history; art reference; artists; carpets; Catalogues Raisonées; ceramics; fine art; gardening; landscape.

Lardanchet, 100, rue Faubourg Saint-Honoré, 75008 Paris.

Dominique de Lattre, Livres, Affiches Anciens, 56 rue de l'Université, 75007 Paris. Tel: 01-45-44-75-30. Fax: 01-45-44-83-53. Est: 1986. Shop; open Monday to Friday 10.30–1 & 2–7. Medium stock. Spec: advertising; aeronautics; antiquarian; archives; art; art history; art reference; artists; aviation; biography; business studies; carpets; children's; colonial; fashion & costume; fine art; industry; interior design; typography; voyages & discovery. PR: Ffr.10–1,000. CC: CB; MC; V. Corresp: French, Spanish, German, Italian. *Also at:* Marché Vernaison, St. Ouen (q.v.).

Librairie Le Bateau Ivre, 89 rue de l'Ouest, 75014 Paris.

Librairie J.M. Le Fell, 16 rue de Tournon, 75006 Paris.

Jacques Lévy, 46 rue d'Alésia, 75014 Paris.

Librairie Les Arcades Lebouc S.A., 8, rue de Castiglione, 75001 Paris. Prop: Monsieur Yves Lebouc. Tel: 01-42-60-62-96. Fax: 01-42-97-43-56. Shop; open Monday to Friday 10–7. Spec: antiquarian; art; art history; art reference; artists; Catalogues Raisonées; illuminated manuscripts; illustrated. CC: V; AE; DC. Corresp: Spanish. VAT No: FR 42 542 038 047.

Lecointre–Drouet, 9, rue de Tournon, 75006 Paris. Tel: 01-43-26-02-92. Fax: 01-46-33-11-40. E-Mail: lecodro@franceantiq.fr. Est: 1980. Shop; open Tuesday to Saturday 10–7. Very small stock. Spec: architecture; photography; typography; avant–garde; 20th century. CC: MC; EC. Cata: 3 a year. Also, a booksearch service and large print books. VAT No: FR 51 321 676 942.

Librairie Jean Lepert, 42 rue Jacob, 75006 Paris. Tel: 01-42-61-42-70. Fax: 01-42-61-46-03. Est: 1976. Storeroom; appointment necessary. Small stock. Spec: travel - Africa, Americas, Asia, Australasia/Australia, Europe, general, Middle East, Polar. CC: V. Cata: 1 a year. Corresp: French, Spanish. Mem: S.L.A.M. VAT No: FR 86 306 563 222.

Lettres Slaves, 18 rue Brillât Savarin, 75013 Paris. Prop: Marc Franciszkowski. Tel: 01-45-81-52-52. Fax: 01-45-81-27-24. Shop: appointment necessary and postal business. Large stock. Spec: general history; autographs; antiquarian; fine & rare; manuscripts (Polish and Slavic). PR: Ffr. 50–20,000. CC: Yes. Cata: 2 or 3 a year and thematic lists as requested. Also, a booksearch service. Corresp: French, Polish, Russian. VAT No: FR 18 398 849 600 11.

J.Y. Lhomond, Stand 11, Allée 1, Marché Vernaison, 99 Rue des Rosiers, 93400 St. Ouen. Tel: 01-45-23-13-80. Fax: 01-45-23-13-84. Est: 1976. Market stand; open Saturday, Sunday, Monday 9–6. Large print books. CC: V. Corresp: French. Mem: S.L.A.M.; S.N.C.A.O. Ordinex. VAT No: FR 09 320 927 312.

Librairie Alain Brieux, 48 rue Jacob, 75006 Paris. Tel: 01-42-60-21-98. Fax: 01-42-60-55-24. Est: 1960. Shop; open Monday to Friday 10–1 & 2–6.30. Spec: medicine; science. CC: AE; DC; MC; EC; V. Cata: periodically. Also, new books in speciality and old scientific and medical instruments. Mem: S.L.A.M. VAT No: FR 83 622 016 921.

Librairie Courant d'Art, 79 rue de Vaugirard, 75006 Paris. Prop: Marie-Jo Grandjean. Tel: 01-45-49-36-41. Fax: 01-45-49-21-16. Est: 1987. Shop; open Monday to Saturday 11-7.30. Very large stock. Spec: antiques; architecture; art; the arts; photography; sculpture; travel - Africa. CC: V; AE; DC; EC; MC. Also, a booksearch service. Corresp: French. VAT No: FR 23 324 016 799.

Librairie de l'Inde S.a.r.l., 20 rue Descartes, 75005 Paris. Prop: André Gauthier. Tel: 01-43-25-83-38. Fax: 01-43-25-79-52. Est: 1985. Shop; open Tuesday, Wednesday, Friday and Saturday 12.30–6.30. Medium stock. Spec: India and other countries on Indian subcontinent. Cata: on India, irregularly. Also, new books on speciality, and publisher on India and Navy. Corresp: French. Mem: S.L.A.M.; U.L.F.; Librairies 5 Alifra. VAT No: FR 39 332 568 971.

Librairie Table d'Émeraude, 21 rue de la Huchette, 75005 Paris.

Loeb–Laroque, 36 rue Le Peletier, 75009 Paris.

Mme. Florence Loewy, 46 avenue René Coty, 75014 Paris. Tel: 01-40-47-06-96. Fax: 01-43-20-06-37. E-Mail: floewy@netlink.co.uk. Shop; appointment necessary. Very small stock. Spec: illustrated; contemporary artists. Cata: 1 or 2 a year. VAT No: FR 64 349 889 170.

Librairie Bernard Loliée, 72 rue de Seine, 75006 Paris.

Librairie Lutèce I, 29, rue Monge, 75005 Paris. Prop: Denni. Tel: 01-43-26-32-16. Est: 1955. Medium stock. Spec: comics in French (only). PR: up to Ffr. 500.

Librairie Lutèce II, 5, rue d'Arras, 75005 Paris. Tel: 01-46-33-33-16. Est: 1955. Shop; open Tuesday to Saturday 2.30–8. Medium stock. Spec: comics in French (only). PR: upto Ffr.500.

Librairie Jean-Jacques Magis, 47 rue St. André des Arts, 75006 Paris. Tel: 01-43-26-50-57. Fax: 01-43-26-11-38. Est: 1925. Storeroom; open Monday to Friday 9.30–12.30 & 2–6.30. Very large stock. Spec: antiquarian; economics; politics; law. Cata: 2 a year. Corresp: Spanish, German, Italian. Mem: S.L.A.M.; Compagnie Nationale des Experts.

Librairie Bernard Maille, 3 rue Dante, 75005 Paris. Tel: & Fax: 01-43-25-51-73. Est: 1979. Shop; open Monday to Friday 2–6 or in the mornings by appointment. Medium stock. Spec: science; medicine; history of medicine; mathematics; physics; astronomy; chemistry; biology; natural sciences. CC: V; MC; EC. Cata: 3 or 4 a year on medicine and sciences. Also, rare books on science & medicine and large print books. Mem: S.L.A.M.; L.I.L.A. VAT No: FR 84 315 584 383.

Maison Charavay Autographs, 3 rue de Furstenberg, 75006 Paris. Prop: Michel Castaing. Tel: 01-43-54-59-89. Fax: 01-43-25-89-31. Est: 1830. Private premises; open Monday afternoons and Tuesday to Friday 10–12 and 2–6. Very large stock. Spec: historical documents. Cata: 4 a year.

Marché du Livre Ancien et d'Occasion du Parc Georges Brassens, c/o Gippe, Rene Froment, 60 rue Dombasle, 75015 Paris. Est: 1987. Book market of 60 dealers at: Pavillons Baltard, rue Brancion, 75015 Paris; open Saturdays & Sundays 9–9, all year. Spec: aeronautics; antiquarian; art; children's; cinema/films; comics; cookery/gastronomy; esoteric; detective, spy, thrillers; science fiction; literature; general fiction; military; periodicals/magazines; occult; philosophy; photography; religion; Jewish religion; social history; travel; women; illustrated; poetry; and many more. PR: Ffr.10–30,000.

Martin, 56, rue St. Georges, 75009 Paris.

Martinez, 21, rue St. Sulpice, 75006 Paris.

Librairie I. Maurel, Marché Vernaison allée 1, Stand 41, 93400 St. Ouen.

Bouquinerie de l'Institut S.A. Mazo Lebouc, 12 rue de Seine, 75006 Paris. Prop: Yves Lebouc. Tel: 01-43-26-63-49. Fax: 01-43-26-81-91. Est: 1954. Shop; open Monday to Saturday 10–1 & 2.30–7. Large stock. Spec: fine arts; modern illustrated; Chagall; Picasso; Miro; Matisse. CC: V. Mem: S.L.A.M.; Chambre Syndicate de L'Estampe, du Dessin et du Tableau. VAT No: FR 14 552 076 309.

R.G. Michel, 17 quai Saint-Michel, 75005 Paris. Tel: 01-43-54-77-75. Est: 1920. Shop; open 9–7. Corresp: German. Mem: S.L.A.M. VAT No: FR 26 775 662 380.

Librairie Monnier, 55 rue de Rome, 75008 Paris.

Librairie Monsieur Le Prince, 49, rue Monsieur Le Prince, 75006 Paris.

de Montbel, 1, rue Paul Cézanne, 75008 Paris.

Librairie Monte–Cristo, 5, rue de l'Odéon, 75006 Paris. Prop: J.M. Embs. Tel: 01-43-26-49-03. Est: 1989. Shop; open 11–1 and 2.30–7. Small stock. Spec: children's; J. Verne; illustrated; romantic. PR: Ffr.1,000–10,000. CC: V; MC. Corresp: French, Norwegian.

Libraire Montfort, 68 Rue Saint Antoine, 75004 Paris. Prop: Gérard Monfort. Tel: 01-40-27-95-54. Fax: 01-40-27-95-60. Est: 1960. Shop; appointment necessary. Medium stock. Spec: archaeology; architecture; art; art history; art reference; the arts. Cata: 2 a year. VAT No: FR 44 384 731 725.

Librairie Montmartroise, 29, rue Durantin, 75018 Paris.

Jean Morel Librairie, 19 rue du Vieux Colombier, 75006 Paris. Tel: 01-45-44-43-26. Est: 1978. Private premises; open Tuesday to Friday 8–6. Very small stock. Spec: applied arts; children's; national culture; education; local history (Normandy); illustrated; memoirs. PR: Ffr.850. Cata: 4 a year. Also, auctions. Corresp: French. Mem: C.N.E.S. VAT No: FR 03 780 993 945 000 10. *Also at:* 33 rue de Dr Caron, 76420 Bihorel–Rouen (q.v.).

La Nef Des Fous, 53, rue Manin, 75019 Paris.

Les Neuf Muses, 41 quai des Grands Augustins, 75006 Paris. Prop: Alain Nicolas. Tel: 01-43-26-38-71. Fax: 01-43-26-06-11. Est: 1980. Shop; open Monday to Friday 2–6.30, mornings by appointment. Small stock. Spec: archives; autographs; calligraphy; Freemasonry; national history; limited editions; literature; manuscripts; signed editions; surrealism. PR: Ffr.500–50,000. Cata: 2 a year. Also, dedicated books and auctions in all fields. Corresp: Spanish, French. Mem: S.L.A.M.; I.L.A.B.; M.S. VAT No: FR 47 320 268 436.

Librairie F. de Nobele, 35 rue Bonaparte, 75006 Paris. Prop: Claude de Nobele & Françoise de Nobele-Smilenko. Tel: 01-43-26-08-62. Fax: 01-46-85-96. Est: 1885. Shop; open Monday to Friday 9–12 and 2–7. Large stock. Spec: fine arts; architecture; archaeology; decorative arts; applied arts. PR: Ffr.100–500,000. CC: V; MC. Cata: irregularly. Corresp: French. Mem: S.L.A.M.; L.I.L.A. VAT No: FR 21 351 949 565.

"L'Or du Temps", 53, rue du Cardinal Lemoine, 75005 Paris. Prop: Pierre R. Ojanski. Tel: 01-43-26-95-18. Est: 1981. Shop; open Monday to Saturday. Medium stock. Spec: cinema/films; limited editions; literature; poetry; surrealism. CC: CB; V. Cata: 3 a year.

Pages d'Histoire, 8 rue Bréa, 75006 Paris.

Librairie du Passage, 111, avenue Victor–Hugo, 75116 Paris.

Le Petit Prince, 121 boulevard St. Michel, 75005 Paris. Tel: 01-43-54-45-60. Fax: 01-40-51-07-52. Est: 1947. Shop; open Monday to Saturday 9.30-7. Spec: French literature, history, fine arts, dictionaries. CC: V. Also, a booksearch service. Corresp: Russian, Armenian.

Pinault, 27 & 36, rue Bonaparte, 75006 Paris.

Plantureux, 61, rue du Faubourg Poissonnière, (3ᵉ étage). 75009 Paris. Prop: Serge Plantureux. Tel: 01-44-79-07-13. Fax: 01-44-79-08-19. Est: 1989. Private premises; appointment necessary. Very small stock. Spec: fine and rare; early imprints; photography; science; children's; erotica. Cata: 1 a year. Corresp: French, German, Italian, Spanish, Russian, Latin. Mem: S.L.A.M. (France), S.V.A.Z. (Czechoslovakia), L.I.L.A.; I.L.A.B. VAT No: FR 76 351 973 995.

Librairie Jean Polak, 8 rue de l'Échaudé, 75006 Paris.

Malo Pollès, 36 rue Vivienne, 75002 Paris.

Pont Traversé, 62 rue de Vaugirard, 75006 Paris. Prop: Marie-Josée Béalu. Tel: 01-45-48-06-48. Est: 1951. Shop; open Tuesday to Saturday 12–7. Medium stock. Spec: poetry; first editions; literature; fine art.

Librairie La Porte Étroite, 10 rue Bonaparte, 75006 Paris. Prop: Claude Schvalberg. Tel: 01-43-54-26-03. Fax: 01-40-46-06-55. Est: 1924. Shop; open Tuesday to Friday 2–7, Saturday 2–6. Small stock. Spec: fine arts; Cata: 2 a year. Corresp: Spanish, German, Italian. VAT No: FR 37 562 125 161.

Poursin, 7, rue des Urslulines, 75005 Paris.

Librairie Puce, 30 rue Bouret, 75019 Paris.

Librairie Musicale Pugno, 19 quai des Grands Augustins, 75006 Paris. Tel: 01-43-26-14-80. Shop; open Tuesday to Saturday 9–12 and 2–6.30. Spec: music. CC: V. VAT No: FR 74 721 074 482.

Librairie Recherches, 238 rue Croix Nivert, 75015 Paris. Prop: André Engel. Tel: 01-45-32-42-72. Est: 1982. Shop; open Monday to Friday 11–2 & 3.15–7, Saturday 10.30–1 & 2.30—7. Small stock. Spec: literature; history; travel. Cata: 2 a year.

Librairie Émile Rossignol, 8 rue Bonaparte, 75006 Paris. Tel: 01-43-26-74-31. Fax: 01-43-29-98-52. Est: 1906. Shop; open Monday to Saturday 9.30–12 & 2–7. Spec: antiquarian; first editions; illustrated; incunabula; manuscripts. Also, bookbinding. Mem: S.L.A.M.

Galerie Rouillon, 27, rue de Seine, 75006 Paris.

Roux Devillas, 12 rue Bonaparte, 75006 Paris. Tel: 01-43-54-69-32. Fax: 01-40-46-91-50. Est: 1935. Shop; open daily 10–12.30 and 2–7 (except Monday mornings and Sundays). Large stock. Spec: aeronautics; antiquarian; archives; astronomy; autographs; countries & continents; documents; history; maritime/nautical; mathematics; science; travel; voyages & discovery. Corresp: French, Swedish (German). VAT No: FR 07 318 450 772.

Galerie Sagot–Le–Garrec, 10, rue de Buci, 75006 Paris.

Librairie Orientale H. Samuelian, 51 rue Monsieur le Prince, 75006 Paris. Tel: 01-43-26-88-65. Est: 1930. Shop; large stock. Spec: Orient; Arabia; Armenia; antiquarian; art; Egyptology; travel - Africa, Asia, Middle East. Also, a booksearch service and new books. Mem: S.L.A.M.

Galerie Saphir, 84 boulevard Saint-Germain, 75005 Paris. Prop: Mrs. F. Szapiro. Tel: 01-43-26-54-22. Fax: 01-43-80-23-49. Shop; open Sunday to Thursday 2–7. Very small stock. Spec: Judaica; Hebraica. PR: Ffr.100–10,000. CC: V; AE; DC; JCB. Corresp: French, Spanish. Mem: S.L.A.M. *Also at:* Dinard & Becherel (q.v.).

Galerie Saphir, 69 avenue de Villiers, 75017 Paris. Prop: Mr. & Mrs. Szapiro. Tel: 01-44-40-26-84. Fax: 01-43-80-23-49. Est: 1979. Shop; open Sunday to Thursday 2–7. Very small stock. Spec: Hebraica; Judaica; history of French Brittany. PR: Ffr.800–80,000. CC: V; AE; JCB; MC. Cata: 1 or 2 a year. Corresp: Spanish. Mem: S.L.A.M. *Also at:* Dinard & Becherel (q.v.).

Sartoni–Cerveau, 15 quai Saint–Michel, 75005 Paris.

Shakespeare & Company, 37, rue de la Bûcherie, 75005 Paris. Prop: George Whitman. Est: 1951. Shop. Large stock. Spec: literature; history; travel; philosophy; foreign (Russian, German, Spanish, Italian); cookery; biography; firsts. PR: Ffr.10–720,000. Also, bargains. Corresp: Russian, Italian, Spanish, German, Chinese.

Librairie du Spectacle, 5 rue de Montfaucon, 75006 Paris. Prop: Francis Garnier Arnoul & Bengt Svensson. Tel: 01-43-54-80-05. Fax: 01-43-54-82-92. Est: 1951. Shop; open Monday to Saturday 11–12.30 & 2–6.30. Large stock. Spec: theatre; music; opera; ballet; circus; mime; puppets and cinema. Cata: 1 a year. Also, new books relating to specialities. Mem: S.L.A.M.

Le Sportsman, 7 bis rue Henri Duchêne, 75015 Paris. Prop: Michel Merejkowsky. Tel: 01-45-79-38-93. Est: 1981. Shop; open Friday 11–8, and at other times by appointment. Medium stock. Spec: sport (16th century to 1990). Cata: irregularly. Also, sporting magazines.

Studio de l'Image, 14 rue des Carmes, 75005 Paris. Prop: Philippe Grand. Tel: 01-43-54-88-73. Fax: 01-43-29-85-04. Est: 1988. Shop; open Monday to Saturday 3–8. Medium stock. Spec: 19th-century books; Paris; film photographs; travel. Also, an art gallery. Corresp: Spanish, Italian, Portuguese, German, Turkish.

Librairie Sylva Sylvarum, 123, rue du Faubourg Du Temple, 75010 Paris. Prop: Christine Reynaud & Emmanuel Camille–Bernard. Tel: 01-42-40-82-81. Fax: 01-42-40-27-72. Est: 1990. Private premises; appointment necessary. Small stock. Spec: academic/scholarly; alchemy; anthropology; antiquarian; banking; bibliography; books about books; business studies; classical studies; dictionaries; economics; fine & rare; history; humanism; incunabula; law; philosophy; politics; social history; social sciences; typography; women. Cata: 2 to 3 a year plus specialised lists on major subjects. Corresp: German, Italian, Portuguese, Spanish. Mem: S.L.A.M; I.L.A.B. VAT No: FR 29 384 125 373.

La Table D'Émeraude, 21, rue de la Huchette, 75005 Paris.

Librairie Historique F. Teissedre, 102 rue du Cherche Midi, 75006 Paris. Prop: M. Teissedre. Tel: 01-45-48-03-91. Fax: 01-45-44-35-52. Shop; open Monday 1.30–7, Tuesday to Friday 10–12 and 1.30–7, Saturday 2–7. Medium stock. Spec: history; economics; social history; military; regional interest; genealogy. Cata: 3 a year. Also, a booksearch service. Corresp: Italian, German. Mem: S.L.A.M. VAT No: FR 84 353 596 646.

Librairie Thomas-Scheler, 19 rue de Tournon, 75006 Paris. Prop: Bernard Clavreuil. Tel: 01-43-26-97-69. Fax: 01-40-46-91-46. Est: 1932. Shop; open 10–1 and 2.30–7. Medium stock. Spec: science; medicine; travel; literature; illustrated; incunabula. PR: Ffr.1,000–30,000. VAT No: FR 93 582 004 974.

Librairie Le Tour du Monde, 9 rue de la Pompe, 75116 Paris. Prop: Jean–Étienne Huret. Tel: 01-42-88-58-06. Fax: 01-42-88-40-57. Est: 1973. Shop; open Tuesday to Saturday 10–1 and 2–7. Very large general stock. Cata: 8 a year. Corresp: Spanish, Italian. Mem: S.L.A.M. VAT No: FR 40 732 078 571 000 13.

Librairie Jean Touzot, 38 rue St. Sulpice, 75278 Paris Cedex 06.

Au Troisième Œil, 37, rue de Montholon, 75009 Paris. Prop: Stéphane Bourgoin. Tel: 01-48-74-73-17. Est: 1972. Shop; open Monday to Friday 1–6.30, Saturday 2–5. Medium stock. Spec: detective, spy, thrillers (major subject); fantasy, horror; science fiction. PR: Ffr.50–800. Also, a booksearch service, new books and fanzines. Corresp: German, Spanish.

Librairie Ulysse, 26, Saint–Louis–en–l'Ile, 75004 Paris. Prop: Catherine Domain. Tel: 01-43-25-17-35. Fax: 01-43-29-52-10. Est: 1971. Shop; open Tuesday to Saturday 2–8, Sundays, occasionally. Very large stock. Spec: travel. PR: Ffr.5–15,000. CC: C.B.; V, fax and mail orders only. Also, a booksearch service, new books and magazines on travel and Cargo Club - livre à la carte. VAT No: FR 68 712 011 576.

Valette, 11, rue de Vaugirard, 75006 Paris.

Librairie Valleriaux, 98 boulevard Voltaire, 75011 Paris. Prop: François Valleriaux. Tel: 01-47-00-50-43. Premises; open Monday to Friday 2–7. Spec: local history; ethnology; folklore; travel - general; architecture; antiquarian; general topography; genealogy; ethnography; illustrated; literature; national languages. Cata: 3 a year on local history and voyages. Corresp: Spanish. Mem: S.L.A.M. VAT No: FR 21 311 544 894.

Josiane Vedrines, 38 rue de Richelieu, 75001 Paris.

Vers et Prose, 23 rue des Boulangers, 75005 Paris. Prop: Christian Vuichoud. Tel: 01-26-00-42. Fax: 01-33-73-41. Est: 1985. Shop; open Tuesday, Thursday and Friday 2–6.30 and by appointment. Small stock. Spec: first editions of 19th-century literature and poetry. Cata: periodically. Corresp: German.

Librairie Henri Vignes, 57, rue St.-Jacques, 75005 Paris. Tel: 01-43-25-32-59. Fax: 01-43-25-30-08. Est: 1996. Shop; open Tuesday to Saturday 1–7. Small general stock. Cata: 4 a year. VAT No: FR 384 988 101. *Also at:* 64 avenue de Général Leclerc, 92340 Bourg La Reine (q.v.).

La Vouivre, 11 rue St. Martin, 75004 Paris. Tel: 01-42-72-37-82 or 01-42-71-32-39. Fax: 42-72-02-83. Est: 1972. Shop; open Monday to Saturday 11–7. Medium general stock. Spec: late 19th- and 20th-century literature; esotericism; tradition; history; theatre. Cata: 10 a year. Corresp: French.

Librairie Jean-Claude Vrain, 12 rue Saint-Sulpice, 75006 Paris. Tel: 01-43-29-36-88. Fax: 01-44-07-22-71. Shop; open Monday to Saturday 9.30–7. Medium stock. Spec: autographs; first editions; illustrated; literature; surrealism; southern France and Provence. PR: Ffr.500–50,000. CC: V. Cata: 1 a year on literature, illustrated and first editions. Corresp: German, Spanish. Mem: S.L.A.M.; I.L.A.B. VAT No: FR 77 343 510 228.

Librairie J. Vrin, 71 rue St. Jacques, 75005 Paris. Prop: A. Paulhac. Tel: 01-43-54-70-49. Est: 1910. Shop; open Monday to Thursday 9–12 & 2–6.30. Large stock. Spec: literature; fine arts; literary studies; French provincial interest. Cata: 5 a year.

Librairie Philosophique J. Vrin, 6 place de la Sorbonne, 75005 Paris. Prop: Andrée Vrin. Tel: 01-43-54-03-47. Fax: 01-43-54-48-18. Est: 1843. Shop; open every day (except Saturday) 9–12 & 2–6.30. Large stock. Spec: philosophy; fine arts; literature; medicine; history; political economics. Cata: on philosophy, medicine and science, and on literature and fine arts, on alternate months. Mem: S.L.A.M.

Friedrich Weissert, 22, rue de Savoie, 75006 Paris. Tel: 01-43-29-72-59. Fax: 01-40-46-85-57. Est: 1988. Shop; open Monday to Friday 10–7. Spec: illustrated. CC: V. Corresp: French, German. Mem: S.L.A.M.; I.L.A.B. VAT No: FR 93 344 196 670.

Le XXᵉ Siècle et ses Sources, 4, rue Aubry le Boucher, 75004 Paris. Prop: Yves Toutut. Tel: 01-42-78-15-49. Fax: 01-42-78-47-90. Est: 1971. Shop; open 10.30–12.30 and 2.30–4.30, closed Saturday morning. Small stock. Spec: fine arts (1870 to date). PR: Ffr.200–3,000. CC: V; MC. Corresp: French. Mem: U.F.E. VAT No: FR 90 306 293 143.

Mme. Dina Zouein, 104 rue de l'Université, 75007 Paris. Tel: 01-45-55-89-72. Fax: 01-44-18-03-54. Est: 1987. Private premises; appointment necessary or postal business. Very small stock. Spec: travel - Middle East. Cata: 2 a year on the Middle East. Also, a booksearch service. Mem: S.L.A.M.; I.L.A.B.

PÉRIGUEUX

Librairie Lamongie Sarl, 2 rue de la Nation, 24000 Périgueux.

Millescamps (Librairie), 7, rue Saint Front, 24000 Périgueux. Prop: Henri-Pierre Millescamps. Tel: 05-53-09-53-25. Fax: 05-53-09-85-38. Est: 1980. Shop; open Monday 2–7, Tuesday to Saturday 10–7. Medium general stock. Mem: S.L.A.M. VAT No: FR 0731 811 4279.

Librairie de Sèze, 52, rue Michel Roulland, 24000 Périgueux.

POITIERS

Libraires Anciennes Brissaud, 162 Grand'rue, 86000 Poitiers. Medium stock. Spec: fine & rare books; law; history of science; travel. *Also at:* 12 rue Magenta, Poiters (q.v.).

Libraires Anciennes Brissaud, 12 Rue Magenta, 86000 Poitiers. *Also at:* 162 Grand'rue, Poitiers (q.v.).

Librairie de l'Escalier, 111, Grand–Rue, 86000 Poitiers. Prop: Edith Andriev. Tel: 05-49-41-32-24. Est: 1981. Shop; open Tuesday to Saturday 11–7. Small general stock. PR: Ffr. 30–40. Corresp: French.

PONTAULT-COMBAULT

Les Oies Sauvages, B.P.16, 77343 Pontault–Combault Cedex. Prop: Marc. Vidal. Tel: & Fax: 01-60-34-72-67. Est: 1991. Private premises; postal business only. Medium stock. Spec: war - WWII (half of stock); literature; esoteric; general history; humour; politics; Holocaust; Freemasonry; history of ideas; occult; French colonies and colonial wars; Germany (1900–1945); French politics. PR: Ffr.50–100. Cata: 4 a year on WWII literature and history and express lists on demand. Also, a booksearch service. Corresp: French.

PUISSERGUIER

John Lyle, 3 Faubourg Saint Roch, 34620 Puisserguier. Tel: 04-67-93-82-44. Est: 1952. Private premises; appointment necessary. Small stock. Spec: gastronomy/cookery; wine; the surrealist movement; curiosa; English and French literature. PR: Ffr.20–20,000, £2–2,000. Cata: irregularly. Corresp: French.

REIMS

Librairie Bibliothême s.a.r.l., 4 rue Colbert, 51100 Reims. Prop: François Goulet. Tel: 03-26-88-43-42. Est: 1983. Shop; open Monday to Saturday 10–12 and 2.30–7. Medium general stock. Spec: Champagne and Ardenne regions. PR: Ffr.100–10,000. Mem: S.L.A.M.; L.I.L.A.

ROCHEFORT SUR MER

La Malle aux Livres, 52, rue de la République, 17300 Rochefort Sur Mer. Prop: Didier Catineau. Tel: & Fax: 05-46-99-34-01. Est: 1992. Shop; open Tuesday to Saturday 10.30–12 and 1–6.45. Small general stock. Spec: aeronautics; antiquarian; art; astrology; author - Pierre Loti; aviation; children's; detective, spy, thrillers; fantasy, horror; science fiction; health; history; illustrated; literature; maritime/nautical; music. Cata: 1 a year. Also, a booksearch service. VAT No: FR 81 388 076 556 (00017).

RODEZ

Librairie Larrouy, 18, rue de la Barrière, 12000 Rodez. Prop: Jean Larrouy. Tel: & Fax: 05-65-42-60-52. Est: 1989. Shop; open Tuesday, Wednesday, Friday and Saturday 2–6. Small stock. Spec: applied art; architecture; archives; art; art reference; artists; ceramics; cookery/gastronomy; crafts; decorative art; Freemasonry; glass; Holocaust; periodicals/magazines; poetry; politics; travel - Europe. PR: Ffr.10–3,000. CC: V. Cata: irregularly.

ROUEN

Librairie Bertran Etienne, 110 rue Molière, 76000 Rouen. Tel: & Fax: 02-35-70-79-96. Est: 1966. Shop; open Tuesday to Saturday 10.30–12 and 2.30-7. Medium stock. Spec: antiquarian from 17th, 18th & 19th centuries; art history; general, local and national history; illustrated; literature; science; travel; voyages & discovery; first editions. PR: Ffr.100–10,000. CC: CB; V. Cata: 1 a year. Mem: S.L.A.M.

Librairie Elisabeth Brunet, 70, rue Ganterie, 76000 Rouen.

FRANCE

ST. CLOUD

Librairie Charles Lucas, 10 rue Armengaud, 92210 St. Cloud.

ST. CYR SUR LOIRE

Librairie Ancienne J.P. Veyssière, 19, rue Victor Hugo, 37540 St. Cyr sur Loire. Tel: 02-47-54-84-54. Fax: 02-47-41-95-77. Est: 1975. Appointment necessary. Medium stock. Spec: fine and rare; humanism; 16th-century. Cata: 4 a year on various subjects. Corresp: French, German, Italian, Spanish. Mem: S.L.A.M.; L.I.L.A. *Also at:* 24 Rue de la Scellerie, 37000 Tours (q.v.).

ST. ÉTIENNE

Le Bouquiniste, 34 rue Michelet, 42000 St. Étienne. Prop: Silvio Cumer-Fantin. Tel: 04-77-32-63-69. Fax: 04-77-32-08-30. Shop; open Tuesday to Saturday 9.30–12 and 2.30–7. Large general stock. Cata: 3 a year. Also, large print books. Mem: S.L.A.M. VAT No: FR 34 398 550 300 014.

L'Odyssée, 15 rue Mi-Carême, 42000 St. Étienne. Prop: Mme. Bonjour. Tel: 04-77-33-21-50. Est: 1976. Shop; open Tuesday to Saturday 10–12 & 3.30–7. Medium general stock. Cata: 1 a year.

ST. GERMAIN EN LAYE

Collections du Passé, 5 rue du Vieil Abreuvoir, 78100 St. Germain en Laye.

ST. JEAN DE LUZ

Chatelard, 1 place Maurice Ravel, 64500 St. Jean de Luz. Tel: 05-59-26-04-09. Fax: 05-59-26-66-09. Est: 1972. Shop. Very small stock.

ST. MARTIN-DE-RÉ

Librairie Ancienne Quillet, Cour du Cinéma, 17410 St-Martin-de-Ré. Prop: Lionel Quillet. Tel: 05-46-09-10-55. Fax: 05-46-29-09-16. Est: 1989. Shop; open every day 10.30–12.30 and 2.30–6.30. Small stock. Spec: maritime/nautical; travel; medicine. PR: Ffr.100–5,000. CC: V; CB. Cata: 1 a year. Also, a booksearch service and large print books. VAT No: FR 92 342 264 074.

ST. OUEN

Mr. D. de Lattre, Marché Vernaison (Allée 1, Stand 47), 99 rue des Rosiers, 93400 St. Ouen. Tel: 01-40-12-68-89 or 01-45-44-75-30. Fax: 01-45-44-83-53. Market stand; open Saturday, Sunday and Monday 9.30–6. Medium stock. Spec: the arts; travel; history; advertising arts. Corresp: Spanish, German. *Also at:* Dominique de Lattre, 56 rue de l'Université, 75007 Paris (q.v.).

SAINTES

Galerie Clémenceau, 4, rue Georges Clémenceau, 17100 Saintes. Prop: Philippe Guillory. Tel: 05-46-93-14-72. Est: 1973. Shop; open Tuesday to Saturday 10–12 and 3–7. Medium stock. Spec: ceramics; local and national history; music - general; numismatics. PR: Ffr.5–3,000. Corresp: French. VAT No: FR 94 300 289 782.

SARZEAU

À la Recherche du Passé, St. Colombier, 56370 Sarzeau. Prop: Robert Chassaniol. Tel: Office: 02-97-26-41-50. Shop: 02-97-26-48-09. Fax: 02-97-26-45-29. Est: 1962. Shop and private premises; open Saturdays and Sundays, public holidays and festivals 3–6.30, and during July and August, Tuesday to Sunday 3–7. Large stock. Spec: French colonies; D.O.M.-T.O.M.; navigation; periodicals/magazines; travel - Africa and Asia; voyages and discovery. Cata: on specialities. Also, large print books. Mem: S.L.A.M.

STRASBOURG

Ancienne Librairie Gangloff, 20 place de la Cathédrale, 67000 Strasbourg. Prop: C. Rebert. Tel: 03-88-32-40-52. Fax: 03-88-22-57-56. Est: 1927. Shop; open Tuesday to Saturday 9–12 & 2–7. Large stock. Spec: Alsace. Cata: 4 a year. Also, new books. Corresp: German. Mem: S.L.A.M. VAT No: FR 12 300 115 672.

TASSIN LA DEMI-LUNE

Librarie Bertrand, 2 Allée des Écureuils, 69160 Tassin la Demi-Lune.

TOULON

Bouquinerie Montbarbon, B.P. 855, 83051 Toulon Cedex. Tel: 04-94-42-46-99. Est: 1974. Shop. Medium general stock. Cata: 5 a year.

Le Passé Retrouvé, 5 rue Corneille, 83000 Toulon. Prop: Ms. Boissier. Tel: & Fax: 04-94-24-20-79. Est: 1994. Shop; open Tuesday to Saturday 9.30–12 and 3–7. Small stock. Spec: maritime/nautical; regionalism; travel. Cata: 3 or 4 a year. Also, a booksearch service. Corresp: Italian, Spanish.

Librairie les Vieux Ordinaires, 8 rue Baudin, 83000 Toulon. Prop: J. Etienne. Tel: & Fax: 04-94-89-59-24. Est: 1976. Shop; open Tuesday to Saturday 2.30–6.30. Very large stock. Spec: regionalism; voyages; medicine; fine illustrated; literature; history; maritime/nautical. Cata: 5 or 6 a year as requested on general or specific subjects. Corresp: Italian, Spanish. VAT No: FR 55 394 072 614.

TOULOUSE

Librairie Champavert, 2 rue du Périgord, 31000 Toulouse. Prop: Roger Roques. Tel: 05-61-21-95-96. Fax: 05-61-12-11-78. Est: 1978. Shop; open Monday to Saturday 10–12 & 2.30–7. Small general stock. Cata: 2 or 3 a year. Also, survey for book auctions in Toulouse and regions and a booksearch service. Mem: S.L.A.M.

Librairie Lestrade, 2, rue Philippe-Feral, 31000 Toulouse. Prop: Michel Lestrade. Tel: 05-61-25-08-80. Est: 1983. Shop; open Tuesday to Friday 10.30–12 and 2.30 to 7, Saturday 2.30–6. Small stock. Spec: biography; books about books; cookery/gastronomy; ex-libris; fine & rare; Freemasonry; heraldry; general and local history; illustrated; limited editions; literature; medicine; memoirs; science; surrealism; general travel; typography; wine. PR: Ffr.100–1,000. Cata: 1 a year. VAT No: FR 83 327 505 715.

Libraire Pierre Marnières, 13 rue de Metz, 31000 Toulouse. Tel: 05-61-21-92-98. Fax: 05-61-21-30-78. Shop; open every day 9–7. Medium stock. Spec: animals; antiquarian; antiques; architecture; art; aviation; calligraphy; carpets; Catalogues Raisonées; ceramics; children's; cinema/films; cookery/gastronomy; costume; countries & continents; dance; decorative art; dictionaries; glass; travel guides; travel and many others. Also, large print books.

TOURS

Bouquiniste, 20, rue Gambetta, 37000 Tours. Prop: Denis Crozatier. Tel: 02-47-46-22-19. Shop; small stock. Spec: alpinism/mountaineering; classical studies; philosophy; comics. PR: £1–100. Corresp: French.

Librairie Veyssière, 24, rue de La Scellerie, 37000 Tours. Prop: Jean Paul Veyssière. Tel: 02-47-47-08-77. Fax: 02-47-55-00-90. Est: 1975. Shop; open Tuesday to Saturday 9.30–12.30 and 2–7. Medium stock. Spec: fine and rare; humanism; 16th-century. Cata: 4 a year on various subjects. Corresp: French, German, Italian, Spanish. Mem: S.L.A.M; L.I.L.A. *Also at:* 19, rue Victor Hugo, 37540 St. Cyr sur Loire (q.v.).

TURCKHEIM

Europe Antic Art, BP 32, 68230 Turckheim. Prop: Jean–Alain Caminade. Tel: 03-89-27-10-97. Fax: 03-89-80-96-24. Est: 1996. Private premises; appointment necessary. Very small stock. Spec: alpinism/mountaineering; architecture; children's; cookery/gastronomy; countries & continents; Alsace; Lorraine; travel guides; medicine; military; photography; technical; textiles; local topography; travel - general, Europe; wine. PR: Ffr.100–10,000. Cata: 3 a year. Corresp: French, German. VAT No: FR 42 408 956 860.

VALENCE

La Bouquinerie, Place de la Pierre, 26000 Valence. Prop: Mme. Adjemian. Tel: 04-75-43-75-71. Fax: 04-75-56-68-16. Est: 1981. Shop; open Tuesday to Saturday 3–7. Medium stock. Spec: modern illustrated. Cata: 4 a year on general and specific subjects. Also, manuscripts and publishers of reprinted antique books.

VÉZELISE

À l'Homme de Fer, 2 rue Jean-Baptiste Salle, 54330 Vézelise.

VENCE

Galerie Librairie de la Basse Fontaine, 2 place Anthony Mars, 06140 Vence. Tel: 04-93-58-30-82. Shop. Medium stock. Spec: fine arts; 19th-century illustrated.

VENETTE

Sciences Nat, 2 rue André-Mellenne, B.P.1, 60280 Venette. Tel: 03-44-83-31-10. Fax: 03-44-83-41-01. Est: 1971. Storeroom; postal business only. Large stock. Spec: natural history & sciences, mainly entomology. PR: Ffr.10–50,000. CC: V; EC; MC. Cata: 1 or 2 a year. Corresp: French. VAT No: FR 38 712 039 502.

FRANCE

VERSAILLES

Librairie des Carrés, 42 rue Royale, 78000 Versailles. Prop: Jean-Pierre & Sue Fouques. Tel: & Fax: 01-39-20-06-32. Est: 1987. Shop; open Tuesday to Saturday 10–12.30 and 2.30–7. Small stock. Spec: antiquarian; earth sciences; illustrated; natural history; science; transport; voyages & discovery. PR: Ffr.100–20,000. Cata: 2 a year on specialities. Also, new books on bibliography, travel and the Paris area. Corresp: French, Spanish, German. Mem: C.L.A.Q.

Librairie Ancienne et Moderne G.-R. Puzin, 30 rue de la Paroisse, 78000 Versailles. Tel: 01-39-50-43-75. Small general stock. Spec: art; history; literature; religion.

VESOUL

Librairie Comtoise, 11 rue d'Alsace-Lorraine, 70000 Vesoul. Prop: C.H. Rebert. Tel: 03-84-76-56-80. Fax: 03-84-75-43-11. Est: 1987. Shop; open 10–12 & 2–7. Small stock. Mem: S.L.A.M.

VICHY

Librairie de la Tour, 16 rue de la Source de l'Hôpital, 03200 Vichy.

Librairie–Galerie le Ver–Vert, 18–20 passage Noyer, 03200 Vichy.

VOIRON

Le Bouquiniste, 13, place Porte–de–la–Buisse, 38500 Voiron. Prop: Dante Logatelli. Tel: 04-76-65-90-63. Fax: 04-76-05-64-68. Est: 1981. Shop; open Tuesday to Saturday 2.30–7. Medium stock. Spec: alpinism/mountaineering; art; cookery/ gastronomy; countries & continents; esoteric; fashion & costume; general fiction; history; horticulture; illustrated; maritime/nautical; mineralogy; natural sciences; navigation; ornithology; travel. PR: FFr.10–10,000. Corresp: French only.

GERMANY

Country dialling code: 49 *Currency:* German mark (DM)

Antiquariat Aix–La–Chapelle, Markt 36, 52062 Aachen. Prop: Eberhard B. Talke. Tel: (0241) 30872. Fax: 20786. Est: 1975. Shop; open Monday to Friday 11–6, Saturday 10–2. Small stock. Spec: rare old books; early printed books. PR: DM100–10,000. CC: V; MC; EC. AE. Corresp: German, Spanish. Mem: V.D.A. VAT No: DE 121 722 693.

AixLibris, Pontdriesch 19, 52062 Aachen. Prop: Dr. Lothar Hennighaus. Tel: (0241) 25340. Fax: 402403. Est: 1986. Shop; open Monday to Friday 11–6, Saturday 10–2. Large stock of antiquarian books. Spec: philosophy; anarchism; socialism; fine and rare; German literature; children's; travels; history of human, social and natural sciences. PR: DM1–30,000. Cata: 2 or 3 a year. Also, a booksearch service. Corresp: German. VAT No: DE 121 670 419.

Antiquariat Schmetz Am Dom, Postfach 3, 52001 Aachen. Prop: Bernhard Schmetz. Tel: (0241) 32528. Fax: 403877. Est: 1981. Shop; open Monday to Friday 10–1 and 3–6, Saturday 10–2. Large stock. Spec: art history; general and local topography; antiquarian; geography. CC: V; EC; AE. Cata: 1 a year. Also, a booksearch service. Corresp: French, German. Mem: V.D.A. VAT No: DE 121 715 900.

AALEN

Scientia Verlag und Antiquariat, Adlerstrasse 65, P.O. Box 1660, 73406 Aalen. Prop: Kurt Schilling. Tel: (07361) 41700. TA: Scientia, Aalenwuertt. Fax: (07361) 45620. Appointment necessary. Spec: law; philosophy. Mainly a publishing company. Mem: V.D.A.

AHLEN

Versandantiquariat Thon, Westrasse 126C, 59227 Ahlen. Tel: (02382) 4413. Fax: 85091. E-Mail: mthon@t-online.de. Est: 1980. Market stand and storeroom. Medium stock. Spec: autographs. Cata: 4 a year. Mem: U.A.C.C.; AdA. VAT No: DE 123 979 824.

ALBSTADT

Antiquariat Gerh. Renner, A.d. Unteren Berg (Fuchsfarm), Postfach 1648. 72439 Albstadt-2-Tailfingen. Tel: (07432) 5114. Fax: 5567. E-Mail: antiquar.renner. mathscience@t-online.de. Est: 1957. Storeroom; open daily 8–6, Saturday 8–12. Large stock. Spec: antiquarian science; mathematics; astronomy; physics. Cata: on mathematics and history of science, 2 a year; general 1 a year. Also, new books, a booksearch service, geodesy, dialling, measure and weight. Corresp: French, Spanish. Mem: B.V.D.B.; Buchhändlervereinigung Frankfurt. VAT No: DE 144 822 334.

ALLMENDINGEN

B.M.C.F. Antiquariat, Hauptstrasse 18 (Postfach 54), 89604 Allmendingen. Prop: Rainer G. Feucht. Tel: (07391) 1276. Fax: 8324. Est: 1975. Private premises; appointment necessary. Medium stock. Spec: censorship; erotica; ethnology; gypsies; homosexuality; miniature books; pharmacy/pharmacology; witchcraft; drug use & abuse. Cata: 10 to 12 a year on avant-garde, bibliography, censorship, erotica, homosexuality, miniature books, occult, pharmacy/pharmacology, Scouting, sexology, witchcraft. Also, a booksearch service and new books relating to specialities. Corresp: French, Spanish. VAT No: DE 145 222 202.

ARNSBERG

Antiquariat und Kunsthandlung Huste, Steinweg 11, 59821 Arnsberg. Prop: Wolfgang and Khamssa Huste. Tel: & Fax: (02931) 4454. Est: 1994. Shop; open 10–1 and 2–6.30. Large stock. Spec: art; literature; graphics; history. PR: DM10–10,000. Also, a booksearch service, large print books and two book auctions a year. Corresp: German, French, Arabic. VAT No: DE 124 676 114. *Also at:* Liebigstrasse 46–48, 44139 Dortmund *and* Goldbergstr. 17, 58095 Hagen (q.v.).

ASCHAFFENBURG

Antiquariat Elfi Duensing, Uhlandstrasse 7, 63741 Aschaffenburg. Tel: (6021) 460825. Est: 1988. Shop. Medium general stock. Spec: animals; art; cinema/films; erotica; esoteric; science fiction; general music; occult; painting; religion; theology; general travel; war. PR: DM1–1,000. Cata: 2 a year. Also, a booksearch service. Corresp: German.

GERMANY

AUGGEN

Antiquariat A. Hirschbihl, Antikhof, 79424 Auggen Baden. Tel: (07631) 8323. Fax: 10539. Est: 1988. Storeroom; appointment necessary. Large stock. Spec: antiquarian; antiques; archaeology; art history; biography; colonial; Egyptology; ethnography; ethnology; geography; history; history of civilization; maritime/nautical; medicine; memoirs; military; occult; religion; general travel; voyages & discovery. PR: DM1–1,000. Cata: 5 a year. Also, a booksearch service. Corresp: German. VAT No: DE 142 489 039.

AUGSBURG

Antiquariat "Die Eule", Annastrasse 32a, 86150 Augsburg. Prop: Joern Uwe & Barbara Woeste. Tel: (0821) 33654. Est: 1988. Shop; open every day 10–6.30 & Saturday 10–2. Medium stock. Spec: antiquarian; the arts; classical studies; Germany, Bavaria; national culture; general fiction; first editions; general and local history; illustrated; landscape; literary criticism; literature; literature in translation; music; philosophy; poetry; politics; psychology/psychiatry; Christian religion; socialism; theology. PR: DM1–500. Also, a booksearch service. Corresp: German, French.

Galerie Hassold, Grottenau 6, 86150 Augsburg.

Margot Loercher, Gartenstrasse 13, 86482 Aystetten (bei Augsburg).

Antiquariat Hartmut R. Schreyer, Ulrichsplatz 12, (Maximilianstrasse), 86150 Augsburg. Tel: (0821) 36468. Fax: 36461. Est: 1976. Shop; open Monday to Friday 10–12 and 2–6, Saturday 10–1. Large stock. Spec: art history; art reference; artists; general and local history; illustrated; literature; photography; local topography. Cata: 2 a year. VAT No: DE 127 437 886.

BAD DÜRKHEIM

Antiquariat Blüm, Weinstrasse Süd 10, 67098 Bad Dürkheim. Tel: (06322) 2846. Fax: 62245. Est: 1973. Shop; open Thursday and Friday 3–6.30, Saturday 9.30–1 or by appointment. Medium stock.

BAD HONNEF

Antiquariat Konrad Meuschel, Hauptstrasse 19a, 53604 Bad Honnef 1. Tel: (02224) 78485. Fax: 5642. Est: 1969. Private premises; appointment necessary. Large stock. Spec: 15th- to 18th-century books and manuscripts. Cata: 3 a year. Also, a booksearch service. Corresp: French. Mem: I.L.A.B. VAT No: DE 123 330 710.

GERMANY

BAD KARLSHAFEN

Antiquariat Bernhard Schäfer, Conradistrasse 2, 34385 Bad Karlshafen.

BAD NEUENAHR

A. Müller–Feldmann, Telegrafenstrasse 21, 53473 Bad Neuenahr. Prop: AnneMarie Müller-Feldman. Tel: (02641) 26339. Fax: 28795. Est: 1967. Shop; open 10–12 and 3–6, Saturday 10–1. Large general stock. Spec: animals; atlases; cartography; decorative art; fashion & costume; geography; general & local topography; wine. PR: DM50–1,500. CC: EC; V; DC.

BAD SODEN

Oliver Klein, Am Carlusbaum 18, 65812 Bad Soden. Tel: (06196) 63983. Fax: 641011. E-Mail: 100517.116@compuserve.com. Est: 1990. Private premises; postal business only. Very small general stock. PR: £10–1,000. CC: EC; V; DC; AE; JCB. Want-lists despatched depending on demand. Primarily a book-locating service for books from more than 90 countries. Corresp: Spanish, French, German. VAT No: DE 175 658 074.

Antiquariat Horst-Joachim von Nolting, Oranienstrasse 16, Postfach 2168, 65803 Bad Soden. Tel: (06196) 23832 or 24892. Fax: 28769. Est 1978. Shop; appointment necessary. Small stock. Spec: applied art; architecture; art history; art reference; artists; illustrated; sculpture. Cata: 5 a year on specialities. Corresp: French. Mem: V.D.A.; I.L.A.B. VAT No: DE 114 296 490.

BAD VILBEL

Dieter W. Berger, Geowissenschaftl. Literatur, Pommernweg 1, 61118 Bad Vilbel. Tel: & Fax: (06101) 84630. Est: 1977. Private premises; appointment necessary. Large stock. Spec: geology; mineralogy; palaeontology; prehistory; mining. Cata: 1 a year. Also, large print books and new books in specialities. Corresp: German. VAT No: DE 112 204 016.

BADEN-BADEN

Valentin Koerner GmbH, H. Sielckenstrasse 36, Postfach 304, 76482 Baden-Baden.

Galerie Elfriede Wirnitzer, Haus Lauschan, Lilienmattstrasse 6, 76530 Baden-Baden.

BADENWEILER

Antiquariat L. Sasse, Kaiserstrasse 1, 79410 Badenweiler. Tel: (07632) 1355. Medium stock.

BAMBERG

Antiquariat Kohr, Zinkenwöerth 9, 96047 Bamberg. Prop: Adolf Kohr. Tel: (0951) 28629. Fax: 22972. Est: 1970. Shop; open Monday, Tuesday, Thursday and Friday 9–1 & 3–6, Wednesday 9–12, Saturday 10–12. Medium stock. Spec: Bavarian topography.

Antiquariat Murr, Karolinenstrasse 4, 96049 Bamberg.

BARGFELD

Das Bücherhaus, Im Beckfeld 48, 29351 Bargfeld/Celle. Prop: Hermann Wiedenroth. Tel: (05148) 1248. Fax: 4232. Shop and storeroom; appointment necessary. Very large stock. Spec: general literature; illustrated; history; memoirs; biographies; art and craft; general science. PR: DM10–30,000. Cata: 8 to 10 a year. Also, publisher (collected works of Karl May, Friedrich Rückert and Hans Wollschläger). Corresp: German. Mem: V.D.A.; I.L.A.B. VAT No: DE 115 113 419:

BAYREUTH

Antiquariat Walter Bösch, Carl–Schüller–Str. 9, 95444 Bayreuth. Tel: (0921) 82196. Est: 1988. Shop; open Tuesday to Friday 12–6, Saturday 10–1. Medium stock. Spec: alpinism/mountaineering; countries; history; history of civilization; music; sport; topography; general travel; biology. PR: DM5–500. Corresp: German.

Uni–Buchladen Peter Kohler, Emil–Warburg–Weg 28, 95447 Bayreuth. Tel: (0921) 58757. Fax: 58331. E-Mail: a1651@freenet.uni-bayreuth.de. Shop; open Monday to Friday 10–6. Spec: science. Mem: B.D.B. VAT No: DE 132 315 092.

GERMANY

BEDBURG-HAU

Antiquariat Gebrüder Haas oHG, Sonnenblick 8a, Postfach 70, Bedburg-Hau.

BEDBURG/ERFT

Marianne Schmidt, Bahnstrasse 10, 50181 Bedburg/Erft. Fax: (02272) 81390. Est: 1990. Private premises. Large stock. Spec: banking; business studies; documents; economics; industrial history; industry; mining; railways; technical. PR: DM15–5,000. Cata: 3 or 4 a year. Corresp: German.

BERGISCH GLADBACH

Bergische Bücherstube Antiquariat u. Versandbuchandel, Hauptstrasse 247, 51465 Bergisch Gladbach. Tel: (2202) 932160. Fax: 932170. Est: 1985. Shop and storeroom; open 10–6. Very large stock. Spec: architecture; archives; art; art history; bibliography; bindings; general & local history; military; paper-making; philosophy; politics; publishers; social history; typography; war. PR: DM50–1,000. Cata: 5–8 a year. Also, a booksearch service. Corresp: German, French. VAT No: DE 122 063 659.

BERLIN

Antiquariat Knut Ahnert, Sybelstrasse 58, 10629 Berlin. Cata: 6 or 7 a year. Mem: B.V.A. VAT No: DE 135 608 733.

Antiquariat der Karl–Marx–Buchhandlung, Karl–Marx Allee 78, 10243 Berlin. Prop: Drs. Kundel & Lenzner. Tel: (030) 2933370. Fax: 29333755. Est: 1953. Shop; open Monday to Friday 10–6.30, Saturday 9–2. Medium stock. Spec: antiquarian; architecture; art; art history; first editions; illustrated; literature; philosophy; politics; psychology/psychiatry; signed editions; social history; social sciences; socialism; technical. PR: DM5–500. Cata: 4 a year. Also, a booksearch service. Corresp: German, Spanish.

Antiquariat Matthias Severin, Meranerstrasse 6, 10825 Berlin. Tel: (030) 8546545. Est: 1982. Shop; open Monday to Friday 12–6.30. Very large stock. Spec: alpinism; the arts; astronomy; botany; broadcasting; chemistry; chess; countries & continents; economics; education; erotica; geography; history; literature; military; natural sciences; politics; religion; sexology; theology; travel.

Antiquariat Mitte, Rungestrasse 20, 10179 Berlin. Prop: F. Martens & O. Zander. Tel: & Fax: (030) 2795355. Est: 1993. Shop; open Monday to Friday 12–6. Large stock. Spec: literature; history; politics; art; geography; philosophy; architecture; criminal history; erotica. Cata: 2 a year. Corresp: German, French, Italian.

Das Arabische Buch–Antiquariat, Horstweg 2, 14059 Berlin. Prop: Schiler & Martin. Tel: (030) 3228523. Fax: 3225183. Est: 1969. Shop; open 10–6. Medium stock. Spec: anthropology; archaeology; calligraphy; carpets; ceramics; colonial; foreign culture; diaries; early imprints; Egyptology; ethnography; ethnology; travel guides; illustrated; foreign languages; mythology; politics; Jewish and Oriental religion - especially Islam; travel - Africa, Asia, Middle East; university texts. PR: £10–500. CC: EC; MC; V; DC. Cata: 2 a year. Also, a booksearch service, publisher and distributor. Corresp: German, Arabic, French, Persian. Mem: B.V.D. VAT No: DE 136 616 403.

Ars Amandi, Poschingerstrasse 10, 12157 Berlin. Prop: Mrs. Gesine Karge. Tel: (030) 8553452. Fax: 79702243. Est: 1993. Storeroom & private premises; open Tuesday to Friday 2–7. Medium stock. Spec: bibliography; criminology; erotica; homosexuality; illustrated; limited editions; miniature books; periodicals/magazines; photography; sexology; women; nudism. PR: DM100–3,000. Cata: 4 illustrated a year, plus lists. Also, a booksearch service, erotic art and objects, pin–up magazines and curiosa. Corresp: German, French. VAT No: DE 175 186 263.

Antiquariat Torsten Baland, Siegmunds Hof 21, 1000 Berlin 21.

Galerie Gerda Bassenge, Erdener Strasse 5a, 14193 Berlin.

Berlin-Antiquariat, Zimmermannstrasse 17, 12163 Berlin - Steglite. Prop: Karl-Heinz Than. Tel: & Fax: (030) 7920520. Est: 1982. Shop; open Monday to Friday 3–6.30 and Saturday 10–2. Very large stock. Spec: architecture; general fiction; fine & rare; history; newspapers; science; topography; travel. PR: £10–10,000. Cata: regularly on general and specific subjects. Also, a booksearch service. Corresp: French. VAT No: DE 136 153 475.

Antiquariat Sibylle Böhme, Am Volkspark 83, 10715 Berlin.

Wolfgang Braecklein, Antiquariat, Ortsteil Friedenau, Dickhardstrasse 48, 12159 Berlin.

Antiquariat Bücherkeller, Hauptstrasse 103, 10827 Berlin.

Bürck (vormals Kohls), Winterfeldtstrasse 44, 10781 Berlin-Schöneberg. Prop: Erick Bürck. Tel: (030) 2164528. Fax: 2154541. Est: 1939. Shop; open Monday to Friday 11–6.30 and Saturday 10–2. Very large stock. PR: DM3–3,000. CC: AE; V; EC; DC. Also, a booksearch service.

Antiquariat an den Ceciliengärten, Rubensstrasse 14, 12159 Berlin (Friedenau). Prop: Volker Kunze. Tel: (030) 8521025. Fax: 8529972. Shop; open Wednesday to Friday 3–6.30. Medium stock. Spec: photography.

Don Vincente – Versand–Antiquariat, Katherinenstrasse 6, 10711 Berlin. Prop: Peter Ober. Tel: & Fax: (030) 8915679. Est: 1985. Private premises; postal business only. Large stock. Spec: literature; Judaica; politics; philosophy; criminology; architecture; science fiction; children's; music; socialism; voyages & discovery. Cata: 2 a year on specialities.

Antiquariat Düwal, Ortsteil Charlottenburg, Schlüterstrasse 17, 10625 Berlin.

Fair Exchange, Dieffenbachstrasse 58, 10967 Berlin. Prop: Ms. Hanson. Tel: (030) 6944675. Est: 1986. Shop; open Monday to Friday 11–6.30, Saturday 10–2. Large stock. Spec: English books. PR: DM1–100. Corresp: German.

Antiquariat Eckhard Fluck, Tegeler Weg 6, 10589 Berlin. Tel: (030) 3441921. Est: 1984. Shop; open Monday to Friday 2–6.30. Medium stock. Spec: author - Carmen Sylva; chemistry; children's; encyclopaedias; national history; motoring; natural sciences; physics; mathematics; railways; horse-riding; technical; travel. PR: DM1–2,500. Corresp: German.

Fontane–Antiquariat, Ebersstrasse 59, 1000 Berlin 62. Prop: Dr. Henning Scheffers. Tel: (030) 7823331. Fax: 7885329. Est: 1985. Shop; open Thursday and Friday 3–6, Saturday 12–2. Large stock. Spec: sets; first editions; German literature; art. Cata: 1 a year. Corresp: French.

Friedenauer Antiquariat, Cranachstrasse 8, 12157 Berlin. Prop: Juergen Klette. Tel: (030) 8556781. Est: 1984. Shop; open Monday to Friday 1–6.30. Very large stock. Spec: circus; feminism; history; geography; illustrated; linguistics; literary criticism; literature; theatre; theology. PR: 50p–£100. Cata: 12 a year. Also, records. Corresp: French, Chinese.

R. Friedländer & Sohn GmbH, Schlesische Strasse 26, Aufg. A., 10997 Berlin.

Antiquariat Bernd Gärtner, Richard-Wagner-Strasse 17, 10585 Berlin. Tel: (030) 3421250. Est: 1969. Storeroom; postal business only. Medium stock. Spec: anthroposophy; bibles; ecclesiastical history & architecture; gnostics; mythology; philosophy; psychoanalysis; psychology/psychiatry; religion - general, Christian, Jewish and Oriental; social sciences; socialism; theology. PR: DM30–5,000. Cata: 2 to 4 a year. Also, a booksearch service.

Antiquariat Gothow und Motzke, Friedelstrasse 52, 12047 Berlin. Prop: Wolfgang Gothow. Tel: & Fax: (030) 7559351. Est: 1981. Shop & storeroom; open Monday to Friday 2–6, Saturday 10–1. Medium stock. Spec: Oriental sciences; Christian, Jewish, Oriental and general religion; travel - Africa, Americas, Asia, Australasia/Australia; Europe, Middle East, Polar and general; foreign and national languages; ethnography; ethnology; linguistics. PR: £5–500. Cata: 3 to 5 a year - regularly on Oriental sciences, linguistics, ethnology (1 a year). Also, a large stock of Soviet/Russian scientific books. Corresp: French, Persian, Arabic, Russian. VAT No: DE 154 390 2930.

Antiquariat in den Hackeschen Höfen, Rosenthaler Str. 40/41, Hof 4, 10178 Berlin. Prop: Oliver Kaemper & Christian Scherfling. Tel: & Fax: (030) 2829027. Shop; open Tuesday to Sunday 12–8. Large stock. Spec: art; circus; local and national history; theatre; local topography; literature. PR: DM10–500. Also, a booksearch service (theatre). Corresp: German, French.

Buch- und Kunstantiquariat Marcus Haucke, Osnabrücker Strasse 26, 10589 Berlin. Tel: & Fax: (030) 3451427. Open Monday to Friday 10–6.30 (Wednesday closed), Saturday 10–2. Large stock. Spec: Marcus Behmer; Georgica; Judaica; the arts; illustrated; fine art; Catalogues Raisonées; graphic art; first editions. PR: DM80–100. Cata: 3 or 4 a year. Also, a booksearch service. VAT No: DE 135 528 194.

Antiquariat H. Hentrich, Plantagenstrasse 21, 12169 Berlin-Steglitz.

Hinterhof–Antiquariat, Czarnikauer Strasse 19, 10439 Berlin. Prop: Abel Doering. Tel: & Fax: (030) 4457891. E-Mail: hinterhof-antiquariat@t-online.de. Est: 1990. Shop; open Tuesday to Friday 12–6.30, Saturday 10–2. Large stock. Spec: philosophy; literature; politics; national history (GDR). PR: DM1–100. Mem: Pirckheimer Gesellscheft e.v. *Also at:* Drièsener Strasse 13, Berlin.

Antiquariat Rolf & Monika Ihring, Winterfeldtstrasse 46 & 56, 10781 Berlin (Schoneberg).

Hans Horst Koch, Kurfürstendamm 216, 10719 Berlin (Charlottenburg).

GERMANY

Antiquariat Lässig & Jeschke, Pariser Strasse 14, 10719 Berlin. Tel: (030) 8835430. Fax: 8852008. Est: 1993. Shop; open Monday to Friday 11–4, Saturday 11–1. Large stock. Spec: antiquarian; bibliography; Jewish religion; war; literature; criminology; Holocaust; travel; history; psychoanalysis; psychology/ psychiatry. PR: DM50–5,000. Cata: 5 or 6 a year. Corresp: German. VAT No: DE 153 642 869.

Antiquariat Lange und Springer GmbH & Co., Otto-Suhr-Allee 26–28, 10585 Berlin.

Antiquariat & Buchhandlung Michael Lehr, Niedstrasse 24, 12159 Berlin.

Antiquariat Mertens & Pomplun, Grossbeerenstrasse 83, 1000 Berlin 61.

Musik Antiquariat, Landschuter Strasse 26, 10779 Berlin. Prop: Dr. Werner Greve. Tel: (030) 2114731. Fax: 2188313. Est: 1992. Private premises. Small stock. Spec: music; dance. PR: DM20–20,000. Cata: 1 or 2 a year. Corresp: German. VAT No: DE 165 523 959.

Galerie Nierendorf, Hardenbergstrasse 19, 10623 Berlin. Prop: Florian Karsch. Tel: (030) 8325013. Fax: 3129327. Open Tuesday to Friday 11–6, Monday and Saturday by appointment. Cata: 2 a year. Also, works by German Expressionists at the beginning of the 20th century. VAT No: DE 135 527 255.

Antiquariat für Occulta und Masonica, Roseggerstrasse 48, 12043 Berlin 44.

Librairie George Omen, Mommsenstrasse 17, 10629 Berlin (Charlottenburg). Tel: & Fax: (030) 3245215. Est: 1965. Shop & private premises; appointment necessary. Large stock. Spec: art; ecology; geography; history; limited editions; literature; military; mythology; occult; pacifism; philosophy; poetry; politics; psychology; science; theology; transport; war; witchcraft; women. PR: DM1–10,000. Cata: 4 a year and on demand. Also, a booksearch service and large print books. Corresp: German, French, Spanish. Mem: Chamber of Trade & Commerce. VAT No: DE 135 527 441.

Gisela Plähn Russica-Slavica, Innsbruckerstrasse 4, 10825 Berlin. Tel: (030) 8543035. Est: 1977. Storeroom; appointment necessary. Medium stock. Spec: Russica and Slavica. Cata: 4 to 6 a year. Corresp: French, Russian, Polish.

Musikalienhandlung Hans Riedel GmbH, Uhlandstrasse 38, 10719 Berlin. Tel: (030) 8827395. Fax: 8832725. Shop; open Monday to Saturday. Very large stock. CC: V; MC; AE; DC. Corresp: French. Mem: B.D.B. VAT No: DE 136 694 133.

Buchhandlung und Antiquariat Rosenfeld, Drakestrasse 35a, 12205 Berlin.

Antiquariat Schomaker, Niedstrasse 24, 12159 Berlin.

Versandantiquariat Schrottmeyer, Königswinterstrasse 12, 10318 Berlin. Tel: (030) 5099382. Est: 1993. Market stand and storeroom; appointment necessary. Very small stock. Spec: architecture; literature; Expressionism; philosophy; first editions. PR: DM25–150. Cata: 1 or 2 a year. Also, a booksearch service and organise flea–markets. Corresp: German.

Bücherhalle Antiquariat Schwarz, Hauptstrasse 154, 10827 Berlin. Tel: (030) 7815669. Fax: 31503403. Est: 1976. Shop; open Monday to Friday 10.30–6.30, Saturday 10.30–2. Very large general stock. PR: DM1–1,000. Cata: 1 a year.

Peter Schwarz Antiquariat, Garmerstrasse 11, 10623 Berlin (Charlottenburg). Tel: (030) 3125654. Fax: 31503403. Est: 1976. Shop; open Monday to Friday 12–6.30, Thursday 12–8, Saturday 10–2. Large stock. Spec: aeronautics; antiquarian; architecture; art; art history; art reference; artists; the arts; autobiography; aviation; bibliography; books about books; carpets; Catalogues Raisonées; children's; cookery/gastronomy; first editions; illustrated theatre. CC: EC. Cata: 1 a year.

Bookstore & Antiquariat Maria Stadnik, Kantstrasse 39/Leibnizstrasse 70, 10625 Berlin (Charlottenburg). Tel: & Fax: (030) 3130430 and 3245215. Est: 1950. Shop; open Monday to Friday 9–6, Saturday 9–1 and by appointment. Very large stock. Spec: almanacs; antiquarian; antiques; art; atlases/cartography; author - George Omen; Catalogues Raisonées; collecting; colonial; firearms; geography; history; limited editions; literture; military; numismatics; philately; science; toys; transport. PR: DM1–20,000. CC: yes. Cata: 4 a year; specials on demand. Also, a booksearch service and large print books. Corresp: German, Spanish, French, Russian. Mem: Chamber of Industry & Commerce. VAT No: DE 135 527 441.

J.A. Stargardt, Clausewitzstrasse 4, 10629 Berlin. Prop: Klaus & Wolfgang Mecklenburg. Tel: (030) 8822542. Fax: 8822466. Est: 1830. Open Monday to Friday 9–5. Medium stock. Spec: autographs; manuscripts; documents; genealogy; heraldry; letters. Cata: 2 or 3 a year on specialities. Corresp: French, German. Mem: I.L.A.B.; V.D.A. VAT No: DE 113 354 098.

Antiquariat Wolfgang Staschen, Potsdamerstrasse 138 10783 Berlin.

Stefan Graf Finck v. Finckenstein, Badensche Strasse 6, 10825 Berlin-Schöneberg. Tel: (030) 8533095. Fax: 8533099. Private premises; appointment necessary. Small stock. Spec: antiques; autographs; genealogy; heraldry. Corresp: German.

Struppe und Winckler, Potsdamerstrasse 103, 10785 Berlin.

Unterwegs– Versandantiquariat M.–L. Surek–Becker, Tieckstrasse 37, 10115 Berlin. Tel: & Fax: (030) 2832932. Storeroom; open Monday to Friday 2–6. Medium stock. Spec: Karl Baedeker; antiquarian; geography; travel guides; photography; travel - general, Africa, Americas, Asia, Australasia/Australia, Europe, Middle East, Polar. PR: DM1–10,000. Cata: 3 to 5 a year. Corresp: German. VAT No: DE 154 212 671.

Antiquariat Elvira Tasbach, Schweinfurthstrasse 76, 14195 Berlin-Dahlem. Prop: Elvira Meran. Tel: (030) 8242289. Fax: 8236463. Est: 1987. Storeroom; appointment necessary. Medium stock. Spec: banking; economics; feminism; industry; law; politics; philosophy; social sciences; socialism. PR: £5–7,000. Cata: 4 a year on economics, political theory, law, socialism, social sciences. Corresp: French. VAT No: DE 135 671 621.

TausendundeinBuch, Gneisenaustrasse 60, 10965 Berlin BRD.

Wasmuth Buchhandlung & Antiquariat GmbH & Co., Postfach 10598 Berlin.

Antiquariat & Buchhandlung Carl Wegner, Martin-Luther-Strasse 113, 10825 Berlin. Prop: Carlos Kühn. Tel: (030) 7822491. Est: 1956. Shop; open Monday to Friday 2–6, Saturday 10–1. Large stock. Cata: occasionally.

Kerstin Weiss Buchhandel (Books & Prints), Reuchlinstrasse 2, 10553 Berlin. Tel: (030) 3453862; (0177) 2317764. Fax: (030) 3453492. Est: 1995. Private premises; appointment necessary. Small general stock. Spec: arts; history; culture of Japan; and highlights on outstanding historical events and persons; literature; literary criticism; translations; travel; explorations; university texts; rare books; periodicals. Cata: 2 or 3 a year on specialities. Also, swordblades, swordfittings, Japanese and Oriental works of art and a booksearch service. Corresp: German. VAT No: DE 167 861 090.

Antiquariat Zerfass & Linke, Apostel Paulus Strasse 30, 10823 Berlin.

Antiquariat Ziegan, Johanna–Stegen–Str. 14, 12167 Berlin–Steglitz. Tel: & Fax: (030) 7715448. Spec: botany; zoology.

GERMANY

BIELEFELD

Antiquariat Granier GmbH, Welle 9, 33602 Bielefeld. Prop: Jochen Granier. Tel: (0521) 67148. Fax: 67146. Est: 1970. Shop; open Tuesday to Friday 10–1 & 3–6, Saturday 10–1. Medium stock. Spec: illustrated; literature; Westphalia. Cata: 2 a year. Also, auctioneers. Mem: V.D.A.

Jochen Granier, Buch- und Kunstauktionen, Otto–Brenner–Str. 186, 33604 Bielefeld. Tel: (0521) 285005. Fax: 285015. E-Mail: buch + kunst@granier.de. Est: 1980. Open Monday to Friday 8–1 and 2–5. General stock. PR: DM200–100,000. Cata: 2 a year. Also, auction sales. Corresp: German. Mem: V.D.A.; B.D.K. VAT No: DE 123 996 457.

Versandantiquariat Theodor Walpurgius, Im Hagen 29, 33739 Bielefeld. Tel: (05206) 8629. Fax: 8615. Est: 1985. Storeroom; appointment necessary. Medium general stock. Spec: military history 1850 to present. PR: DM1–1,000. Cata: 10 a year.

BOCHOLT

Bücher Mammut, Antiquariat Rainer Heeke, Haus Woord, Münsterstrasse 13, 46397 Bocholt. Tel: (02871) 183218. Fax: 225106. Shop; open Monday to Saturday 10–1 and 3–7. Medium stock. Spec: Oriental; literature; art; religion. PR: all prices. Cata: 2 a year. Corresp: German, Dutch. Mem: Boekenstad Bredevoort.

BOCHUM

Psychologie–Antiquariat Dr. Hermann Feuerhelm, Rautenbergstrasse 7a, 44797 Bochum. Tel: (0234) 797217. Fax: 793841. Est: 1989. Storeroom and private premises. Fax orders: 24 hours, no shop or regular times. Medium stock. Spec: psychology, especially academic psychology. Cata: several thematic quoting lists a year. Also, a booksearch service. Corresp: German. VAT No: DE 126 894 164.

Antiquariat Lorych, Willy-Brandt-Platz 8, 44787 Bochum. Prop: Susanne Lorych. Tel: (0234) 682421. Shop; open Monday to Friday 11–5.30, Saturday 10–1. Spec: German literature; history; children's; geography; sport; travel guides; antiquarian. Always interested in any Struwwel Peter editions. PR: 50p–£1,000. Cata: 4 a year. Mem: P.B.F.A. VAT No: DE 126 702 298.

BONN

Antiquariat–Buchhandlung–Verlag, Postfach 150104, 53040 Bonn. Prop: Wolfgang Habelt. Tel: (0228) 232015; 232016. Fax: 232017. Est: 1948. Storeroom; open Monday to Friday 8–5. Very large stock. Spec: archaeology; classical philology. PR: DM1–1,000. CC: MC; V. Cata: 6 a year. Mem: B.D.B. VAT No: DE 122 113 397.

Auktionshaus Bödiger, Franziskanerstrasse 17–19, 53113 Bonn. Prop: Walter Fischer. Tel: (0228) 604200. Fax: 6042099. E-Mail: 73563.271@compuserve.com. Est: 1947. Shop; open Monday to Friday 9–1 and 2.30–6. Very small stock. Spec: antiques; art; art history; art reference. Cata: 2 a year. Also, antiques and East Asian art. Corresp: German. Mem: B.D.K.; R.K.V.; Z.I.N.O.A.; B.D.K.A.

Versandantiquariat Dr. Rainer Brockmann, Ginsterweg 28, 53757 Sankt Augustin. (•) Tel: (0228) 330713. Fax: 343788. Est: 1984. Private premises; appointment necessary. Small general stock. PR: DM10–1,000. Cata: 1 a year. Also, a booksearch service. Corresp: German, French, Dutch, Spanish. VAT No: DE 153 264 272.

Bücher–Etage, Martinsplatz 1, 53113 Bonn. Prop: Manfred Nosbüsch. Tel: (0228) 638761. Est: 1976. Shop; open Monday to Friday 10–6.30, Saturday 10–2. Very large general stock. Corresp: French. *Also at:* Antiquariat Manfred Nosbüsch, Bonn (q.v.).

Antiquariat Clement, Rathausgasse 18, 53111 Bonn. Prop: Catherine Clement. Tel: (0228) 636622. Fax: 657570. Est: 1979. Shop; open Monday to Friday from 10am. Very large general stock. Spec: local topography; literature; transport; art; gnostics; foreign languages. CC: AE. Corresp: French, Spanish, German. Mem: P.B.F.A.

Buchladen Linz, Alte Bahnhofstrasse 20, Postfach 20 08 54, 53138 Bonn. Prop: Franz W. Moersch. Tel: & Fax: (0228) 362448. Shop; open Monday to Friday 9–12.30 and 2.30-6.30, Saturday 9–1.

Buchhandlung am Bundeshaus. Maderspacher, Hermann Ehlers Str. 20, 53113 Bonn. Prop: Ben Maderspacher. Tel: (0228) 215420. Fax: 263651. Est: 1949. Shop; open Monday to Friday 8–4. Very small stock. Spec: politics; almanacs. Corresp: French, German. Mem: B.D.B. VAT No: DE 178 685 508.

Antiquariat Manfred Nosbüsch, Bonner Talweg 14, 53113 Bonn. Tel: (0228) 229251. Fax: 217591. Est: 1979. Shop; open Monday to Friday 11–6.30, Saturday 10–2. Very large stock. Spec: 18th- to 20th-century literature; humanities; travel; science. Cata: 1 or 2 a year. Corresp: French. Mem: V.D.A. *Also at:* Bücher-Etage, Bonn (q.v.).

Buchhlandung-Antiquariat Sawhney, Reuterstrasse 4a, 53113 Bonn. Prop: Christiane & Jagdev S. Sawhney, PhD. Tel: (0228) 216622. Est: 1986. Shop; open Monday to Friday 9–6.30, Saturday 9–1 (first Saturday in month 9–6). Very large stock. Spec: agriculture; biography; biology; architecture; fine printing; natural sciences; history; travel. CC: AE; EC; V. Cata: irregularly. Corresp: German. Mem: Book Dealers Association of Germany and North Rhein Westfalen. VAT No: DE 122 175 621.

Hanno Schreyer, Euskirchener Strasse 57–59, 53121 Bonn. Prop: Georg Schreyer. Tel: (0228) 621059. TA: Buchschreyer, Bonn. Fax: (0228) 613029. Est: 1953. Shop; appointment necessary. Very large stock. Spec: atlases/cartography; graphic art; illustrated; topography; travel. Corresp: French. Mem: V.D.A. VAT No: DE 122 179 145.

BREMEN

Antiquariat Beim Steinernen Kreuz GmbH, Beim Steinernen Kreuz 1, 28203 Bremen. Prop: Udo Seinsoth. Tel: (0421) 701515. Fax: 72171. Est: 1980. Shop; open Tuesday to Friday 10–1 & 3–6.30, Saturday 10–2. Large stock. Spec: 20th-century literature; art; social history. Cata: 2 a year. Mem: V.D.A. VAT No: DE 114 397 943.

Antiquariat Götz – R. Schmidt, Nernstrasse 16, 28357 Bremen.

Antiquariat im Schnoor, Hinter der Balge 1, 28195 Bremen. Prop: Kurt Lammek. Tel: (0421) 323416. Shop; open Tuesday to Friday 10–1.30 & 3–6, Saturday 10–2. Medium general stock. Cata: 2 a year.

BRUNSWICK (BRAUNSCHWEIG)

W. Brandes, Postfach 1461, Wolfenbüttelerstrasse 12, 38102 Braunschweig. Tel: (0531) 75003. Fax: 75015.

Antiquariat Im Hopfengarten, Hopfengarten 3, 38102 Braunschweig. Booksearch service.

Leseratte Buchladen, Hopfengarten 40, 38102 Braunschweig.

Antiquariat Rabenschwarz, Wendenstrasse 48, 38100 Braunschweig. Prop: Reinhard Denecke. Tel: (0531) 124064. Est: 1990. Shop and storeroom; open Monday to Friday 10–1 and 3–6, Saturday 10–1. Medium stock. Spec: industrial history; books about books; industry; anthroposophy; 20th century literature; philosophy; socialism; university texts (history). PR: DM1–1,000. Cata: 2 a year. Also, a booksearch service and large print books. Corresp: German.

Antiquariat A. Klittich-Pfankuch, Kleine Burg 12, 38100 Braunschweig.

CHEMNITZ

Antiquariat Max Müller, Postfach 229, 09002 Chemnitz. Prop: Gottfried Müller. Tel: (0371) 62416. Fax: 671437. Est: 1913. Shop at: Reitbahnstr. 23a, 09111 Chemnitz; open Monday to Friday 9–18, Saturday 9–1. Medium stock. Spec: art; the arts; history; history of civilisation; theology; philosophy. Cata: 3 a year on theology, art, history, history of civilisation and philosophy. Also, new books and craft items. Mem: Börsenverein des Deutschen Buchhandel.

COBURG

Antiquariat am Markt. Siegfried-H. Hirsch, Steingasse 4, 96450 Coburg. Tel: (0956) 192996. Fax: 190535. E-Mail: buechersuchdienst@t-online.de. Shop. Small stock. Spec: House of Coburg. PR: DM10–1,000. CC: V; DC; AE; EC. Also, a booksearch service and large print books. Corresp: German. VAT No: DE 132 417 623.

COLOGNE (KÖLN)

Versandantiquariat Bogdanou & Siebert, Inh. Maria Bogdanou, Krefelder Strasse 97 a, 50670 Köln. Prop: Maria Bogdanou. Tel: (0221) 7391881. Fax: 728976. E-Mail: Bogdanou@link-lev.dinoco-de. Est: 1993. Medium stock. Spec: Eastern and South Eastern Europe; gypsies. PR: DM18–28. Cata: 24 a year. Corresp: German, Russian, Greek, French, Polish, Belarusan, Ukrainian. Mem: B.D.B. VAT No: DE 161 539 593.

Buch Gourmet, Buchhandlung & Antiquariat fur Kochen, Essen & Trinken, Hohenzollernring 16–18, 50672 Köln. Prop: Dieter K. Eckel. Tel: (0221) 2574072. Fax: 255305. E-Mail: 100732.1756@compuserve.com. Est: 1987. Shop; open Monday to Friday 9–6.30, Saturday 9–2. Small stock. Spec: only cookery/gastronomy. PR: DM30–1,000. CC: V; EC; AE; DC. Cata: 4 a year. Also, new books from all over the world on specialist subject and a booksearch service. Corresp: French. Mem: B.V.D.B. VAT No. DE 122 743 759.

Antiquariat Buchholz, Neuen Dumontstrasse 17, 50667 Köln. Prop: Daniel Buchholz. Tel: (0221) 2576251. Fax: 253351. Est: 1968. Shop; open Monday to Friday 10–6.30, Saturday 10–2. Large stock. Spec: art; children's; cookery/ gastronomy; illustrated; tobacco; literature; medicine; general and local topography. PR: DM5–20,000. CC: All. Cata: 3 a year. Corresp: German. VAT No: DE 169 881 230.

Jürgen Dinter, Buchholzstrasse 8–10, 51061 Köln. Tel: (0221) 646001. Fax: 646018. Est: 1982. Private premises; appointment necessary. Small stock. Spec: philosophy; incunabula. Cata: 2 or 3 a year. Corresp: French, Italian. Mem: I.L.A.B.

Antiquariat Gundel Gelbert, St.-Apern-Strasse 4, 50667 Köln. Tel: (0221) 2576131. Fax: 254885. Premises; open Monday to Friday 11–6.30, Saturday 10–2. Small stock. Spec: 18th- to 20th-century literature in first editions and sets; fine and illustrated; art; history of civilisation. Cata: 1 a year. Mem: V.D.A. VAT No: DE 122 763 138.

Kunstandlung Goyert, Hahnenstrasse 18, 50667 Köln.

Antiquariat Heuberger, Postfach 21 04 46, 50530 Köln.

Antiquariat Kleinsorge, Dürener Strasse 92, 50931 Köln. Prop: Reinhard Kleinsorge. Tel: & Fax: (0221) 407566. Est: 1993. Shop. Small stock. Spec: literature; philosophy; art. PR: DM10–1,000.

Antiquariat Lésabendio, Gereonswall 5, 50668 Köln. Prop: Gertrud Klefisch & Helmuth Kahle. Tel: (0221) 136303. Est: 1992. Shop; open Monday to Friday 2–6.30, Saturday 11–2. Small stock. Spec: literature; art. Corresp: German, Italian.

Versandantiquariat Hans–Joachim Loose, Vor den Siebenburgen 38–42, 50676 Köln. Tel: (0221) 324545. Fax: 324746. Est: 1978. Private premises; open 3–6. Small stock. Spec: academic; fencing; university texts. PR: DM10–10,000. Cata: 1 a year. Corresp: German. Mem: IHK Köln (Industrie- und Handelskammer).

Mare Balticum, Inh. Helker Pflug, Huhnsgasse 39–41, 50676 Köln. Tel: & Fax: (0221) 214996. Est: 1990. Shop & storeroom; open Monday to Friday 9–6. Small stock. Spec: Baltic states (Estonia, Latvia, Lithuania); Eastern Europe; antiquarian; art; art history; atlases/cartography; dictionaries; ecclesiastical history & architecture; first editions; foreign texts; genealogy; travel guides; general & national history; Holocaust; foreign languages; literature; literature in translation; memoirs; Middle Ages; photography; poetry; politics; Christian & Jewish religion; social history; travel - Europe; university texts. CC: V. Cata: 6 a year. Also, a publishing house. Corresp: German. VAT No: DE 126 269 9937.

Maternus Buchhandel & Verlag GmbH & Co. KG, Severinstrasse 76, 50678 Köln.

Galerie Orangerie-Reinz GmbH, Helenenstrasse 2, 50667 Köln.

C. Roemke & Cie., Apostelnstrasse 7, 50667 Köln. Tel: (0221) 2573717. Fax: 2584565. Est: 1865. Shop; open Monday to Friday 10–6. Spec: theology (Protestant); Iceland. Cata: 1 a year. VAT No: DE 122 776 087.

Antiquariat Memoria Schumann, Kiefernweg 11, (-Efferen), 50354 Hürth, Near Köln. Prop: R. Schumann. Tel: (02233) 67282. Est: 1986. Private premises; appointment by telephone only (in the afternoon). Medium stock. Spec: literature; literature in translation; art; travel; illustrated; almanacs; architecture; autobiography; autographs; caricature; cartoons; feminism; first editions; travel guides; history; music; philosophy; poetry; psychoanalysis; psychology/psychiatry; signed editions; socialism; technology. PR: DM20–500. Cata: 2 a year. Also, publishers of German exile literature 1533–45. Corresp: German, French.

Siegfried Unverzagt, Limburger Strasse 10, 50672 Köln. Tel: (0221) 251515. Fax: 251344. E-Mail: buchsuche@aol.com. Est: 1982. Shop; open Tuesday to Friday 11–6.30, Saturday 11–2. Very large general stock. PR: DM10–2,000. Cata: 1 or 2 a year plus special catalogues on request. Also, a booksearch service and information on the Internet http://members.aol.com/buchsuche/info.html.

Venator & Hanstein KG, Cäcilienstrasse 48, (Haus Lempertz), 50667 Köln. Prop: Rolf Venator, H.R. Hanstein & K.H. Knupfer. Tel: (0221) 2575419. Fax: 2575526. Shop; open Tuesday to Friday 10–1 and 2.30–6, Saturday 10–1. Very small stock. Cata: 1 or 2 a year for auctions. VAT No: DE 122 649 294.

Versandantiquariat Peter Weber, Mauritiussteinweg 108, 50676 Köln. Tel: (0221) 241384. Fax: 249193. Shop; open Monday to Friday 10–6.30, Thursday until 8.30, Saturday 10–2. Very large stock. Spec: aviation; books about books; ethnology; general and industrial history; Holocaust; sport; travel - general, Asia; voyages & discovery; hunting. Cata: 10–15 catalogues/small lists a year. Corresp: written Japanese only. VAT No: DE 122 893 163.

Versandantiquariat Gertrud Weiermüller, Beethovenstrasse 24, 50674 Köln.

CONSTANCE (KONSTANZ)

Patzer & Trenkle, Postfach 10 15 41, 78415 Konstanz. Tel: (07531) 21337. Fax: 16256. Est: 1986. Shop at: Hussenstr. 45, 78462 Konstanz; open Monday to Friday 10–6.30, Saturday 10–2. Large stock. Spec: aeronautics; astronomy; aviation; children's; South Western Germany; local history; juvenile. PR: DM30–2,000. Cata: 8 a year. Corresp: German. Mem: I.L.A.B.; V.D.A. VAT No: DE 142 307 223.

DARMSTADT

Elisabeth Wellnitz, Sachsenstrasse 35, 64297 Darmstadt. Tel: & Fax: (06151) 54716. Est: 1959. Private premises; appointment necessary. Very small stock. Spec: history; politics; military. Cata: 2 a year.

DETTINGEN

Antiquariat Banzhaf, Neuffener Strasse 34, 72581 Dettingen. Prop: Michael Banzhaf. Tel: (07073) 4786. Fax: 4567. Est: 1988. Private premises; appointment necessary. Very small stock. Spec: atlases/cartography; bibliography; children's; books about books; printing; fine and rare. PR: £50–3,000. Cata: 2 a year on children's, atlases and bibliography. Corresp: German, French. VAT No: DE 147 148 385.

DIESSEN

Versandantiquariat Otto H. Bauer, Buzallee 43, Postfach 11 33, 86907 Diessen. Prop: Otto Heinrich Bauer. Tel: (08807) 1819. Est: 1987. Private premises. Large stock. Spec: antiquarian; alpinism/mountaineering; art; children's; first editions; travel guides; illustrated; literature; travel. PR: DM10–2,000. Cata: 2 or 3 a year. Corresp: German, French, Italian.

DORTMUND

Reiseantiquariat Dietmar Hübner, Stolzestrasse 23/25, 44139 Dortmund. Tel: (0231) 103071. Est: 1989. Market stand and storeroom; open at weekends (market events). Small general stock. Spec: cultural history; technical; topography. PR: DM5–500. Cata: small lists, irregularly. Corresp: French, Spanish.

Antiquariat & Kunsthandlung Huste, Liebigstrasse 46–48, 44139 Dortmund. Prop: Wolfgang & Khamssa Huste. Tel: & Fax: (0231) 122638. Est: 1988. Shop; open 10–1 and 2–6.30. Large stock. Spec: art; literature; graphics; history. PR: DM10–10,000. Also, a booksearch service, large print books and two book auctions a year. Corresp: German, French, Arabic. VAT No: DE 124 676 114. *Also at:* Steinweg 11, 59821 Arnsberg *and* Goldbergstr. 17, 58095 Hagen (q.v.).

Kunsthandlung Kirchner, Hoher Wall 30, 44137 Dortmund. Prop: Rainer Kirchner. Tel: & Fax: (0231) 149957. Est: 1980. Shop; open Tuesday to Friday 10–1 and 3–6, Saturday 10–1. Small general stock. PR: DM5–2,000. Corresp: German, Portuguese. VAT No: DE 124 647 582.

DRESDEN

Antiquariat Hamm, Stephensonstrasse 35, 01257 Dresden. Prop: Mr. Helge Hamm. Tel: (0351) 2021771. Est: 1990. Shop; open Monday to Friday 2–6. Medium stock. Spec: authors - Karl May and Zane Grey; cookery/gastronomy; geography; history; juvenile; local topography; travel; voyages & discovery; adventure books in German (Indians, Wild West). PR: DM20–500. Also, a booksearch service.

Historica–Antiquariat Bert Wawrzinek, Helgolandstrasse 17, 01097 Dresden. Tel: (0351) 4114757. Est: 1990. Shop; open Monday to Friday 10–1 and 3–6. Large stock. Spec: aeronautics; art; biography; general, local and national history; history of civilization; military; politics; general and local topography; travel. Corresp: German. VAT No: DE 140 285 525.

DÜSSELDORF

Antiquariat Ahrens & Hamacher, Friedrichstrasse 104, 40217 Düsseldorf. Tel: (0211) 318960. Fax: 334563. Est: 1986. Shop; open Monday to Friday 10–6, Saturday 10–2. Large stock. Spec: biography; general, local and national history; literature; literature in translation; Christian religion. PR: DM1–200. CC: EC. Cata: 3 a year. Also, a booksearch service. Corresp: German, French.

Bender Antiquariat KG, Trinkaus–Galerie, Königsallee 21–23, 40212 Düsseldorf.

Antiquariat Daras & Gilbert GbR, Marktstrasse 11, 40213 Düsseldorf. Prop: Patrice Daras & Marie–Christine Gilbert. Tel: (0211) 131913. Fax: 328488. Est: 1982. Shop; open Monday to Wednesday 11–6, Thursday & Friday 11–8, Saturday 11–4. Very large stock. Spec: literature; history; art; photography; travel; geography; philosophy. PR: DM20–5,000. Also, a booksearch service. Corresp: German, French. VAT No: DE 154 062 259.

Antiquariat Eickhoff, Germaniastrasse 28, 40223 Düsseldorf. Prop: Peter Eickhoff. Tel: (0211) 1375809. Fax: 1370807. Est: 1986. Private premises; appointment necessary. Small stock. Spec: antiquarian; art reference; autographs; avant-garde; bibliography; Catalogues Raisonées; first editions; foreign texts; illustrated; foreign languages; limited editions; literature; surrealism. PR: DM100–1,000. Cata: 3 a year. Corresp: German, French. VAT No: DE 119 406 693.

Antiquariat M. & R. Fricke, Poststrasse 3, 40213 Düsseldorf. Prop: Marion & Roswitha Fricke. Tel: (0211) 323234. Fax: 329569. Est: 1979. Shop; open Tuesday to Friday 11–6.30, Saturday 11–2. Very small stock. Spec: avant–garde 20th century and rare books. Cata: 1 to 3 a year. Also, contemporary art gallery. Mem: V.D.A. VAT No: DE 119 246 011.

Hofladen-Antiquariat Ganseforth, Hohe Strasse 47, 40213 Düsseldorf. Prop: Ludwig & Ingrid Ganseforth. Tel: (0211) 131676. Fax: 3238716. Est: 1970. Shop; open Monday to Friday 10–6, Saturday 10–2. Medium stock. Spec: Westphalia and Rhineland; history of civilisation; fine and rare; literature.

Das Graphik-Kabinett, Humboldtstrasse 80, 40237 Düsseldorf.

Zeitungs–Antiquariat W. Koop, Florastrasse 9, 40217 Düsseldorf.

Lustenberger & Schäfer OHG, Citadellstrasse 9, 40213 Düsseldorf. Tel: (0211) 132612. Fax: 322257. Est: 1991. Shop; open Monday to Friday 11–6.30, Saturday 11–2. Large stock. Spec: antiquarian; art; bibliography; biography; books about books; ceramics; children's; author Heinrich Heine; glass; history of ideas; limited editions; literature; miniature books; printing; private press; sets of books; travel; typography. PR: DM1–10,000. Cata: 2 a year. Also, a booksearch service and French and Spanish wines. Corresp: French, Spanish. Mem: B.D.B. VAT No: DE 119 246 757.

Buch- und Kunstantiquariat Hans Marcus, Ritterstrasse 10, 40213 Düsseldorf. Prop: Ange Marcus. Tel: (0211) 325940. Fax: 327633. Shop; appointment necessary. Spec: pre-1870 illustrated. Cata: 1 a year. Also, large print books. Mem: V.D.A.; I.L.A.B. VAT No: DE 119 207 471.

Antiquariat Stefan Müller, Hildesbrandstrasse 11, 40215 Düsseldorf. Tel: (0211) 330652. Fax: 330550. Est: 1994. Storeroom and private premises; appointment necessary. Very small stock. Spec: incunabula; books printed before 1520; manuscripts; documents; autographs before 1520. Cata: 1 a year. Also, books etc. on Maximilian I (1459–1519). Corresp: German. VAT No: DE 119 479 482.

Graphik–Salon Gerhart Söhn KG, Robert Reinick Str. 2, 40474 Düsseldorf. Tel: (0211) 4380092. Fax: 4350889. Est: 1969. Shop; open daily. Very small stock. Spec: art; art reference. PR: DM1–1000. Cata: 2 a year. Also, graphics of 20th century. Corresp: German, French. VAT No: DE 119 246 298.

Stern–Verlag Janssen & Co., Friedrichstrasse 24–26, P.O. Box 101053, 40001 Düsseldorf. Prop: Horst & Klaus Janssen. Tel: (0211) 38810 Fax: 3881200. E-Mail: 100704.2104@compuserve.com. Est: 1900. Shop; open Monday to Friday 9–6.30, Saturday 9–2 (but first Saturday each month open 9–6). Very large stock. Spec: the arts. Cata: on the arts, 3 a year. Also, new books, library services, and a booksearch service. Corresp: German, French. Mem: B.V.D.B. VAT No: DE 119 420 520.

Dr Helmut Vester, Friedrichstrasse 7, 40217 Düsseldorf.

Galerie Vömel KG, Königsallee 30, (Kö–Center), 40212 Düsseldorf.

DUISBURG

Dieter Drier, Wedauer Str 314, 47279 Duisburg.

Antiquariat Sabine Keune, Friedrich-Alfred-Strasse 79, 47226 Duisburg. Tel: (02065) 59619. Fax: 56827. Est: 1987. Private premises; appointment necessary. Small stock. Spec: children's; illustrated; literature. Cata: 2 a year on antiquarian children's and illustrated. Corresp: French, German. Mem: I.L.A.B.; V.D.A.; Börsenverein des Deutschen Buchandel. VAT No: DE 121 351 886.

EBERBACH AM NECKAR

Polygraphicum Peter A. Helm, Backgasse 1, 69412 Eberbach am Neckar. Prop: Peter August Helm. Tel: & Fax: (06271) 1387 or (06263) 276 (answering system). Est: 1980. Shop and private premises; open Monday to Friday 10–12 and 3–6, Saturday 10–1 (closed Wednesday). Very small general stock. Spec: art; art history; art reference; decorative art; fine & rare; printing; general & local topography; travel - Europe. PR: DM100–10,000. Also, paintings, drawings and watercolours. Corresp: French, Italian. VAT No: DE 144 054 731.

EICHSTÄTT

Armin Jedlitschka, Postfach 1211, 85066 Eichstätt. Tel: (08421) 80521. Fax: 3219. Est: 1991. Private premises; appointment necessary. Very small stock. Spec: fine and rare; manuscripts. VAT No: DE 131 748 660.

ERFURT

Akademische Buchhandlung und Antiquariat Hierana GmbH, Wenigemarkt 2, 99084 Erfurt. Manager: Paul Schindegger. Tel: (0361) 5611711. Fax: 5611717. Est: 1983. Private premises; appointment necessary. Very small stock. Spec: literature; politics; social sciences; economics; jurisprudence and contemporary history. Mem: V.D.A.; I.L.A.B. VAT No: DE 179 283 861.

GERMANY

ERLANGEN

Buch– und Kunstantiquariat Heinz Wünschmann, Wasserturmstrasse 14, 91054 Erlangen.

ERLENBACH AM MAIN

Keip Periodicals GmbH, Am Sportplatz 2, 63906 Erlenbach am Main.

ESSEN

Die Gravüre, Rüttenscheider Strasse 56, 45130 Essen.

Das Kleine Antiquariat, Bredeneyer Str. 83, 45133 Essen. Prop: Thomas Jenisch. Tel: (0201) 425111. Fax: 425131. Est: 1986. Shop; appointment necessary. Small stock. Spec: Judaica; architecture; art; cookery/gastronomy; illustrated; law; pharmacy/pharmacology; psychoanalysis; travel. PR: DM20–250. Corresp: German, Dutch, Spanish. VAT No: 174 162 315. *Also at:* Bredevoort, The Netherlands (q.v.).

Antiquariat Medizin & Naturwissenschaften, Hufelandstrasse 32, 45147 Essen. Prop: Dr. L. Goetzhaber. Tel: (0201) 701344. Fax: 707351. Est: 1981. Shop. Very large stock. Spec: medicine; natural sciences. Cata: 5 a year.

Skandinavisches Versand–Antiquariat Ulrich F. Meysenburg, Rombergweg 34, 45138 Essen. Tel: & Fax: (0201) 283243. Est: 1990. Storeroom; postal business only. Small stock. Spec: academic/scholarly; children's; Scandinavia; local history; Scandinavian language; linguistics; Scandinavian literature; literature in translation; travel - Polar; university texts. PR: DM1–500. Cata: approximately 4 a year. Also, a specialised import bookstore. Corresp: all Scandinavian languages, German. VAT No: DE 158 561 570.

Steeler Antiquariat, Eickelkamp 11, 45276 Essen. Prop: Mr. Arnd Hepprich & Mr. Dirk Franken. Tel: (0201) 516060. Fax: (069) 4692863. E-Mail: 100760.2273@compuserve.com. Est: 1988. Shop; open Thursday 3–8.30, Friday 3–6.30, Saturday 10–2. Large stock. Spec: biographies; regional: Rührgebiet; mining; fiction (only German books). PR: DM10–500. Cata: 2 or 3 a year. Also, mail order, a booksearch service and information on Internet: http://ourworld.compuserve.com/homepages/steeler. Corresp: German.

Antiquariat Eckhard Wünnenberg, Hollestrasse 1, 45127 Essen.

ESTENFELD

Versandantiquariat Gisela Gottschalk, Grünewaldstrasse 27, 97230 Estenfeld. Tel: (09305) 8269. Fax: 1742. Small stock. Spec: astronomy; horology; railways. Cata: 3 or 4 a year. VAT No: DE 134 081 034.

FRANKFURT AM MAIN

Eric T. Brück – Antiquariat Metropolis, Leerbachstrasse 85, 60322 Frankfurt am Main. Tel: (069) 559451. Est: 1986. Storeroom; appointment necessary. Medium to large stock. Spec: literature; Judaica; art; politics; social sciences; private press; illustrated. PR: DM100–10,000. Corresp: German. Mem: P.B.F.A.

Galerie Brumme Frankfurt, Braubachstrasse 34, 60311 Frankfurt am Main.

Bücher–Kreth GmbH, Friedberger Anlage 14, 60316 Frankfurt am Main. Prop: Andreas S. Brahm & Roland Kreth. Tel: (069) 497223. Fax: 497826. E-Mail: frogbook alo.com. Est: 1990. Shop and market stand; open Monday to Friday 8–6.30, Saturday 8–2, Thursday 8–8.30. Medium stock. Spec: herpetology; arachnology; Frankfurt; old and rare. PR: DM20–20.000. CC: V; MC; EC. Cata: 4 a year on herpetology and arachnology. Corresp: French, German. Mem: B.D.B. VAT No: DE 112 013 166.

China Antiquaria, Weilbacher Strasse 38, 65439 Flörsheim. (•) Prop: Elke Mueller-Risse. Tel: (6145) 53536. Fax: 53587. Est: 1991. Storeroom and private premises; appointment necessary. Small stock. Spec: all kinds of books on China in German, English and French, and Chinese languages and Chinese books. Cata: 4 a year on speciality, including antiquarian, rare and some new editions. Also, a booksearch service. Corresp: German, French. Mem: Börsenverein des Deutschen Buchandel.

Antiquariat Christo, Alte Gasse 67, 60313 Frankfurt am Main. Prop: Chr. Missirloglou. Tel: (069) 283579. Est: 1956. Shop; open Monday to Saturday 10–6.30. Large stock. Spec: art; architecture; children's; history; rare pre-1920.

Antiquariat Georg Ewald, Grosse Bockenheimerstr. 29, 60313 Frankfurt am Main. Tel: (069) 287413. Fax: 288447. Est: 1982. Shop; open Monday to Friday 11–7, Saturday 10–4. Large stock. Spec: 20th-century German literature; exile literature 1933–1948; Reclams Universal-Bibliothiek. Also, a booksearch service. Corresp: French. Mem: B.V.D.B.; Hessischer Buchhändlerverband. VAT No: DE 111 897 072.

Galerie und Kunstantiquariat Joseph Fach oHG, Fahrgasse 8, 60311 Frankfurt am Main.

Zeil–Antiquariat Henle, Zeil 24, 60313 Frankfurt am Main.

Antiquariat Günther Parschau, Letzter Hasenpfad 42, 60598 Frankfurt am Main. Tel: & Fax: (069) 632220. Est: 1994. Private premises; appointment necessary. Medium stock. Spec: agriculture; architecture; bibles; bindings; children's; cookery/gastronomy; Germany; Europe and other countries; early imprints; fine & rare; forestry; travel guides; illustrated; hunting; theology; local topography and topography of Germany and Europe etc.; travel; voyages & discovery; wine. PR: DM20–2,000. Cata: 4 a year. Also, a booksearch service and book restoration. Corresp: German, Spanish, Portuguese. VAT No: DE 162 617 014.

Versandantiquariat Wolfgang Rueger, Dreieichstrasse 52, 60594 Frankfurt am Main. Tel: (069) 615638. Fax: 625974. Est: 1992. Large stock. Spec: signed first editions; literature of the 20th century; children's; history; travel. Cata: 4 a year. Also, a booksearch service.

Kunsthandlung Helmut H. Rumbler, Börsenplatz 13–15, 60313 Frankfurt am Main. Tel: (069) 291142. Fax: 289975. Est: 1971. Shop; open Monday to Friday 10–6, Saturday 9–1. Very small stock. Spec: art; art reference. Cata: on prints reference. Corresp: French. Mem: V.D.A. VAT No: DE 112 063 719.

Frankfurter Bücherstube Schumann und Cobet, Lindenstrasse 30, 60325 Frankfurt am Main.

Tresor am Römer, Braubachstrasse 15, 60311 Frankfurt am Main. Prop: Hans Beyerle. Tel: (069) 281248. Fax: 282160. Est: 1977. Shop; open Monday to Friday 10–1 & 2–6, Saturday 10–1. Small stock. Spec: valuable books of 16th to 19th centuries. Cata: 1 a year. Mem: V.D.A.

Frankfurter Kunstkabinett Hanna Bekker vom Rath GmbH, Braubachstrasse 15, 60311 Frankfurt am Main.

FRASDORF

Musikantiquariat Emil Katzbichler, Wilhelming 7, 83112 Frasdorf. Tel: (8051) 2595. Fax: 64113. E-Mail: 101700.2401@compuserve.com. Est: 1964. Very large stock. Spec: music only. Cata: 4 to 5 a year. Also, music publisher and publications on musicology and a booksearch service. Corresp: German, French. Mem: I.L.A.B. VAT No: DE 131 071 986.

FREIBURG

Foto–Versandantiquariat Silvia Fahl, Unterer Mühlenweg 31, 79114 Freiburg. Tel: (0761) 4764767. Fax: 482586. Est: 1976. Storeroom; open every day, telephone first. Very small stock. Spec: photographic literature of all kinds. PR: DM15–1,000. Cata: 2 a year. Corresp: German.

Versandantiquariat Stefan Feickert, Ziegelhofstrasse 58, 79110 Freiburg. Booksearch service.

Forster & Kaner, Antiquare in Freiburg GmbH, Grünwälderstrasse 6, 79098 Freiburg im Breisgau. Prop: Heinrich Forster & Margot Kaner. Tel: (0761) 35479. Fax: 32290. Est: 1975. Shop; open Monday to Friday 9.30–6.30 and Saturday 9.30–2 (first Saturday in month 9.30–6). Medium general stock. Corresp: French, Turkish. Mem: Verband der Verlage und Buchhändler in Baden-Württemberg; Börsenverein des Deutschen Buchhandels. VAT No: DE 142 106 135.

Musikantiquariat zum grossen C. Hinner Bauch, Silberbergstrasse 7, 79254 Oberried–Hofsgrund. (•) Tel: & Fax: (07602) 514. Est: 1985. Shop and private premises; appointment necessary. Large stock. Spec: music (all aspects). PR: DM20–5,000. Cata: 2 a year. Corresp: French. Mem: Musikhandel Bonn. VAT No: 142 007 886.

Antiquariat Uwe Kolb, Schutternstrasse 2, 79112 Freiburg.

Buchhandel Labyrinth, Gartenstrasse 8, 7800 Freiburg im Breisgau.

Antiquariat Peter Mulzer, (Guntramstr. 46), Postfach 1072, 79010 Freiburg. Tel: (0761) 277689 or 2021928. Est: 1975. Storeroom. Very large stock of 35,000. Spec: (only books printed 1800–1945): academic/scholarly; atlases/cartography; children's; esoteric; romance; health; Holocaust; law; Nazism (only for historical purposes); newspapers; periodicals/magazines; politics; Christian religion (Catholicism); science; social history; university texts; war. PR: DM30–120. Cata: 4 a year. Also, a booksearch service. Corresp: French, German. VAT No: DE 142 053 542.

Antiquariat Armin Schneider, Littenweiler Strasse 13, 79117 Freiburg. Tel: & Fax: (0761) 60293. Est: 1995. Private premises. Very small stock. Spec: travel; literature; geography; history. PR: DM10–1,500. Cata: 4 a year.

GERMANY

Antiquariat am Siegesdenkmal, Friedrichring 11, 79098 Freiburg. Prop: Michaela Weiers. Tel: (0761) 280393. Fax: (07665) 51996. Shop; open Tuesday to Friday 2–6.30, Saturday 10–1. Small general stock. Cata: 2 a year.

Antiquariat Peter Uhl, Werthmannplatz 2, 79098 Freiburg. Est: 1981. Shop; open Tuesday to Friday 2–6.30, Saturday 10–1. Small general stock. PR: DM20–500. Corresp: German, French.

FRIEDBERG

Antiquariat Karel Marel, Benrathweg 36a, 61169 Friedberg.

FRIEDRICHSDORF

Buch- und Kunstantiquariat Heidrun Schiffmann, Spessartring 24, 61381 Friedrichsdorf. Tel: & Fax: (06007) 80136. Private premises; open 6–8. Small stock. Spec: pharmacy; medicine; rare books on chess; Americana; Canadiana; Judaica; geography; travels; cookery; children's; whaling; sport; botany; Freemasonry; Red Indians; typography; ceramics. PR: DM1–1,000. Cata: 6 a year. Also, a booksearch service and pharmacy antiques. Corresp: French. VAT No: DE 111 258 213.

FRONHAUSEN

Buch- und Kunstantiquariat E. Schenk zu Schweinsberg, Giessenerstrasse 4, 35112 Fronhausen/Lahn. Tel: (06426) 6343. Fax: 5804. VAT No: DE 113 334 607.

FÜRTH

Antiquarian Bookshop, Hornschuch Promenade 17, 90762 Fürth.

Briefmarken Arie Duits, Robert–Schumann–Str. 9, 90768 Fürth. Tel: (0911) 722379. Fax: 722587. Est: 1981. Storeroom; open Monday to Saturday 8–8. Small stock. Spec: atlases/cartography; autographs; aviation; censorship; collecting; documents; industrial and local history; humour; history of ideas; industry; letters; maritime/nautical; military; numismatics; philately; photography; printing; technology; needlework; railways. PR: DM1–10,000. CC: V. Cata 3 or 4 a year. Also, a booksearch service. Corresp: German, Dutch. Mem: of the research project "Postal History of Great Britain".

Antiquariat Klaussner, Hornschuchpromenade 17, 90762 Fürth. Tel: (0911) 709331. Fax: 709341. Est: 1974. Private premises; appointment necessary. Medium stock. Spec: literature in first and complete editions (18th–20th century); illustrated; caricature; art; art history; philosophy; psychoanalysis; psychology/psychiatry; socialism. PR: DM30–5,000. Cata: 4 or 5 a year. Also, a booksearch service and ordering of available books. Corresp: German, French. Mem: B.D.B. VAT No: DE 157 402 700.

FULDA

Buchhandlung Ulenspiegel, Löherstrasse 13, 36037 Fulda.

GEHRDEN

H. Preidel, Antiquariat für Medizin, Bismarckstrasse 20, Postfach 11 28, 30983 Gehrden. Tel: (05108) 4766. TA: Preidelbuch, Gehrden. Fax: 8501. Est: 1959. Private premises; appointment necessary. Medium stock. Spec: antiquarian medicine. Mem: V.D.A. VAT No: DE 115 491 395.

GERLINGEN

Antiquariat Les–Art Günther Veit, Burgklinge 33, (Schillerhöhe), 70839 Gerlingen. Est: 1980. Storeroom; appointment necessary. Small stock. Spec: antiquarian; art; art history; avant–garde; cinema/films; dance; first editions; Holocaust; illustrated; limited editions; literature; literature in translation; photography; socialism; theatre. PR: DM20–20,000. CC: AE. Cata: 4 to 6 a year. Corresp: French. VAT No: DE 145 960 7792.

GIESSEN

Versandantiquariat Frank Mihm–Speiser, Wilhelmstrasse 46, 35392 Giessen. Est: 1989. Appointment necessary. Small general stock. PR: DM1–1,000. Also, a booksearch service. Corresp: German.

GLASHÜTTEN

Detlev Auvermann KG, Zum Talblick 2, 61479 Glashütten 1. Tel: (06174) 96520. Fax: 965230. Est: 1961. Shop; appointment necessary. Very large stock. Spec: economics; early imprints; natural history; law; art; art history. Cata: 1 a year on general periodicals. Corresp: German, French, Italian, Spanish. Mem: V.D.A.; S.L.A.M.; I.L.A.B.; L.I.L.A. VAT No: DE 176 681406.

GLEICHEN

Antiquariat und Versandbuchhandlung Heinz–Jörg Ahnert, Hainbundstrasse 2, 37130 Gleichen. Tel: (05508) 8589. Est: 1985. Shop and storeroom; hours irregular. Very large stock. Spec: artists; biography; economics; erotica; feminism; history; juvenile; music; philosophy; photography; psychoanalysis; psychology/ psychiatry; sexology; sport; theatre; theology; travel - general, Africa, Americas, Asia, Europe. PR: DM3–200. Cata: irregularly. Also, a booksearch service. Corresp: German, Dutch.

GÖTTINGEN

Antiquariat Swen Alpers, P.O. Box 11 01 06, 37046 Göttingen. Tel: & Fax: (0551) 74995. Est: 1990. Storeroom; postal business only. Small stock. Spec: antiquarian; art; carpets; colonial; countries; foreign culture; Egyptology; ethnography; ethnology; fine & rare; folklore; geography; gypsies; landscape; maritime/nautical; mythology; photography; general & Oriental religion; all categories of travel. PR: DM30–3,000. Cata: 3 a year. Also, a booksearch service. Corresp: German, Spanish, Norwegian, Danish, French.

Atrium Antiquariat, Burgstrasse 33, 37073 Göttingen. Prop: Gert Schroeder. Tel: & Fax: (0551) 59387. E-Mail: AtriumAnt@aol.com. Est: 1989. Shop; open Monday to Friday 10–1 and 3–6, Saturday 10–1. Large stock. Spec: applied art; architecture; art; art history; art reference; artists; books about books; children's; fine printing; history; illustrated; literature; literature in translation; natural sciences; photography; private press; science; history of science; general travel. PR: DM20–2,000. Cata: 12 a year. Also, a booksearch service and Internet catalogue: http://members.aol.com/AtriumAnt.

Wissenschaftliches Antiquariat Ernst Geibel, Burgstrasse 11, 37073 Göttingen. Tel: (0551) 58705. Est: 1898. Shop; open Monday to Friday 3.30–6.30, Saturday 10–1. Medium general stock.

Göttinger Antiquariat Erich Gross, Mauerstrasse 16/17, 37073 Göttingen. Tel: (0551) 57503. Fax: 57500. Est: 1946. Shop; open Monday to Friday 9–12 and 3–6, Saturday 9–12. Very large stock. Spec: sciences. PR: DM1–5,000. Cata: 4 a year on different sciences. Corresp: German. Mem: V.D.A. VAT No: DE 115 265 822.

Buchhandlung und Antiquariat Robert Peppmüller, Barfüsserstrasse 11, 3400 Göttingen. Prop: Rainer Schmidt. Tel: (0551) 56800 or 56809. Est: 1872. Shop; open Monday to Friday 11–1 & 3–6. Medium general stock. Spec: university literature. Corresp: French. Mem: B.V.D.B.; Landesverband der Buchhändler und Verleger in Niedersachsen; Arbeitsgemeinschaft Wissenschaftlicher Sortimenter. VAT No: DE 115 311 986.

Antiquariat Peter Pretzsch, Kurze Strasse 16, 37073 Göttingen. Tel: (0551) 43355. Est: 1995. Shop; open Tuesday to Friday 10–1 and 2–6, Saturday 10–1. Small general stock. Spec: children's from 1900 to today; literature; literature in translation. PR: DM1–1,000.

GOLDBACH

Antiquariat und Verlag Keip GmbH, Bayernstrasse 9, 63773 Goldbach. Prop: Ulrich Keip. Tel: (6021) 59050. Fax: 590542. Est: 1958. Storeroom; open Monday to Friday 8–5.30. Very large stock. Spec: academic/scholarly; antiquarian; dictionaries; early imprints; economics; history - general, industrial, local and national; journals; law; military; politics; social history; social sciences; general & local topography; voyages & discovery. PR: DM200 plus. Cata: 6 to 8 a year. Also, a booksearch service. Corresp: German, French, Italian. Mem: B.V.D.B; I.L.A.B.; V.D.A.

GÜTERSLOH

Buch- und Kunstantiquariat Ursula Dempwolf, Elbrachtsweg 46, 33332 Gütersloh.

HAGEN

Antiquariat und Kunsthandlung Huste, Goldbergstrasse 17, 58095 Hagen. Prop: Wolfgang and Kamssa Huste. Tel: & Fax: (02331) 183934. Est: 1994. Shop; open 10–1 and 2–6.30. Spec: literature; art; history. PR: DM10–10,000. Also, a booksearch service, large print books and two book auctions a year. Corresp: German, French, Arabic. VAT No: DE 124 676 114. *Also at:* Liebigstrasse 46–48, D-44139 Dortmund *and* Steinweg 11, 59821 Arnsberg (q.v.).

HALLE (WESTFALEN)

G. Lohmann, Postfach 1337, 33778 Halle (Westfalen), Talstrasse 10.

GERMANY

Antiquariat J. Reinhardt, Postfach 11 53, 33776 Halle (Westfalen). Prop: Paul E. Erdlen. Tel: (05201) 665393. Fax: 665303. Est: 1949. Shop at: Bredenstrasse 15, 33790, Halle/Westfalen; appointment necessary. Very large stock. Spec: Judaica; Masonica; occulta; historica; alchemy; anthroposophy; antiquarian; architecture; art history & reference; astrology; bibles; bibliography; books about books; children's; cookery; culture; dictionaries; documents; encyclopedias; erotica; esoteric; fine & rare and many others. Cata: on specialities. Also, a booksearch service & large print books. Mem: V.D.A.; I.L.A.B. VAT No: DE 127 049 869.

HAMBURG

Abc–Antiquariat, Hohe Bleichen 20, 20354 Hamburg. Prop: Hans Rohscheid. Tel: (040) 352334. Est: 1978. Shop; open Monday to Friday 10–6.30, Saturday 10–2. Small stock. Spec: German history; German literature. PR: DM10–800. Also, paintings. Corresp: French.

Barthowiaks Forum Book Art, Körnerstrasse 24, 22301 Hamburg. Prop: Heinz Stefan Bartkowiak. Tel: (40) 2793674. Fax: 2704397. Est: 1983. Storeroom; appointment necessary. Very small stock. Spec: artists' books; book objects; portfolios. PR: £20–1,000. Cata: occasionally on speciality. Also, exhibitions and book presentations. Corresp: German, French. VAT No: DE 118 790 421.

Das Bücherkabinett, Emkendorfstrasse 1, 22605 Hamburg. Prop: Dr. Maria Conradt. Tel: (040) 882055. Fax: 8801342. Est: 1931. Appointment necessary. Spec: valuable books up to 1850. Cata: irregularly. Corresp: French. Mem: V.D.A. VAT No: DE 118 945 078.

Antiquariat an der Bundestrasse, Bundersstrasse 27, 20146 Hamburg. Prop: Gerhard Ryks & Sabina Varma. Tel: (040) 4107281. Est: 1984. Shop; open Monday to Friday 11–8, Saturday 11–4. Very large stock. Spec: academic/scholarly; antiquarian; biology; cinema/films; cookery/gastronomy; general fiction; general & local history; literature; literature in translation; mathematics; music; natural sciences; ornithology; philosophy; politics; physics; travel; photography. PR: DM1–1,000. Also, a booksearch service. Corresp: German, French, Spanish, Italian.

Kunsthandel Thomas le Claire, Elbchaussee 156, 22605 Hamburg.

Antiquariat Dr. Jörn Güntheer, Reichskanzlerstrasse 6, 22609 Hamburg.

Antiquariat Halkyone, P.O. Box 50 18 28, 22718 Hamburg. Prop: Detlef Gerd Stechern. Tel: (040) 389714. Fax: 38610997. E-Mail: 100433.1156@ compuserve.com. Est: 1993. Shop at: Lamp'lweg 10, 22767 Hamburg; open Monday to Friday 9.30–6.30, Saturday 11–2. Medium stock. Spec: autographs; bibliography; fine & rare; first editions; reference. PR: DM200 and up. Cata: 4 a year. VAT No: DE 156 367 155.

Antiquariat Paul Hennings, Altstädterstrasse 15, 20095 Hamburg. VAT No: DE 118 902 125.

Antiquariat Susanne Koppel, Parkallee 4, 20144 Hamburg. Tel: (040) 454407. Fax: 453013. Est: 1986. Private premises; appointment necessary. Very small stock. Spec: German literature in first editions; 18/19th century travel. Cata: 2 a year. Mem: V.D.A. VAT No: DE 118 292 544.

Libresso, Antiquariat an der Universität, Binderstrasse 24, 20146 Hamburg 13.

Kunstantiquariat Joachim Lührs, Michaelisbrücke 3, 20459 Hamburg. Tel: (040) 371194. Fax: 371103. Est: 1992. Shop; open Monday to Friday 11–6.30, Medium stock. Spec: applied art; architecture; art; art history; art reference; the arts; photography. Cata: 2 a year and 4 lists on architecture, artists, art history and photography. Also, a booksearch service and exhibitor at Quod Libet Jut. Antiquarian Book Fair, Hamburg. Corresp: German, French, Italian.

Antiquariat Reinhold Pabel, Krayenkamp 10b, 20459 Hamburg. Prop: Gottwalt Pankow. Tel: (040) 364889. Fax: 374391. Est: 1974. Shop; open Monday to Saturday 9–6, Sunday 10–5. Large stock. Spec: antiquarian; northern Germany local history; juvenile; art; illustrated. Cata: 2 or 3 a year; small lists. Also, a booksearch service and organiser of International Antiquarian Book Fair "Quod Libet", Hamburg. Corresp: French, Russian. Mem: B.V.D.B.

Punctum. Fotobuch–Versandantiquariat O. Paulssen, Klosterbergenstrasse 34, 21465 Reinbek/Hamburg. Prop: Olaf Paulssen. Tel: (040) 7222626. Fax: 7227534. Est: 1986. Private premises; appointment necessary. Medium stock. Spec: photography - literature; picture books; theory; technique; magazines; famous photographers; how-to-do books. Cata: 1 a year plus several lists. Also, a booksearch service and new book orders. Corresp: German. VAT No: DE 300 373 1778.

Antiquariat Der Rabe, Heinrich Barth-Str. 4a, 20146 Hamburg. Prop: Ellinor Lang & Antje Gärtner. Tel: (040) 4500920. Fax: 4500944. Est: 1990. Shop; open Monday to Friday 11–6 (Wednesday 11–8 and Saturday 10–2). Medium stock. Spec: children's; general fiction; detective, spy, thrillers; history; history of civilisation; Holocaust; humanities; literature; literature in translation; philosophy; psychology/psychiatry; Jewish religion; theology. PR: DM1–100. Cata: 2 a year. Also, a booksearch service. Corresp: German, French.

Versandantiquariat Renate Riepen, Raamstieg 8, 22397 Hamburg. Tel: (040) 6080216; 6072669. Fax: 6080368. Shop; open Wednesday and Friday. Medium general stock. Also, large print books. Corresp: German, Danish. VAT No: DE 118 410 320.

GERMANY

Antiquariat und Buchhandlung Barbara Schöningh, Ottenser Marktplatz 15, 22765 Hamburg. Tel: (040) 3906949. Fax: 397160. Est: 1989. Private premises; appointment necessary. Small stock. Spec: architecture; applied art; gardening; town–planning; canals/inland waterways. Cata: 3 a year. Also, special lists and offers. Corresp: German, French. VAT No: DE 117 965 478.

Antiquariat Jürgen Stammerjohann, Hohenzollernring 27, 22763 Hamburg.

Max Wiedebusch Buchhandlung-Antiquariat, Dammtorstrasse 20, 20354 Hamburg 36. Prop: Helmi Chelala. Tel: (040) 345001. Fax: 3480117. Est: 1936. Shop; open Monday to Friday 9–6, Saturday 9–1. Medium general stock. PR: DM10–5,000. Also, a booksearch service. VAT No: DE 118 946 802.

Buchhandlung & Antiquariat Dr. Robert Wohlers & Co., Lange Reihe 69–70. 20099 Hamburg St. Georg. Tel: (040) 247715. Shop; open Monday to Friday 9–6.30, Saturday 9–1. Medium general stock. Mem: Norddeutscher Buchhändler und Verleger Verband; B.V.D.B. VAT No: DE 118 872 657.

HANOVER (HANNOVER)

Galerie Jens-Heiner Bauer, Holzmarkt 4, 30159 Hannover.

Antiquariat & Filmbuchhandlung Heinz Gärtner, Marienstrasse 105–7, 30171 Hannover.

Antiquariat die Silbergäle, Ferdinand Wallbrechtstr. 50, 30163 Hannover. Prop: Thomas Mahr & Georg Wiesing–Brandes. Tel: (0511) 9805723. Fax: 884853. Est: 1984. Private premises. Small stock, only major subjects. Spec: architecture; art; autographs; avant–garde; first editions; literature; philosophy; photography; surrealism; Dada & Expressionism. PR: DM100–10,000. Cata: 1 or 2 a year. Also, a booksearch service and an office in Paris. Corresp: German, French. VAT No: DE 115 743 543.

HEBERTSHAUSEN

Verlag für Filmschriften C. Unucka, Am Kramerberg 7a, 85241 Hebertshausen. Prop: Christian Unucka, Dipl. Psychology. Tel: (08131) 13922. Fax: 10075. Est: 1975. Shop; postal business. Small stock. Spec: only cinema/films. Cata: actual film book lists, every 6 weeks. Also, archives on film literature. Mem: B.D.B. VAT No: DE 127 683 057.

HEIDELBERG

Ernst Dieter Fischer Buchhandlung und Antiquariat, Postfach 251160, 69079 Heidelberg.

Galerie Olaf Greiser, Schröderstrasse 14, 69120 Heidelberg.

Antiquariat Hatry, Hauptstrasse 119, 69117 Heidelberg. Prop: Thomas Hatry. Tel: (06221) 26202. Fax: 26226. Est: 1985. Shop; open Monday to Friday 10.30–8, Saturday 10–4. Very large stock. Spec: German literature; philosophy; music; fine arts; books about books; economics. PR: DM1–50,000. CC: V. Cata: 1 a year. Corresp: German. Mem: I.L.A.B.; V.D.A.

Antiquariat Richart Kulbach, Neugasse 19, 69117 Heidelberg. Prop: Sabine Rahlf. Tel: (06221) 23614. Fax: 12113. Est: 1933. Shop; open Monday 2–6, Tuesday to Friday 10–1 and 2–6, Saturday 10–1. Very large stock. Spec: geography; history; literature. Cata: 1 or 2 a year. Corresp: German, French.

Antiquariat Rolf Schwing, Gaisbergstrasse 29, 69115 Heidelberg.

Bibliographicum E. Tenner, Hauptstrasse 194, 69117 Heidelberg. Prop: H.-Herm. Lindner. Tel: (06221) 26252. Est: 1951. Shop; open Monday to Friday 9–1 and 2–6.30, Saturday 9–2 or 4. Spec: literature. PR: DM30–8,000. CC: all major cards. Corresp: German. Mem: V.D.A. VAT No: DE 175 996 371.

HEILBRONN

Antiquariat Gerhard Gruber, Neuwiesenstrasse 16/1, 74078 Heilbronn.

HERFORD

Antiquariat in der Radewig, Löhrstrasse 3, 32052 Herford. Prop: Ruediger Laüg, M.A. Tel: (05221) 53455. Est: 1985. Shop; open Tuesday to Saturday 9-1 and 2.30–6. Medium general stock. PR: DM1–1,000.

HILDESHEIM

Georg Olms Verlag, Hagentorwall 7, 31134 Hildesheim. Prop: Dr. N.C. Malt & W. Georg Olms. Tel: (05121) 15010. Fax: 150150. E-Mail: olms@georg-olms.hi.cunct.de. Est: 1945. Storeroom; open 9–4. Medium stock. Spec: antiquarian; art history; bibliography; biography; chess; classical studies; cookery/gastronomy; early imprints; Egyptology; fine & rare; foreign texts; geography; history; humanities; foreign languages; limited editions; Middle Ages; music; philosophy; travel; university texts. PR: DM10–1,000. Cata: 2 a year. Corresp: French, German. Mem: B.D.B. VAT No: DE 115 971 094.

GERMANY

Antiquariat Vree, Orleansstrasse 26, 31135 Hildesheim. Prop: Hans-Günter Vree. Tel: (05121) 55429 and 32423. Fax: 55459. Est: 1975. Shop at: Hoher Weg 32.33 (Andreas Kirchplatz), 31134 Hildesheim; open Monday to Friday 2–6, Saturday 10–1. Very large stock. Spec: regional and local history of Lower Saxony (especially Hildesheim). Cata: 1 a year on pedagogics & criminology. Also, Modernes Antiquariat at Orleaustrasse 26; open from 2–6. Corresp: German.

HÖCHBERG

Buchversand und Antiquariat Matthias Flury, Eduard–Buchner–Strasse 17, 97204 Höchberg. Tel: & Fax: (0931) 405486. Est: 1990. Shop at: Hauptstrasse 73 (opp. Rathaus) Höchberg; open Tuesday 8.30–6.30 and by phone or written appointment. Medium stock. Spec: art; autographs; bibliography; Egyptology; encyclopedias; esoteric; fine art; first editions; Freemasonry; genealogy; glass; graphic art; general, local and national history; homeopathy; illustrated; limited editions; numismatics; occult; religion; history of science; technology; travel; witchcraft; City address books. PR: DM1 and up. Cata: 4 a year on modern antiquarian. Also, a booksearch service and large print books. Corresp: German. VAT No: DE 134 074 703.

HOLZMINDEN

Antiquariat Ursula Hinrichsen, (37671) Twierweg 23, Postfach 1451, 37594 Holzminden.

JOERNHAGEN

Versandantiquariat Robert A. Mueller Nachf., Bothfelder Strasse 11, 30916 Joernhagen.

KAISERSLAUTERN

Antiquariat Peter Winkelmann, Rud.-Breitscheid-Strasse 45, 67655 Kaiserslautern. Tel: (0631) 18605 or 60304. Est: 1984. Shop; open Monday to Friday (except Thursday) 11–12.30 & 3–6 and Saturday 11–1. Medium stock. Spec: illustrated; Rhenish palatinate; incunabula; exile literature; botanical. Also, paintings.

KARLSRUHE

Antiquariat am Basler Tor, Amthausstr. 33, 76227 Karlsruhe–Durlach. Prop: Carla & Denis Western. Tel: & Fax: (0721) 405058. E-Mail: 100571.3470@ compuserve.com. Shop; open Monday to Friday 10–1 & 3–6.30, Saturday 10–2, Wednesday closed. Large general stock. Spec: local topography - Durlach, Karlsruhe, Baden, Rhineland–Palatinate. Cata: several a year. VAT No: DE 169 430 695.

Antiquariat Kurt–Dieter Götz, Moltkestrasse 61, 76133 Karlsruhe. Tel: (0721) 859716. Fax: 859717. Est: 1985. Shop; open Monday to Friday 9–5.30, Saturday 10–1. Medium stock. Spec: antiques; applied art; art; carpets; Catalogues Raisonées; ceramics; crafts; decorative art; embroidery; fashion & costume; firearms; glass; interior design; jewellery; lace; stained glass. CC: EC; V; DC; AE. Also, art & decorative art. VAT No: DE 143 525 008.

Versandantiquariat Pia Oberacker–Pilick, Amthausstrasse 3, 76227 Karlsruhe. Tel: & Fax: (0721) 41675. Est: 1980. Storeroom; business by telephone & fax only. Medium stock. Spec: journeys/travels/expeditions; German literature; children's; socialism/revolution 1848; philosophy; theology; religious sciences. PR: DM80–4,000. Cata: 2 a year. Also, a booksearch service. Corresp: Spanish, French, German.

KASSEL

Archiv der deutschen Frauenbewegung e.V., Gottschalkstrasse 57, 34127 Kassel.

Horst Hamecher, Göthestrasse 74, 34119 Kassel. Prop: Dr. Volker Wendland. Tel: (0561) 13179. Est: 1947. Shop; open Tuesday to Friday 9–12 & 3–5, Saturday 9–12. Very large stock. Spec: anthroposophy; architecture; art; children's; classical studies; esoteric; forestry; general & national history; foreign & national languages; literature in translation; maritime/nautical; medicine; military; philosophy; psychology/psychiatry; history of science; theology. Cata: 10 a year. Corresp: French. Mem: B.V.D.B.

Antiquariat Günter Hochgrebe, Königstor 53, 34119 Kassel. Tel: (0561) 1710378. Est: 1988. Shop; open Monday to Saturday 10–1 and 3–6, Saturday only 10–1. Medium general stock. Also, a booksearch service. Cata: 1 a year. Corresp: French.

Achim Makrocki GmbH, Harleshauser Strasse 86, 34130 Kassel. Tel: (0561) 61000. Fax: 61011.

KEHREIN

Bücher-Kehrein, Engerser Strasse 40, 56564 Neuwied. Prop: Peter Kehrein. Tel: (02631) 98830. Fax: 988369. Est: 1896. Shop; open Monday to Friday 8.30–6.30, Saturday 8.30–1 or 4. Small stock. Spec: Rhineland; Carmen Sylva; Friedrich Wolf; Fr. W. Raiffeuseu; Maximilian zu Wied; Neuwied; Wied; Herruhuter; violin/cello. PR: DM1–2,000. CC: MC; V. Also, a booksearch service, specialise on D. & A. Roentgen - cabinet makers and new books. Mem: B.V.D.B.; Landersverband der Verleger und Buchhändler Rheinland-Pfalz. VAT No: DE 149 485 445.

GERMANY

KELTERN

Antiquariat Goecke & Evers, Sportplatzweg 5, 75210 Keltern 3. Prop: Erich Bauer. Tel: (07236) 7174. Fax: 7325. Est: 1928. Private premises; postal business only. Medium stock. Spec: zoology and entomology. CC: MC; V; AE. Cata: 1 or 2 a year. Also, new books on entomology. Corresp: French. Mem: Verband der Verlage und Buchhandlungen in Baden- Württemberg. VAT No: DE 144 087 112.

KÖNIGSTEIN

Antiquariat Reiss & Sohn, Adelheidstrasse 2, 61462 Königstein. Prop: Godebert & Clemens Reiss. Tel: (06174) 1017. Fax: 1602. Est: 1970. Shop; open Monday to Friday 9–1 and 2–6. Very small stock. Cata: 2 a year with English notes. Also, auction sales. Mem: V.D.A. VAT No: DE 167 515 897.

KONSTANZ

Bücherstube Am See, Kreuzlinger Strasse 11, 78462 Konstanz.

Antiquariat E. Erdmann, Zähringerplatz 15, 78464 Konstanz. Prop: Erika Erdmann. Tel: (07531) 51920. Est: 1987. Shop; open Monday to Friday 3–6, Saturday 10–1. Small stock. Spec: antiquarian; local history and national history; health; literature; maritime/nautical; aeronautics; travel; voyages & discovery; war; military. PR: DM1–250. Corresp: German.

Lingua Franca Christa Neureiter, Ringstrasse 109, 78465 Konstanz. Tel: & Fax: (075331) 6882. Est: 1991. Private premises; open every day of the week, in the afternoon. Medium stock. Spec: antiquarian; art; art history; artists; books about books; calligraphy; Catalogues Raisonées; collecting; diaries; erotica; ex–libris; fine & rare; first editions; illustrated; journals; limited editions; miniature books; occult; philosophy; religion; war. PR: DM1–1,000. Cata: 1 a year. Also, a booksearch service. Corresp: German. VAT No: DE 114 130 036.

Buch und Kunst Georg Scheringer, Münzgasse 16, 78462 Konstanz.

KORNWESTHEIM

Brockhaus Antiquarium, Kreidlerstrasse 9, Postfach 1220, 70803 Kornwestheim. Tel: (07154) 132751. Fax: 132713. Telex: 722794 bro d. Est: 1856. Storeroom; appointment necessary. Very large stock. Spec: geography; ethnology; Africana; Americana; Asiatica; Arctica; antiquarian travel in distant lands. PR: DM50–50,000. Cata: 7 or 8 a year. Also, exporter of new German books and periodicals. Corresp: French, German. Mem: V.D.A.; B.V.D.B. VAT No: DE 146 124 076.

KOTTGEISERING

Antiquariat Walter Ricke, Villenstrasse Süd 30, 82288 Kottgeisering. Tel: (08144) 94043. Fax: 1309. VAT No: DE 128 172 526.

LAHR

Der Antiquar in Lahr, Buch & Kunst, Schützenstrasse 31, 77933 Lahr. Prop: Werner Engelmann. Tel: (07821) 38247. Est: 1987. Open Monday, Tuesday, Thursday & Friday 2.30–6.30. Medium stock. Spec: Badenia; travel; children's; juvenile; literature; art. PR: DM1–5,000. Cata: 1 year, approximately 80 pages. Also, a booksearch service, paintings and graphics. Corresp: German, French.

LANDAU

Antiquariat Mühlan, Storchengasse 3, (-Wollmesheim), 76829 Landau. Small stock. Spec: alchemy; astrology; esoteric; geography; homeopathy; magic & conjuring; mysticism; mythology; natural health; occult; parapsychology; supernatural; local topography; travel; voyages & discovery; witchcraft. PR: DM40–300. Cata: 3 a year. Corresp: French.

LANDSHUT

Antiquariat Moser, Kirchgasse 241, 84028 Landshut. Prop: Roland Moser. Tel: & Fax: (0871) 29498. Est: 1984. Shop; open Thursday to Saturday. Small stock. Spec: art; local history; architecture. PR: DM30–300. Cata: lists on request. Also, a booksearch service and large print books.

LEER

Buchhandlung, Verlag und Antiquariat T. Schuster, Muhlenstrasse 17, 26789 Leer.

LEIPZIG

Antiquariat Dieter Trier, Tschaikowskistrasse 9, 04105 Leipzig.

LEUTKIRCH

Antiquariat Roland Gögler, Vorderreischach 1, 88299 Leutkirch. Tel: (07561) 912255. Fax: 912257. E-Mail: 07561912255-0001@t-online.de. Est: 1990. Storeroom. Medium stock. Spec: antiquarian; applied art; architecture; art; art history; art reference; artists; bibliography; bindings; books about books; Catalogues Raisonées; fine & rare; first editions; illustrated; limited editions; literature; private press; signed editions. Cata: approximately 4 a year. Corresp: German. VAT No: DE 173 708 073.

LICHTENFELS

H.O. Schulze, Marktplatz 15, 96215 Lichtenfels. Prop: Hermann D. Schulze. Tel: (09571) 78010. Fax: 78055. Est: 1865. Shop; open Monday to Friday 2–6, Saturday 9–1. Small stock. Spec: Franconica; literature. Cata: 12 a year on Franconica, literature, art, theology, philosophy and history. Also, new books. Mem: B.V.D.B.

LINDAU

Dr. Klaus Robert Zeller, Fischergasse 13, 88131 Lindau.

LÜBECK

Arno Adler, Postfach 2048, 23508 Lübeck. Prop: Kurt Adler. Tel: (0451) 74466. Fax: 7063762. Est: 1932. Shop at: Hüxstrasse 55, 23552 Lübeck; open Monday to Friday 9–6, Saturday 9–1. Very large stock. Spec: economics; general and local history; literature; maritime/nautical; politics; social sciences; Hanseatic history. Cata: 2 a year on specialities. Also, new books. Mem: V.D.A.; I.L.A.B.; B.D.B. VAT No: DE 135 031 295.

Buch- und Kunstantiquariat Peter Babendererde, Grosse Burgstrasse 35, 23552 Lübeck. Prop: Jürgen Babendererde. Tel: (0451) 7060666. Fax: 706755. Est: 1840. Shop; open Monday to Friday 9–1 and 2–6, Saturday 10–1. Very large general stock. Spec: botany; carpets; children's books; decorative art; geography; illustrated; navigation; general and local topography; town-planning; travel - general, Africa, Americas, Asia, Australasia/Australia, Europe, Middle East, Polar; voyages & discovery; zoology. CC: EC; MC. Cata: 8–10 lists a year. Also, a booksearch service. Mem: V.D.A. VAT No: DE 135 031 480.

St. Juergen Antiquariat, Ratzeburger Allee 40, 23562 Lübeck. Prop: Christa Knippschild-Straetz. Tel: (0451) 596262. Fax: 593079. Est: 1989. Shop; open Tuesday to Friday 3–6, Saturday 10–1. Medium stock. Spec: literature; cookery/gastronomy. PR: £4–200. Cata: 2 a year. Corresp: German.

LÜNEBURG

Antiquariat Ruthild Jäger, (21335) Steinweg 17, Postfach 18 61, 21308 Lüneburg.

LUDWIGSBURG

Antiquariat Althoheneck, Untere Gasse 29, 71642 Ludwigsburg. Prop: Heiner Bouttler. Tel: (07141) 506144. Fax: 59725. Est: 1980. Shop; open Wednesday, Thursday & Friday 3–6.30, Saturday 10–2. Medium general stock. PR: DM30–100. Cata: approximately 1 a year. Also, during the second weekend in September about 150 dealers attend a bookmarket at the store. Corresp: German, French.

MAINBURG

Antiquariat Hans Lindner, Sandolfstrasse 32C, 84048 Mainburg. Tel: (08751) 5617. Fax: 5418. Est: 1982. Storeroom; appointment necessary. Medium stock. Spec: antiquarian; illustrated; children's picture books; letterpress-printed books; first editions; curiosa; literature; private press. PR: £50–20,000. Cata: 2 a year. Corresp: German, French. Mem: V.D.A.; I.L.A.B. VAT No: DE 129 890 160.

MAINZ

Siegfried Brumme, Buch- und Kunstantiquariat, Kirschgarten 11, 55116 Mainz.

Sammlerstudio Phileurope, Postfach 3645, 55026 Mainz. Fax: (06131) 237342.

Wilfried Sellin – Antiquariat am Fischtor, Fischtorstrasse 4–8, 55116 Mainz. Tel: (06131) 221962. Shop. Medium general stock. Corresp: French, Italian. Mem: B.V.D.B. VAT No: DE 149 003 460.

MARBURG

N.G. Elwert, Universittsbuchhandlung GmbH & Co. KG, Reitgasse 7–9, 35037 Marburg.

Fritz–Dieter Söhn, Renthof 8, 35037 Marburg. Tel: (06421) 66002. Fax: 62977. Est: 1983. Storeroom; appointment necessary. Very large stock. Spec: medicine; microscopy. Cata: 2 a year. Corresp: German. Mem: I.L.A.B.

MECKENHEIM

Urbs et Orbis Klaus Semmel, Ortsteil Merl, Göddertzgarten 42, 53340 Meckenheim.

GERMANY

MEERSBURG

Antiquariat List & Francke, Stettener Strasse 33, 88709 Meersburg, Postfach 14 60, 88704 Meersburg.

Kunsthandel Ph. Mathias, Mülhofer Strasse 2, 88718 Daisendorf. Tel: (07532) 7872. Fax: 49672. Est: 1950. Shop at: Daisendorfer Strasse 8, 88709 Meersburg. Very small stock. Spec: antiquarian; art; art history; art reference; artists; atlases/ cartography; autographs; Catalogues Raisonées; early imprints; fine art; graphic art; illustrated; incunabula; manuscripts; painting; general & local topography; travel - general, Africa, Americas, Asia, Australasia/Australia, Europe, Middle East, Polar; typography. PR: DM20–20,000. Also, oil paintings, watercolours and drawings. Corresp: French, Dutch, Italian, Japanese. Mem: Verband der Kunst- und Antiquitätenhändler.

MEITINGEN

Versandantiquariat Dr. Wolfgang Wanzke, Mendelstrasse 11a, 86405 Meitingen. Tel: & Fax: (08271) 41710. Est: 1991. Private premises. Small stock. Spec: aeronautics; antiquarian; biology; botany; chemistry; children's; earth sciences; economics; first editions; history of civilisation; illustrated; industry; literature; medicine; natural sciences; pharmacy/pharmacology; printing; technical technology; zoology. PR: DM10–1,000. Cata: 1 or 2 a year. Corresp: German.

METTMANN

Antiquariat Dietlind Unterberg, Fontanestrasse 20, (-Metzkausen) 40822 Mettmann. Tel: (02104) 53357. Storeroom and private premises; open only on demand. Very small stock. Spec: children's picture books. Cata: occasionally. Corresp: German. VAT No: DE 121 622 147.

MICHELSTADT

Antiquariat am Neuthor, Friedrich–Ebert–Strasse 8, 64720 Michelstadt.

MINDEN

Antiquariat W. Graf, Simeonstrasse 7, 32423 Minden. Tel: & Fax: (0571) 25343. Shop; open 10–1 and 3–6. Medium stock. Spec: topography; travel; Baedeker & Murray Travel Guides; aeronautics; encyclopedias. Also, a booksearch service.

MÖSSINGEN

Musikantiquariat Ulrich Schwarz, Sternbergstrasse 55, 72116 Mössingen. Tel: (07473) 23440. Est: 1994. Private premises; small stock. Spec: music - stringed instruments. PR: DM10–5,000. Corresp: French. VAT No: DE 167 773 032.

MORSUM

Cicero Presse, 25980 Morsum/Sylt. Prop: Timm Zenner. Tel: (04651) 890305. Fax: 890885. Est: 1965. Private premises; appointment necessary. Very large stock. Spec: bibliographies; Catalogues Raisonneés; encyclopaedias. Cata: 1 or 2 a year. Corresp: French, Spanish. Mem: V.D.A.; I.L.A.B. VAT No: DE 134 974 814.

MÜLHEIM

Buch- und Schallplattenantiquariat Gross, Kappenstrasse 5, 45473 Mülheim. Est: 1980. Storeroom; appointment necessary. Small general stock. PR: DM50–5,000.

MÜNSTER

Commedia, Frauenstrasse 9, 48143 Münster. Prop: F.W. Bitzhenner. Tel: (0251) 46000. Fax: 46745. Est: 1980. Shop; open Monday to Friday 10–6 and Saturday 10–1. Large stock. Spec: fiction; science. Cata: 9 to 12 a year. Also, a booksearch service. *Also at:* Medium Buchmarkt, Münster (q.v.).

Delibrium Antiquariat, Hörsterstrasse 35/36, 48143 Münster. Prop: Eugen Kuepper. Tel: (0251) 518870. Fax: 511419. Est: 1970. Shop; open Monday to Friday 2–6.30, Saturday 10–2. Very large stock. Spec: advertising; architecture; art; books about books; first editions; history; illustrated; literature; periodicals/magazines; philosophy; photography; typography. PR: DM5–1,000. Also, a booksearch service. Corresp: German, French.

Winfried Geisenheyner, Postfach 480155, 48078 Münster. Tel: (02501) 7884. Fax: 13657. E-Mail: rarebooks@geisenheyner.de. Est: 1981. Private premises; appointment necessary. Small stock. Spec: science; technology; medicine; travel; children's; illustrated literature. Cata: 4 a year. Also, a booksearch service. Mem: V.D.A.

Antiquariat Andreas Grundmann, Ottostrasse 5, 48155 Münster. Tel: & Fax: (0251) 663395. Est: 1991. Postal business only. Very large stock. Spec: the arts; national culture; ecclesiastical history & architecture; fine & rare; folklore; Christian religion. PR: DM5–10,000. Cata: 2 a year. Corresp: French, German, Dutch.

Antiquariat Bernhard Hüning, Grevener Strasse 343, 48159 Münster. Tel: (0251) 211668. Fax: 215640. Est: 1889. Private premises; postal business only. Medium general stock. Spec: trade; professions; towns; landscapes etc. PR: DM1–10,000. Also, the local history of Münster and Münsterland. Corresp: Dutch.

Antiquariat Hans-Jürgen Ketz, Scharnhorststrasse 92, 48151 Münster. Tel: (0251) 521082. Fax: 525851. Est: 1978. Appointment necessary. Spec: horology; science; technology; medicine; travel. Cata: every 2 or 3 years. Corresp: French. Mem: V.D.A.

Medium Buchmarkt, Rosenstrasse 5–6, 48143 Münster. Prop: Friedrich W. Bitzhenner. Tel: (0251) 46000. Fax: 46745. Est: 1980. Shop; open Monday to Friday 10–6.30, Saturday 10–1.30. Large stock. Spec: fiction; art; design; architecture; photography. CC: EC; MC: V; AE. Cata: 9 to 12 a year. Also, a booksearch service and secondhand records. Corresp: German. VAT No: DE 158 655 245. *Also at:* Commedia, Münster (q.v.).

Antiquariat Ortwin Rüttger, Alter Fischmarkt 8, 48143 Münster.

MUDERSHAUSEN

Edmund Hertling Buchhändler und Antiquar, Taunusblick 4, 65623 Mudershausen. Tel: (06430) 6242. Est: 1976. Storeroom; postal business only. Large stock. Spec: topography of Germany and former German territories; political science; folklore; voyages. Cata: on Hassiaca, Nassovica, Rhenania, World Wars, conservatism and folklore, 8 a year. Mem: V.D.A.; B.V.D.B.

MUNICH (MÜNCHEN)

Antiquariat Theodor Ackermann, Ludwigstrasse 7, 80539 München. Prop: Christoph Sebald. Tel: (089) 284787. Fax: 280172. Est: 1865. Shop; open Monday to Friday 9–6, Saturday 10–1. Medium stock. Spec: astronomy; botany; chemistry; early imprints; economics; fine & rare; incunabula; natural history; natural sciences; philosophy; physics; science; travel; zoology. Cata: 4 a year. Mem: V.D.A.; I.L.A.B. VAT No: DE 129 794 618.

Alpen–Antiquariat, Postfach 810528, 81905 München. Prop: Ingrid Koch. Tel: (089) 931516. Fax: 9305821. Est: 1987. Mail order or by appointment. Small stock. Spec: alpinism; travel. PR: DM10–1,000. Cata: 2 a year. Also, a booksearch service. Corresp: German. VAT No: DE 129 818 567.

Avalun Antiquariat, Postfach 10 01 53, 80075 München.

Hermann Beisler, Antiquariat, Oskar–von–Miller–Ring 33, 80333 München.

Galerie Siegfried Billesberger, Billesberger Hof, 85452 Moosinning/München.

Buchhandlung Georg Blendl GmbH & Co. KG, Pacellistrasse 5, 80333 München.

Kunstantiquariat Klaus von Brincken, Salvatorstrasse 2, 80333 München.

Carussell Verlag, Am Haselweg 13, 85599 Parsdorf. (•) E-Mail: tschik@aol.com. Est: 1979. Very small stock. Spec: erotica; esoteric; illustrated; cookery/gastronomy. PR: DM1–100. Corresp: German.

Ursula Haeusgen, Kaiserstrasse 8, 80801 München.

Hartung & Hartung Antiquariat-Auktionen, Postfach 20 09 25, 80009 München.

Galerie am Haus der Kunst, Franz-Josef-Strauss-Ring 4, 80539 München. Prop: Monika Schmidt. Tel: (089) 222315. Fax: 2800044. Est: 1985. Shop; open Wednesday to Friday 10.30–6, Saturday 10.30–1. Very small stock. Spec: Japanese books. Mem: V.D.A. VAT No: DE 130 555 450.

Hans Höchtberger, Postfach 860404, 81631 München. Tel: (089) 983686. Est: 1969. Private premises; appointment necessary. Medium stock. Spec: art; books about books; illustrated; first editions of German literature. Cata: 2 or 3 a year. Also, literary and art periodicals. Corresp: French. VAT No: DE 130 435 055.

Buchhandlung H. Hugendubel GmbH & Co. KG, Postfach 10 07 52, 80081 München.

Versandantiquariat Richard Husslein, Dompfaffweg 7, 82152 Plannegg (bei München). Tel: (089) 5234732. Private premises. Medium stock. Spec: autographs; art; books about books; cinema/films; first editions; illustrated; limited editions; printing. PR: DM40–1,200. Cata: 2 a year on cinema/films. Corresp: Italian, Greek.

Alte Graphik Julia F. Iliu, Barerstrasse 46, 80799 München.

Versandantiquariat MGM Joker KG, Stiglmaierplatz 2, 80333 München. Tel: (089) 5233660. Fax: 525393. Est: 1980. Shop; open Monday to Friday 9–6, Saturday 9–1. Small stock. Spec: numismatics; jewellery; antiquarian; antiques. PR: DM1–5,000. Cata: 2 a year. Corresp: French. Mem: V.D.A. VAT No: DE 130 006 976.

Karl & Faber, Amiraplatz 3, 80333 München. Prop: Louis Karl. Tel: (089) 2218865-66. Fax: 2283350. Est: 1923. Open Monday to Friday 9–1 & 2.30–6. Small stock. Spec: art; art reference; artists; fine art - 15th–20th century; travel. PR: DM300 and up. Cata: 2 a year, plus exhibition catalogues. Also, works of art, Old Masters, 19th century contemporary art, Post Impressionists, drawings, watercolours, paintings, valuations, consultancy, private sales and auctions. Corresp: French, German, Italian, Spanish. Mem: B.D.K.; V.D.A.; I.L.A.B.; S.S.L.A.E. VAT No: DE 129 772 566.

J. Kitzinger, Schellingstrasse 25, 80799 München. Prop: Raimund & Bernhard Kitzinger. Tel: (089) 283537. Fax: 281394. Est: 1892. Shop; open Monday to Friday 9–6, Saturday 9–1. Large stock. Spec: humanities; art; literature; history; theology. Cata: irregularly. Also, new books. Corresp: French, Italian. Mem: V.D.A.; B.V.D.B. VAT No: DE 811 143 716.

Antiquariat Rainer Köbelin, Schellingstrasse 99, 80798 München. Tel: (089) 285640. Fax: 5237404. Shop; open Monday to Friday 10–1 and 3.30–6.30, Saturday 10.30–1. Spec: fencing; sport; military; Bavarica; cookery/gastronomy; children's.

Antiquariat Lutz-Peter Kreussel, Occamstrasse 10, 80802 München. Tel: (089) 395121. Fax: 390907. Est: 1982. Shop; open Monday to Friday 12–6.30, Saturday 10–2. Medium stock. Spec: literature; history; art; sciences; travel; Baedeker; 20th century first editions of literature & art; geography; illustrated; cookery; architecture. PR: DM1–10,000. Cata: 2 to 4 a year. Also, a booksearch service. Corresp: French, Italian, German.

Kubon & Sagner, Buchexport-Import GmbH, 80328 München. Tel: (089) 542180. TA: Buchsagner, München. Fax: 54218218. E-Mail: postmaster@kubon-sagner.de. Est: 1946. Shop at: Hess–Strasse 39/41, München; open Monday to Friday. Very large stock. Spec: Slavic and Finno–Ugric studies; Romania; Baltica; Sudetica; Silesiaca. CC: V; EC. Cata: weekly. Also, new books and periodicals from Eastern Europe. Cata: yearly. Corresp: Russian, Czech, Slovak, Polish. Mem: B.V.D.B. VAT No: DE 811 194 845.

Kunstantiquariat Stephan List, Barerstrasse 39/Rückgeb, 80799 München.

Numismatik Lanz München, Maximilianspl. 10, 80333 München.

Almuth Petersen-Roil, Münchener Freiheit 24, 80802 München 40. Tel: (089) 390704. Est: 1981. Private premises; appointment necessary. Small stock. Spec: ethnology (particularly Asia, Indonesia, Oceania and north-west-coast Indians). Also, publisher of series "Island-Bibliographies". Cata: 4 a year. Corresp: Netherlands, Spanish. Mem: B.V.D.B.

Dr. Karl H. Pressler, Römerstrasse 7, 80801 München. Tel: (089) 341331 or 398430. Est: 1954. Storeroom; appointment necessary. Very large stock. Spec: literature; history; bibliography; fine and rare. Mem: B.V.D.B.; V.D.A.; A.B.A. (UK).

Rauhut Rainer Philographikon, Pfisterstrasse 11, 80331 München. Tel: (089) 225082. Fax: 225791. Est: 1974. Shop; open Monday to Friday 10–6, Saturday 10–2. Very large general stock. Spec: botany; sport; topography. CC: All major. Also, illuminated manuscripts. Corresp: French, German, Spanish, Dutch. Mem: Association of German Antiquarian Dealers. VAT No: DE 130 100 034.

Antiquariat G. Scheppler & M. Müller, Giselastrasse 25, 80802 München. Prop: Matthias Müller. Tel: (089) 348174. Fax: 398214. Shop; open Monday to Friday 10.30–6.30, Saturday by appointment. Medium stock. Spec: art; geography; history; medicine; occult; philosophy; science; theology. Cata: 4 a year. Mem: V.D.A.

Kunstantiquariat Monika Schmidt, Türkenstrasse 48, 80799 München. Tel: (089) 284223. Fax: 2800044. Est: 1970. Shop; open Monday to Friday 10–6, Saturday by appointment from 10–1. Very small stock. Spec: atlases; travel; illustrated 15th-century to 1860. Mem: V.D.A. VAT No: DE 130 555 450.

Antiquariat Schneider-Henn, Galeriestrasse 2b, 80539 München.

Schweitzer Sortiment, 80295 München. Tel: (089) 55134280. Fax: 55134100. Shop; open Monday to Wednesday. Medium stock. Spec: law. Cata: 1 or 2 a year.

Antiquariat Michael Steinbach, Demollstrasse 1/I, 80638 München. Tel: (089) 1571691. Fax: 1577096. Est: 1972. Private premises; appointment necessary. Small stock. Spec: illustrated; literature in first and early editions; bibliophily; art; arts and crafts. PR: DM10–10,000. Cata: 1 or 2 a year. Also, a booksearch service. Corresp: Spanish, French, German. Mem: V.D.A. DE 130 208 178.

Antiquariat Turszynski, Sperlstrasse 28, 81476 München. Prop: Uwe Turszynski. Tel: (089) 7552598. Fax: 7552596. Est: 1986. Private premises. Very small stock. Spec: alchemy; chemistry; colonial; cookery/gastronomy; early imprints; fine & rare; foreign texts; history of ideas; foreign languages; occult; travel - Africa, Americas, Asia, Australasia/Australia; Europe; Middle East; Polar; voyages and discovery; whaling. PR: £100–10,000. Cata: 4 a year. Corresp: Italian. VAT No: DE 131 534 877.

Buch- und Kunstantiquariat Robert Wölfle, (80799) Amalienstrasse 65, Post Box 40 19 80, 80719 München 40.

Buch- und Kunstauktionshaus F. Zisska & R. Kistner, Unterer Anger 15, 80331 München. Tel: (089) 263855. Fax: 269088. Est: 1983. Shop; open Monday to Friday 9–1 & 2–6. Spec: old and rare; manuscripts; autographs; topography. Cata: 2 a year for auctions. Also, auctioneers. Mem: I.L.A.B.; V.D.A. VAT No: DE 129 732 689.

NETTETAL

Hans K. Matussek, Buchhändler & Antiquariat, Postfach 12 65, 41302 Nettetal.

NEU-ULM

Pallas Antiquariat Rudolf Mayrhofer, Weserstr. 8, 89231 Neu-Ulm. Est: 1994. Private premises. Small stock. Spec: illustrated; literature; literature in translation; national culture. Cata: 4 a year. Corresp: French, Italian.

NEUSS

Harald Hildebrandt, Tiberiusstrasse 12, 41468 Neuss. Tel: (02131) 120149. Fax: 103083. Est: 1980. Private premises; appointment necessary. Small stock. Spec: antiquarian; art; bibliography; colour-plate; fine & rare; illuminated manuscripts; illustrated; travel. PR: £50–3,000. Also, large print books. Corresp: French, German. VAT No: DE 120 720 020.

Buch- und Kunstantiquariat Brigitta Kowallik, Klarissenstrasse 5 & 10, 41460 Neuss.

Wolfgang Symanczyk, Buchhandlung und Antiquariat, Hubertusweg 32, 41466 Neuss.

NUREMBERG (NÜRNBERG)

Antiquariat G. Grauer, Kornmarkt 8 - Maximum, 90402 Nürnberg. Prop: Godela Grauer. Tel: (0911) 2448425. Fax: 2448427. Est: 1935. Shop; open Tuesday to Friday 9–1 and 2–6, Saturday 9–2. Large general stock. Spec: antiquarian; art; art history; art reference; late 19th and 20th century literature; philosophy; history. Also, new books (including facsimiles), and a booksearch service. Corresp: German. Mem: B.V.B.V. VAT No: DE 811 922 528.

GERMANY

Antiquariat Gerhard Hofner, Emmericher Str. 21, 90411 Nürnberg. Tel: (0911) 523234. Fax: 525675. Est: 1982. Shop; appointment necessary. Small stock. Spec: old and rare; humanities; the arts; literature; bibliography; books about books. Cata: on specialities, 3 or 4 a year. Mem: V.D.A. VAT No: DE 133 285 513.

Antiquariat Peter Kessler, Fürther Strasse 89, 90429 Nürnberg. Tel: (0911) 289977. Fax: 2879027. Est: 1985. Shop; open Tuesday to Friday 2–6. Medium stock. Spec: Franconica; antiquarian; art; local history; national languages; music; natural sciences; photography; local topography. PR: DM1–1,000. Cata: 2 to 4 a year. Corresp: French, Dutch.

OBERHAUSEN

Reise–Antiquariat Dieter Kuhlmann, Gellertstrasse 13, 46049 Oberhausen. Tel: (0208) 854466. Est: 1986. Appointment necessary. Medium stock. Spec: antiquarian; art; artists; children's; circus; countries & continents; fables; general fiction; graphic art; illustrated; literature; politics; travel. Also, a booksearch service. Corresp: French, German.

OBERURSEL

WL–Handels–Service Waltraud Löbel, Gerhart–Hauptmann–Strasse 4, 61440 Oberursel. Prop: Waltraud & Karlheinz Löbel. Tel: (06171) 24326. Est: 1973. Private premises; appointment necessary. Very small stock. Spec: Bohemia and Hessia, including graphic art and historical. PR: DM1–2,000. CC: MC. Corresp: German. Mem: Industrie- u. Handelskammer Frankfurt a.M. VAT No: DE 111 299 099.

OBING

Antiquariat Dr. Reto Feurer, Postfach 1230, 83119 Obing. Tel: (08624) 1604. Est: 1980. Storeroom; appointment necessary. Medium stock. Spec: first editions; dedicated copies; illustrated; art; film and photography; periodicals. PR: DM10–5,000. Cata: 2 or 3 a year on literature, art, photography, illustrated etc. Also, a booksearch service. Corresp: French, Italian. VAT No: DE 131 478 863.

ODENTHAL

Guenther Leisten, St.-Engelbert-Strasse 24, 51519 Odenthal. Tel: (02202) 78540. Est: 1951. Appointment necessary. Small stock. Spec: autographs; cookery/gastronomy; crafts; fine and rare; paper-making; pharmacy/pharmacology; history of science; teaching. Corresp: French. Mem: V.D.A.; I.L.A.B. VAT No: DE 122 057 239.

OFFENBURG

Antiquariat Ottmar Müller, Zellerstrasse 14, 77654 Offenburg. Tel: (0781) 38996. Est: 1994. Storeroom; appointment necessary, and market stand. Small general stock. PR: DM1–1,000. Cata: 2 or 3 a year. Also, a booksearch service.

OLPE/BIGGESEE

Kunstantiquariat Dr. Gerhard Schneider, Rhode–Goldsiepen 12, 57462 Olpe/ Biggesee.

OSNABRÜCK

Antiquariat Harlinghausen, Arndtstrasse 5, 49078 Osnabrück. Tel: (0541) 433929. Est: 1973. Private premises; appointment necessary. Spec: portraits. Mem: V.D.A.

Antiquariat Kraemer & Hansen GmbH, Laischaftsstrasse 17a, 49080 Osnabrück.

Buch- und Kunstantiquariat Reinhard Kuballe, Sutthauser Strasse 19, Postfach 26 63, 49016 Osnabrück.

H. Th. Wenner Antiquariat, Heger Strasse 2-3, 49074 Osnabrück. Tel: (541) 3310366. Fax: 201113. Est: 1939. Shop; open Monday to Friday 10–1 and 3–6. Very large general stock. Corresp: German. Mem: V.D.A.; L.I.L.A. VAT No: DE 117 658 455.

OSTERODE

Buch- und Kunstantiquariat Alice Elchlepp, Schillerstrasse 14a, 37520 Osterode.

PADINGBUETTEL

Jan Hendrik Niemeyer, Dorfstrasse 4, 27632 Padingbuettel. Tel: & Fax: (04742) 2117. Est: 1992. Storeroom; open Monday to Friday 9–6.30, Saturday 9–2. Very small stock. Spec: maritime/nautical; shipbuilding. Cata: 2 or 3 a year on specialities. Also, a booksearch service. Corresp: French. VAT No: DE 153 227 071.

Ridinger Gallery Niemeyer, Dorfstrasse 4, 27632 Padingbuettel, Near Bremerhaven. Tel: & Fax: (04742) 2117. Est: 1959. Storeroom; open Monday to Friday 9–6.30, Saturday 9–2, or by appointment. Spec: animals; atlases/cartography; dogs; fables; fine & rare; forestry; gardening; graphic art; Beethoven; ornithology; painting; zoology; hunting; riding; fishing; Johann Elias Ridinger and family; Joseph Georg Wintter (1751–1789). PR: DM100–150,000/200,000. Cata: 4 to 10 a year on specialities. Also, a booksearch service. Corresp: French. VAT No: DE 122 210 824.

PATTENSEN

Horst Wellm, Bennigser Weg 1, 30982 Pattensen (Han.). Tel: (05101) 13361. Est: 1967. Private premises; appointment necessary. Medium stock. Spec: bibliography; regional and local history; sciences. Cata: 2 a year. Also, a booksearch service.

PFORZHEIM

Antiquariat Angelika Hofmann, Theodor–Heuss–Strasse 52, 75180 Pforzheim. Tel: (07231) 765152. Fax: 765242. Est: 1990. Storeroom; open Monday to Friday 9–12 and 2–6. Very large general stock. Cata: 2 or 3 a year. Also, an out of print book service. Corresp: German.

Antiquariat Peter Kiefer, Buch-und Graphikauktionen, Kaiser-Friedrich-Strasse 10, 7530 Pforzheim.

POTSDAM

Antiquariat Harmut König, Schulstrasse 1, 14641 Markee/Havelland. (•) Tel: (03321) 49034. Est: 1973. Storeroom; open Wednesday 9–6. Large stock. Spec: architecture; art; autobiography; cinema/films; foreign & national culture; first editions; general & national history; Holocaust; illustrated; limited editions; literature; pacifism; photography; politics; private press; signed editions; socialism; general & local topography. PR: DM1–1,000. Cata: 6 to 8 a year. Also, a booksearch service. Corresp: Danish, Dutch, German. VAT No: DE 138 647 416.

QUICKBORN

Antiquariat Heinz Tessin, Harksheider Weg 138, 25451 Quickborn. Tel: & Fax: (04106) 2453. Est: 1977. Shop; appointment necessary. Medium stock. Spec: books about books; botany; ex-libris; geography; illustrated; literature; medicine; natural sciences; science; socialism; space travel; technical; general & local topography; travel; voyages & discovery; zoology. PR: DM20–500. Cata: 1 or 2 a year. Corresp: German. VAT No: DE 134 462 940.

RAUENBERG

Antiquariat Franz Siegle, Postfach 11 14, 69227 Rauenberg.

REGENSBURG

Buch und Kunstantiquariat Reinhold Berg, Wahlenstrasse 6, 93047 Regensburg. Tel: & Fax: (0941) 52229. E-Mail: bergbook@donau.de. Est: 1977. Shop; open Monday to Friday 9–12.30 and 2–6, Saturday 9–1. Spec: travel; illustrated 16-20th century; plate books. Cata: 1 a year. Corresp: German. Mem: V.D.A. VAT No: DE 133 586 877.

Ch. Hackel M.A., Regensburger Antiquariat, Hinter der Grieb 2, 93047 Regensburg.

RENNEROD

Westerwald–Antiquariat Helmut R. Lang, Hauptstrasse 71, 56477 Rennerod. Tel: (0611) 376931. Fax: 300850. Est: 1982. Shop; open daily 10–8. Medium stock. Spec: antiquarian; archaeology; architecture; art; art history; autographs; avant–garde; bibliography; bindings; biography; books about books; Catalogues Raisonées; cookery/gastronomy; early imprints; ethnography; ethnology; ex–libris; fine printing; first editions; history; illustrated; limited editions; literature; philosophy; printing; private press; signed editions; general topography & travel; typography. PR: DM1–20,000. Cata: 12 a year. Also, a booksearch service, book object service and large print books. Mem: Gutenberg–Gesellschaft, Ges.d. Bibliophilen. VAT No: DE 177 435 615. *Also at:* Rheinstrasse 104 *and* Hochstättenstrasse 2-10, Wiesbaden (q.v.).

RENNINGEN

Fonsblavus Antiquariat, Grabenstrasse 3, 71272 Renningen. Prop: Hans-Guenter Bilger. Tel: (07159) 2260. Fax: 18314. E-Mail: fonsblavus@compuserve.com. Est: 1985. Storeroom; appointment necessary. Small stock. Spec: antiquarian; fine & rare; early imprints; first editions; natural sciences; mathematics; medicine; literature; physics; general travel; astronomy - Kepler. PR: DM50–10,000. Cata: irregularly. Also, a booksearch service and book fairs. Corresp: German, French. Mem: B.D.B. VAT No: DE 145 980 734.

REUTLINGEN

Auktionshaus Antiquariat Heck, Kaiserstrasse 64, 72764 Reutlingen. Prop: Thomas Leon Heck. Tel: (07121) 370911. Fax: (07071) 87408. Est: 1982. Shop. Very large stock. Spec: first editions; literature. Corresp: French, Spanish, Italian. VAT No: DE 146 478 807. *Also at:* Hafengasse 10, 72070 Tübingen (q.v.)

Antiquariat Karl Knödler, Postfach 20 51, 72710 Reutlingen.

RIEDLINGEN

Buchantiquariat u. Verlag Genth, 88525 Heudorf am Bussen/Riedlingen, Breite 13. Prop: Hannelore Genth. Tel: (07371) 96096. Fax: 96098. Shop; open Monday to Friday 9–6, Saturday 9–12. General stock. Also, a booksearch service and large print books. Corresp: German, Italian.

RODGAU

Buch- und Kunstantiquariat Hubert Niesen, Postfach 300447, 63091 Rodgau. Tel: (06106) 733164. Fax: 79667. Est: 1976. Storeroom and private premises; appointment necessary. Large stock. Spec: aeronautics; atlases; cartography; aviation; children's; cookery/gastronomy; fine & rare; literature; natural sciences; space travel; topography; transport; travel. PR: DM20–5,000. Cata: 5 to 10 lists a year. VAT No: DE 114 051 359.

ROSENHEIM

Antiquariat Eigl, Schmellestrasse 1, 83022 Rosenheim. Prop: Ralf Eigl. Tel: (08031) 33504. Fax: 12911. Est: 1985. Very small stock. Spec: travel & exploration only. PR: DM500–15,000. Cata: 3 a year. Corresp: German. VAT No: DE 152 140 394.

Antiquariat Kurz, Schmettererstrasse 20, (im 'Mail–Keller) am Roxyberg, 83022 Rosenheim. Tel: (08031) 12817. Fax: 380256. Est: 1980. Open Monday to Friday 10–6. Large stock. Spec: hunting; aeronautics; alpinism/ mountaineering; art; art history; children's; cookery/gastronomy; geography; history; household management; literature; motoring; needlework; photography; sport; textiles. Cata: 4 a year. Also, a booksearch service. Corresp: German.

Antiquariat Schwarzfischer, Hochgernstr. 47, 83026 Rosenheim. Prop: Elfriede Schwarzfischer. Mgr: Helmut Schwarzfischer. Tel: (08031) 44457. Fax: 43944. Est: 1990. Storeroom and private premises; open Monday to Friday 9–8, Saturday 9–1. Small stock. Spec: anthropology; antiquarian; atlases; foreign culture; ethnography; ethnology; fine & rare; geography; natural history; travel - general, Africa, Asia, Middle East, Polar; voyages & discovery. PR: DM100– 35,000. Cata: 2 a year. Corresp: German. Mem: B.D.B.; Froschauer Genossenschaft Zürich/Switzerland. VAT No: DE 131 130 946.

ROTTHALMÜNSTER

Antiquariat Heribert Tenschert, Kirchplatz 14–15, 94094 Rotthalmünster.

SAARBRÜCKEN

Antiquariat Martin Barbian, Türkenstrasse 11–13, 66111 Saarbrücken. Prop: Martin Barbian & Ina Grund. Tel: & Fax: (0681) 31877. Est: 1990. Shop; open Monday to Friday 10–6, Saturday 10–2. Medium stock. Spec: geography; general and local history; literature; art; art history; military. PR: DM10–1,000. Cata: 4 to 6 a year. Corresp: German. Mem: V.D.A. VAT No: DE 162 500 563.

Der Buchladen-Antiquariat, Försterstrasse 14, 66111 Saarbrücken. Shop. Very small stock.

Jura Buchhandlung, Talstrasse 58, Postfach 101563 66119 Saarbrücken. Prop: Gerhard Hasslocher. Tel: (0681) 5846116. Fax: 581591. E-Mail: jurabuch@aol.com. Est: 1982. Shop; open Monday to Saturday 9–6.30. Small stock. Spec: law. Cata: 6 a year. Also, a booksearch service. Corresp: French, Spanish, Italian, German. Mem: Buchhandlervereinigung. VAT No: DE 138 103 990.

Kunstantiquariat Peter H. Köhl, St. Johanner Markt 20, 66111 Saarbrücken. Tel: & Fax: (0681) 33242. Est: 1962. Shop; open Monday to Friday 10–1 and 2–6, Saturday 10–1. Medium general stock. Spec: Saar; Lorraine; Alsace; Luxemburg; Moselle. PR: DM1–1,000. Cata: 1 or 2 a year. Corresp: French, German, Italian. Mem: V.D.A.; Verband Saarländischer Kunst & Buchhandler.

ST. GOAR

Reichl Verlag, Auf dem Hänchen 34, 56329 St. Goar. Tel: (06741) 1720. Fax: 1749.

SCHMITTEN IM TAUNUS

Dominik Auvermann GmbH, Ortsteil Niederreifenberg, Hauptstrasse 86, 61389 Schmitten im Taunus. Prop: Dominik Auvermann. Tel: (06082) 930044. Fax: 930045. Est: 1992. Shop; appointment necessary. Small stock. Spec: periodicals/magazines; limited editions; literature and collected works. PR: DM500–25,000. Corresp: German, French, Italian, Spanish. Mem: German Antiquarian Assn. VAT No: DE 154 344 913.

SCHRIESHEIM

Antiquariat Frank Albrecht, Panoramastrasse 4, 69198 Schriesheim. Tel: (06203) 65713. Fax: 65311. Est: 1985. Private premises; appointment necessary. Medium stock. Spec: 20th-century literature; politics; history; illustrated. PR: DM100–10,000. Cata: 10 a year. Also, publisher of 20th-century political bibliography. Corresp: German. Mem: V.D.A.; P.E.N. International. VAT No: DE 144 468 306.

GERMANY

SCHWÄBISCH HALL

Bücher-Gebhard, Schwatzbühlgasse 7, 74532 Schwäbisch Hall.

SCHWANAU

Pharmazeutisches Antiquariat Waldemar Dürr, Kürzeller Strasse 13, 77963 Schwanau. Tel: (07824) 2400. Fax: 2088. Est: 1972. Private premises. Spec: pharmacy; botany.

SCHWERIN

Schweriner Antiquariat, Puschkinstrasse 59, 19055 Schwerin.

SINDELFINGEN

Sindelfinger Kabinett Brigitte Strehler, Postfach 429, 71063 Sindelfingen.

STOLBERG-ZWEIFALL

Globetrott–Zentrale Bernd Tesch. Reise–Ausrüstungen, Zur Fernsicht 18, 52224 Stolberg–Zweifall. Tel: & Fax: (02402) 75375. Est: 1977. Postal business only. Very small stock. Spec: world travel; motorcycle; survival. Cata: 2 a year. Also, expert on motorcycle world tours. Corresp: German.

STRAUBING

Buchhandlung Stöcker, Ludwigsplatz 4, 94315 Straubing. Prop: Wolfgang Stöcker. Tel: (09421) 10120. Fax: 81791. Est: 1969. Shop; open Monday to Friday 9–6, Saturday 9–1. Medium general stock. Cata: 2 a year. Mem: Börsenverein des Deutschen Buchandel.

STUTTGART

Antiquariat Petra Bewer, Haussmanstrasse 20, 70188 Stuttgart. Tel: (0711) 2348526. Fax: 2348627. Est: 1994. Private premises; appointment necessary. Medium stock. Spec: architecture; art; art history; the arts. PR: DM1–1,000. Cata: 2 a year. Also, organisation of the Antiquaria, annual antiquarians' fair in Ludwigsburg, Germany. Corresp: German. VAT No: DE 169 495 888.

Musikantiquariat Dr. Ulrich Drüner, Ameisenbergstrasse 65, 70188 Stuttgart.

Antiquariat Engel & Co. GmbH, (70184) Alexanderstrasse 11, Postfach 10 12 41, 70011 Stuttgart. Tel: (0711) 240413. Fax: 2360021. Est: 1964. Shop; open Monday to Friday 9–6.30, Saturday 9–1. Large stock. Spec: anthroposophy; art; biology; geography; literature; medicine; natural sciences; philosophy. Cata: 3 a year and lists on natural sciences, medicine, geography, art, literature, philosophy/bibliophily. Mem: V.D.A.

Antiquariat Th. & M. Held, Schlostrasse 94/1, 70176 Stuttgart. Prop: Thomas & Marianne Held. Tel: (0711) 626032. Fax: 628798. Est: 1985. Shop; open Wednesday to Friday 2–6 and by appointment. Medium stock. Spec: applied art; carpets; colonial; decorative art; embroidery; ethnography; ethnology; fashion & costume; jewellery; knitting; lace; needlework; Oriental religion; tapestry; textiles; travel - Africa, Asia, Australasia/Australia, Middle East, Polar. Cata: 4 a year. Also, a booksearch service. Corresp: German, French. VAT No: DE 147 486 494.

Antiquariat Wilhelm Hohmann, Rotenwaldstrasse 41, 70197 Stuttgart. Tel: (0711) 6572328. Fax: 6572914. Est: 1990. Shop; open Monday to Friday 9–1 and 2–6. Medium stock. Spec: business history of all branches - advertising; banking; bibliography; biography; business studies; caricature; cartoons; economics; industrial history; industry; political economy; social history; social sciences. PR: DM20–5,000. Cata: 4 or 5 a year. Also, a booksearch service. Corresp: French, German. Mem: B.D.B. VAT No: DE 147 496 899.

Antiquariat Fritz Keller, Alexanderstrasse 32, 70184 Stuttgart. Tel: (0711) 241272. Fax: 2360441. Est: 1989. Shop; open Monday, Tuesday, Thursday & Friday 2–6.30, Saturday 10–12. Medium stock. Spec: children's; industrial history; motoring; military; general & local topography; toys. Corresp: German. VAT No: DE 951 792 6259.

H. Lindemanns Buchhandlung, Nadlerstrasse 10, 70173 Stuttgart. Prop: Werner Götze. Tel: (0711) 233499. Fax: 2369672. Est: 1852. Shop; open 9.30–6. Medium stock. Spec: photography; cinema; film. CC: MC; V. Cata: 2 a year. Also, new books on photography. Mem: B.V.D.B. VAT No: DE 147 465 425.

Antiquariat Fritz Neidhardt, Fleckenweinberg 12, 70192 Stuttgart. Tel: (0711) 8567173. Fax: 8178870. Est: 1952. Shop; appointment necessary. Very small stock. Spec: fine & rare; botany; art; colour-plate; early imprints; fine printing; illustrated; natural history; natural sciences; history of science; technology; zoology; entomology; herbalism. Also, large print books. Corresp: German, French, Dutch. VAT No: DE 147 599 366.

J.F. Steinkopf, Antiquarian und Buchhandlung, Postfach 10 43 54, 70038 Stuttgart.

J. Voerster, Relenbergstrasse 20, 70174 Stuttgart.

TEETZ

Antiquariat Hennwack, Ganzer Strasse 8, 16866 Teetz. Prop: Harald Hentrich & Holger Wagner. Tel: & Fax: (033) 976 50549. Est: 1981. Cata: 1 a year.

TRIER

Antiquariat Am Dom, Sternstrasse 4, 54290 Trier. Prop: P. Fritzen & P. Schwarz. Tel: (0651) 48425. Fax: 45971. Est: 1987. Shop; open Monday to Friday 10–6, Saturday 9–4. Large general stock. Spec: art history; philosophy; theology. PR: £10–1,000. Cata: periodically. Corresp: French. VAT No: DE 149 770 617.

TÜBINGEN

Baders Tübinger Antiquariat, Wilhelmstrasse 3, 72074 Tübingen. Prop: Winfried Bader. Tel: & Fax: (07071) 51427. Est: 1995. Shop; open Monday to Friday 10–6, Saturday 10–4. Very large general stock. Spec: sciences. PR: DM1–100. Cata: 2 a year. Also, a booksearch service. VAT No: DE 147 052 135. *Also at:* Antiquariat Bader, Herrenkellergasse 14, 89073 Ulm. (q.v.).

Auktionshaus Antiquariat Heck, Hafengasse 10, 72070 Tübingen. *Also at:* Kaiserstrasse 64, 72764 Reutlingen (q.v.).

J.J. Heckenhauer oHG, Postfach 1728, 72007 Tübingen. Prop: Roger & Alfred Sonnewald. Tel: (07071) 23018. Fax: 23651. Est: 1823. Shop at: Holzmarkt 7, Tübingen; open Monday to Friday 10–1 & 2–6.30, Saturday 10–2. Very large stock. Spec: antiquarian; art; author - Hesse; bibles; Russia, Poland, Czech Republic and Byzantinism; foreign languages; photography; religion. PR: DM1–5,000. Cata: 1 or 2 a year. Corresp: French, Italian, Russian. Mem: I.L.A.B. VAT No: DE 146 947 401.

TUTZING

Hans Schneider, Mozartstrasse 6, 82327 Tutzing. Tel: (08158) 3050. TA: Musikantiquar, Tutzing. Fax: 7636. Est: 1949. Storeroom; appointment necessary. Very large stock. Spec: music. Cata: 8 a year. Corresp: French. Mem: V.D.A.; B.V.D.B.; Gesellschaft für Musikforschung. VAT No: DE 131 360 693.

ULM

Buch- und Kunstantiquariat Aegis, Breite Gasse 2, 89073 Ulm. Tel: (0731) 64051. Fax: 6021276. Est: 1958. Shop; open Monday to Friday 9–6, Saturday 9–2. Medium stock. Cata: 3 a year. Mem: B.D.B. VAT No: DE 147 053 197.

Antiquariat Bader, Herrenkellergasse 14, 89073 Ulm. Prop: Winfried Bader. Tel: & Fax: (0731) 618618. Est: 1995. Shop; open Monday to Friday 10–6, Saturday 10–4. Medium general stock. PR: DM1–100. Cata: 2 a year. Also, a booksearch service. VAT No: DE 147 052 135. *Also at:* Baders Tübinger Antiquariat, Wilhelmstrasse 3, 72074 Tübingen. (q.v.).

DENEB, Fischergasse 6, 89073 Ulm. Prop: U. Krauss. Tel: & Fax: (0731) 610995. Est: 1991. Storeroom and private premises; open Monday to Friday 10–3. Medium general stock. PR: DM10–1,000. Cata: 1 a year. Also, a booksearch service.

VAREL

Antiquariat Lehmann & Cons., Osterstrasse 8, 26316 Varel. Prop: Stephan Lehmann-Özyurt. Tel: (04451) 83151. Fax: 83151. Est: 1977. Private premises; appointment necessary. Medium stock. Spec: 20th-century art and literature; maritime history; northern Germany. Cata: 1 or 2 a year. Corresp: Turkish. Mem: B.V.D.B.

VETTWEISS

Antiquariat Dieter van Reimersdahl, Amswelweg 16, 52391 Vettweiss.

VÖLKLINGEN

Buch–Galerie Silvia Umla, Kühlweinstr. 101, 66333 Völklingen. Tel: & Fax: (06898) 294822. Est: 1992. Private premises; appointment necessary. Small stock. Spec: antiquarian; art; art history; art reference; artists; bibliography; books about books; botany; calligraphy; children's; education; herbalism; illustrated; literature; printing; private press; theology; typography. PR: DM10–1,000. CC: EC. Cata: 2 a year. Also, a booksearch service, large print books and antiques. Corresp: French, German. Mem: B.V.A. VAT No: DE 160 457 566.

WALTROP

Antiquariat & Fachbuchversand Hartmut Spenner, Stratmannsweg 10, 4355 Waltrop. Tel: (02309) 75572. Fax: 75532. Est: 1982. Shop; appointment necessary. Large stock. Spec: theology. Cata: 4 to 6 a year. Corresp: German. Mem: B.V.D.B. VAT No: DE 126 433 689.

GERMANY

WEDEMARK

Antiquariat Harro von Hirscheydt, Neue Wiesen 6, 30900 Wedemark. Storeroom. Very large stock. Cata: 10 to 12 a year. Corresp: German, Latvian, Swedish. Mem: B.D.B.

WEEZE

Luftfahrt Antiquariat, Brückerhöfe 1, 47652 Weeze. Prop: H.-P. Kopetsch. Tel: & Fax: (02837) 381. Est: 1993. Storeroom; appointment necessary or 24 hours by telephone. Medium general stock. Spec: aeronautics; astronautics; aviation. PR: DM15–200. Cata: 4 a year. Also, a booksearch service. Corresp: German, Dutch.

WEIDEN

Buchhandlung und Antiquariat Hubert Schlegl, Max–Reger–Strasse 18, 92637 Weiden. Tel: (0961) 481580. Fax: 4815870.

WEIDENTHAL

Rudolf Patzer, Mainzer Berg 23, 67475 Weidenthal. Tel: (06329) 362. Est: 1698. Private premises; appointment necessary. Large stock. Spec: bibliography. Cata: 4 a year. Also, human science periodicals. Mem: V.D.A.

WENTORF

WVA Antiquariat, Gärtnerstrasse 5a, 21465 Wentorf. Prop: Barbara & Wolfgang Eymer. Tel: & Fax: (040) 7204392. Est: 1982. Private premises. Medium stock. Spec: almanacs; antiquarian; architecture; art; children's; fables; fine art; geography; graphic art; illustrated; limited editions; literature; photography; surrealism; general travel; typography; voyages & discovery. PR: DM10–1,200. Cata: 1 or 2 a year plus occasional lists. Corresp: French, German. VAT No: DE 135 318 476.

WESEL

Buchhandlung und Antiquariat Uta Hülsey, Postfach 101034, 46470 Wesel. Spec: applied art; art reference; carpets; tapestry; textiles. VAT No: DE 120 987 860.

WIESBADEN

Otto Harrassowitz, (65183) Taunusstrasse 5, Postfach 29 29, 65019 Wiesbaden.

Christa Hemmen Verlag, Grillparzerstrasse 22, 65187 Wiesbaden. Prop: Christa & Jens Hemmen & Christina & Klaus Groh. Tel: (0611) 805649. Fax: 807671. Est: 1986. Appointment necessary. Medium stock. Spec: molluscs and marine invertebrates. PR: DM2–12,000. CC: V; AE. Cata: 2 a year. Also, publishing. Corresp: German. VAT No: DE 113 897 825.

Buchantiquariat Matthias Hill, Westendstrasse 23, 65195 Wiesbaden. Est: 1986. Shop; open Monday to Friday 10–6, Saturday 10–2. Very large stock. Spec: encyclopaedias; illustrated; architecture; technical; natural history; chromolithography. PR: DM1–20,000. Also, large print books. Corresp: German, French, Italian. Mem: P.B.F.A. VAT No: DE 113 787 914.

Antiquariat Helmut R. Lang, Mauritius–Einkaufs–Galerie, Hochstättenstr. 2–10, 65183 Wiesbaden. Tel: (0611) 300756. Fax: 300850. Est: 1982. Shop; open daily 10–8. Medium stock. Spec: antiquarian; archaeology; architecture; art; art history; autographs; avant–garde; bibliography; biography; books about books; Catalogues Raisonées; cookery/gastronomy; early imprints; ethnography; ethnology; ex–libris; fine printing; first editions; history; illustrated; limited editions; literature; philosophy; printing; private press; signed editions; general topography & travel; typography. PR: DM1–20,000. Cata: 12 a year. Also, a booksearch service & book object service and large print books. Mem: Gutenberg–Geselschaft, Ges.d. Bibliophilen. VAT No: DE 177 435 615. *Also at:* Hauptstrasse 71, 56477 Rennerod *and* Rheinstrasse 104, 65185 Wiesbaden (q.v.).

Antiquariat Helmut R. Lang, Rheinstrasse 104, 65185 Wiesbaden. Tel: (0611) 376931. Fax: 300850. Est: 1982. Shop; open daily 10–8. Medium stock. Spec: art; antiquarian; archaeology; architecture; autographs; cookery; bibliography; bindings; biography; books on books; Catalogues Raisonées; early imprints; ethnography/ethnology; ex–libris; fine printing; first, limited & signed editions; history; literature; philosophy; printing; private press; topography; travel; typography. PR: DM1–10,000. Cata: 12 a year. Also, booksearch, large print books & book market organiser. Mem: Gutenberg - Gesellschafts Ger.d. Bibliophilen. VAT No: DE 177 435 615. *Also at:* Hochstättenstrasse 2–10, 65183 Wiesbaden *and* Hauptstrasse 71, 56477 Rennerod (q.v.).

Musikantiquariat Heiner Rekeszus, Herrngartenstrasse 7, 65185 Wiesbaden. Tel: (0611) 3082270. Fax: 3081262. Est: 1986. Storeroom and private premises. Large stock. Spec: music only (books, scores etc.); musical instruments. PR: DM25–1,000. Cata: 2 or 4 a year and special lists. Also, a booksearch service. Corresp: German. VAT No: DE 113 952 269.

Antiquariat & Antiquitäten C. Rinnelt, Taunusstrasse 36, 65183 Wiesbaden. Tel: (0611) 523307. Fax: 9590951. Est: 1945. Shop; open Monday to Friday 9–1 & 2–6.30, Saturday 10–2. Large stock. Spec: children's; Germany, especially Hessen & Nassau; fine and rare; literature; technology. PR: DM20–500. Cata: 1 to 3 a year. Also, antiquities and Fine Arts. Corresp: French, German. Mem: V.D.A.; I.L.A.B.; B.D.K.A. VAT No: DE 113 953 735.

Dr. Martin Sändig GmbH, Postfach 51 20, 65041 Wiesbaden.

Elmar Sändig. Dipl.-Kfm, Sonnenberger Strasse 71, 65191 Wiesbaden. Tel: (0611) 565528. Est: 1973. Private premises; open any time. Medium stock. Spec: artists; colour–plate; Nassau; fine & rare; fine printing; illustrated; photography; golf; local topography. PR: DM50–1,000. Cata: 2 a year. Corresp: German, French. VAT No: DE 113 644 009.

Wertpapier–Antiquariat Bernd Suppes, Am Schlosspark 121, (-Biebrich), 65203 Wiesbaden. Tel: (0611) 9600830. Fax: 692309. Est: 1986. Open Monday to Friday 8.30–6. Medium stock. Spec: antiquarian; autobiography; autographs; banking; colonial; documents; economics; industrial history; industry. PR: DM1–2,000. Cata: 2 a year. Corresp: German. Mem: V.H.W.; Börsenverein. VAT No: DE 113 961 069.

Antiquariat & Buchhandlung M. Zimmerschied, P.O. Box 6240, 65052 Wiesbaden. Tel: (0611) 441040. Fax: 9490033. Est: 1951. Shop at: Blücherstrasse 24, 65195 Wiesbaden; open Monday to Thursday 9–12 and 2–6.30, Friday 9–6.30, Saturday 10–1. Very large stock. Spec: antiquarian. Cata: 2 or 3 a year. Also, CDs, Videos, LPs, video games, PC tools and games.

WORPSWEDER

Worpsweder Antiquariat, Alte Molkerel, Osterweder Strasse 21, 27726 Worpsweder. Prop: Uta Migge & Ian Bild. Tel: (04792) 7072 or 7885. Fax: 4559. Est: 1987. Shop; open Tuesday to Sunday 11–6. Medium stock. Spec: Worpsweder; Judaica; psychology; German children's. PR: DM5–5,000. Cata: regular lists available. Also, an English & German booksearch service. VAT No: DE 116 221 251.

WÜRZBURG

Becker Verlag und Antiquariat, Am Rubenland 13, 97084 Würzburg.

Antiquariat Hermann E. Bub, Oberthuerstrasse 9, 97070 Würzburg.

Antiquariat A. Meixner - **"Autographs"**, Spessartstrasse 27a, 97082 Würzburg. Tel: (0931) 42249. Est: 1973. Private premises; open Monday to Friday 3–7. Medium stock. Spec: autographs; manuscripts; signed editions; documents. Cata: 3 a year.

Antiquariat und Verlag Daniel Osthoff, Martinstrasse 19, 97070 Würzburg. Tel: & Fax: (0931) 572545. Est: 1988. Shop; open Monday to Friday 10–6, Saturday 10–1. Medium stock. Spec: literature; general & local history; classical studies. PR: DM5–10,000. Cata: 4 a year. Corresp: German. VAT No: DE 134 116 708.

WUNSIEDEL

Buchhändler Böhringer, Ludwigstrasse 33, 95632 Wunsiedel. Prop: Heinrich Böhringer. Tel: (09232) 2117. Fax: (09231) 1774. Est: 1919. Shop; open Monday to Friday 7.45–6.15, Saturday 8.45–1. Small stock. Spec: antiquarian; bibliography; foreign & national culture; dictionaries; fashion & costume; first editions; folklore; general, local and national history; foreign and national languages; literature; literature in translation; memoirs; Bavaria and Bohemia, and their folk music. PR: DM20,000 - purchaser's price. CC: EC. Also, a booksearch service and large print books. Corresp: Spanish, Czech. Mem: B.D.B. VAT No: DE 134 190 441.

WUPPERTAL

Friedrich Burchard, Fachbuchhandlung & Antiquariat, P.O. Box 144127, 42310 Wuppertal. Prop: Manfred Burchard. Tel: (0202) 740337 or 742696. Fax: 742185. Est: 1907. Shop at: Sonnbornerstrasse 144, 42327 Wuppertal (Sonnborn); open Monday, Tuesday, Thursday and Friday 8–1 & 3–6 and Wednesday and first Saturday of each month 8–1. Very large stock. Also, new academic books. Mem: V.D.A. VAT No: DE 121 119 073.

Antiquariat Graeff & Heinrich, Flensburger Str. 11, 42107 Wuppertal. Prop: Max Christian Graeff & Michael Heinrich. Tel: (0202) 4598421. Est: 1990. Private premises. Small general stock. Spec: art history; the arts; literature; history; biography. PR: DM1–500. Also, a booksearch service. Corresp: German.

Clemens Müller "Bouquiniste", Kapellenweg 59, 42285 Wuppertal.

Kunsthandel Schmidt & Green, Herbringhausen 10, 42399 Wuppertal. Prop: Lutz & Marianne Schmidt. Tel: (0202) 612061. Fax: 613740. Est: 1972. Private premises; appointment necessary. Very large stock. Spec: classical modern; decorative graphics; topographical subjects; trades and professions. PR: DM100–20,000. Cata: 1 a year. Corresp: German. Mem: RKV eu. VAT No: DE 157 220 002.

GREECE

Country dialling code: 30   *Currency:* Drachma (Dr)

Parousia Bookshop, 94 Solonos Street, 10680 Athinai.

Pharos/Athens, P.O. Box 18246, Athinai 11610.

Stavros E. Stavridis, 18 Panaghitsas, 145 62 Kifisia, Athinai. Tel: (01) 8017079. Est: 1972. Shop; open daily 10–6. Large stock. Spec: Greece; Cyprus; Turkey; archaeology; Near East history; art. Cata: 1 or 2 a year. Corresp: French. Mem: Association of Greek Antique Dealers.

HUNGARY

Country dialling code: 36 *Currency:* Forint

Font Antikvárium, 1062 Andrássy út 56, Budapest.

Legenda Antikvàrium, Ferenciek Tere 3, 1053 Budapest. Prop: Aranka Kerenyi & Tekla Benkö. Tel: & Fax: (01) 1174924. Est: 1993. Shop; open 10–6. Medium general stock. Also, large print books.

ICELAND

Country dialling code: 354 *Currency:* Icelandic krona (IKr)

AKUREYRI

Fródi Fornbókabúd, Kaupangsstraeti 19, Box 169, 602 Akureyri. Prop: Olga 'Agústsdóttir. Tel: 6-26345. Est: 1971. Shop; open 2–6. Medium stock. PR: £1–1,000. Corresp: German, Swedish, Danish. Mem: The Trade Organisation of Akureyri.

REYKJAVIK

Bragi Kristjonsson, Antikvariat, P.O. Box 775, 121 Reykjavík.

ISRAEL

Country dialling code: 972 *Currency:* Shekel (Sh)

HOD-HASHARON

R. Livny Books, P.O. Box 276, Hod-Hasharon 45263. Prop: Reuven Livny. Tel: (09) 405193. Est: 1981. Private premises; postal business only. Medium stock. Spec: Hebraica; Judaica; Palestinia; Near East travel; archaeology; art. PR: US$15–1,000. Also, a booksearch service & new books published in Israel. Corresp: German.

JERUSALEM

Ludwig Mayer (Jerusalem) Ltd., P.O. Box 1174, Jerusalem 91010. Prop: Marcel & Jana Marcus. Tel: & Fax: (02) 625-26-28. Est: 1908. Shop at: Shlomzion Hamalka Street 4, Jerusalem 91010; open Sunday to Thursday 8–1 & 3–7, Friday 8–1. Spec: academic/scholarly; archaeology; dictionaries; education; gnostics; general & national history; history of civilisation; Holocaust; humanities; history of ideas; international affairs; the Middle Ages; mysticism; philosophy; politics; psychology/psychiatry; general, Christian & Jewish religion; social history; social sciences. CC: V; MC. Cata: 1 a year. Corresp: German, French, Russian, Hebrew.

TEL AVIV

Dugit Messianic Outreach Centre, 43 Frishman, Tel Aviv. Tel: (03) 5237586. Fax: 5228738. Remodelled: 1993. Shop and Evangelistic Outreach; open 10–7. Small stock. Spec: art; bibles; children's; decorative art; ecclesiastical history & architecture; fine art; graphic art; general, local and national history; history of civilisation; Holocaust; Christian & Jewish religion; travel - Europe, Middle East; war. PR: $3–45. Also, music and video tapes and materials in Hebrew, English, Russian & other languages. Corresp: Hebrew.

קונים ומוכרים
ספרים משומשים

HALPER'S BOOKS

BUYING & SELLING
QUALITY USED BOOKS

87 Allenby St. Tel-Aviv, Tel/Fax: 03-6299710 :אלנבי 87 ת"א טלפקס

171

J. Halper - Books, 87 Allenby, Tel Aviv. Prop: James Halper. Tel: & Fax: (03) 6299710. Est: 1989. Shop; open 9.30–7, closed Saturday. Very large stock. Spec: antiquarian; archaeology; autographs; books about books; ex–libris; general history; Holocaust; illustrated; mysticism; philosophy; Jewish religion; Islam; military history; travel - Middle East. PR: £1–100. Cata: 4 a year. Also, a booksearch service and large print books.

Landsberger, 9 Ben Yehuda, Tel Aviv. Prop: Esther Parnes. Tel: (03) 5176330. Fax: 5222646. Est: 1934. Shop. Medium stock. CC: V. Corresp: German, Hebrew.

Nun–Bet Books (Postscriptum), 6 Ben Yehuda, 63801 Tel Aviv. Prop: Michal & David Ben Ami. Tel: (03) 6207818. Fax: 5259333. Est: 1986. Shop; open Sunday to Thursday 9.30–7, Friday 9.30–2.30. Large stock. Spec: academic/scholarly; antiquarian; Holocaust; literature; Jewish religion. CC: V; EC; DC; MC. Corresp: German, French, Hebrew.

M. Pollak - Antiquariat, 36 & 42 King George, Tel Aviv 63298. Prop: Cornel Pollak. Tel: (03) 5288613; 5281336. Fax: 6297346. Est: 1899. Shop; open Sunday to Friday 9–1.30, Tuesday also 4–7. Saturday closed. Very large stock. Spec: German books; Judaica & Hebraica; Palestine Travel; art. Cata: 2 a year on German books and Judaica. Corresp: German, French, Hebrew. Mem: A.B.A. (Int.); V.D.A. VAT No: 064 702 673.

Robert's Antique Prints, 84 Ben Yehuda St., Tel Aviv, 63435. Prop: Robert Pollak. Tel: (03) 5236461. Fax: 5237739. Est: 1965. Shop; open daily 10–1.30 and 4–7, Saturday closed. Large stock. Spec: Holy Land travel before 1900. Corresp: French, Spanish, German. Mem: P.B.F.A. VAT No: 064 702 681.

ITALY

Country dialling code: 39 *Currency:* Italian lira (Lr)

ASTI

Libreria Coenobium di A. Santero, Via Q. Sella, 20, 14100 Asti.

BIASSONO

Pasina Maurizio, Via Cavour, 19, I-20046 Biassono (MI).

BOLOGNA

Garisenda Libri & Stampe S.a.S., Strada Maggiore 14a, 40125 Bologna. Prop: Maria Fiammenghi. Tel: (051) 231893. Est: 1959. Shop; open Monday to Saturday 9.30–12.30 & 4–7 (Thursday 9.30–12.30). Very small stock. Spec: geography; fine arts; illustrated. Cata: 2 a year. VAT No: IT 002 822 503 72.

Libreria Naturalistica, s.n.c., C.P. 2224, Via Valdonica, 11, 40100 Bologna. Prop: Piero Piani. Tel: & Fax: (051) 233567 or Tel: 220344. Est: 1982. Shop; appointment preferable. Medium stock. Spec: natural history and related subjects. Cata: 2 a year. Also, new scientific books and magazines, a book search service and large print books. Corresp: French. Mem: A.L.A.I. VAT No: IT 041 170 403 70.

E. Sermoneta - Studio Bibliografico, Via C. Battisti, 2, 40123 Bologna.

Libreria F. Veronese, Via de' Foscherari 19, 40124 Bologna. Prop: Ruggero Carnevali. Tel: & Fax: (051) 236492. Est: 1888. Shop; open Monday to Saturday 10–1 & 4–7.30 (closed Saturday afternoon from June to August). Medium stock. Spec: Bologna; humanities. Also, new books on Bologna. Cata: 2 a year.

Orfeo Vigarani, Via Magnani N.6, 40134 Bologna. Tel: (051) 6144086. Est: 1981. Private premises; appointment necessary. Small general stock. Spec: classical studies; fine & rare; occult; history of science. Cata: 2 a year. Corresp: French. Mem: A.L.A.I.; L.I.L.A.

Studio Bibliografico Zanasi, Via Brizio 12, 40134 Bologna. Tel: (051) 6142384. Fax: 6140330. Est: 1986. Private premises; appointment necessary. Medium stock. Spec: illustrated; art deco; art nouveau; children's. Cata: 1 a year. Also, large print books. Corresp: French, German. Mem: A.L.A.I.

ITALY

BOZEN (BOLZANO)

Buchmarkt Athesia, Silbergasse 21/E, 39100 Bolzano. *Also shops in:* Brixen, Bruneck, Meran, Schlander *and* Sterzing (q.v.).

Verlagsanstalt Athesia GmbH, Lauben 41, Casella Postale 417, 39100 Bolzano-Bozen.

Athesiabuch, Papierhandlung, Goethestrasse 5, 39100 Bolzano. *Also shops in:* Brixen, Bruneck, Meran, Schlander *and* Sterzing (q.v.).

Ferrari & Auer, Buchhandlung, Waltherplatz 12, 39100 Bolzano.

BRIXEN (BRESSANONE)

Athesiabuch, Weissenturmgasse 1, 39042 Bressanone. *Also shops in:* Bozen, Bruneck, Meran, Schlander *and* Sterzing (q.v.).

BRUNECK (BRUNICO)

Athesiabuch, Stadtgasse 60, 39031 Brunico. Tel: (0474) 554424. *Also shops in:* Bozen, Brixen, Meran, Schlander *and* Sterzing. (q.v.).

BUSTO ARSIZIO

Insubria Libreria Antiquaria s.a.s., Via Roma, 8, 21052 Busto Arsizio.

CAGLIARI

NANA' s.a.s., Casella Postale 248, 09100 Cagliari. Prop: Sergio Zuddas. Tel: (070) 655995. E-Mail: serzu@mbox.vol.it. Est: 1990. Shop at: via La Marmora, 63 Cagliari; open 5pm–8.30pm. Small general stock. Cata: 2 a year. Corresp: French, Spanish.

CASALE MONFERRATO

Ivano Cancellier, Via Comello, 5, 15033 Casale Monferrato. Tel: & Fax: (0142) 782278 & Tel: (0338) 6190152. Est: 1992. Storeroom; appointment necessary. Medium stock. Spec: alpinism/mountaineering; aviation; children's; industry; literature; military; socialism; transport. PR: £2–200. Corresp: French, Italian. VAT No: IT 016 051 900 63.

COMO

Dominioni Alessandro - Libraio Antiquario, Via Dottesio 5, 22100 Como.

CREMONA

Libreria Turris Editrice, Corso Garibalbi, 215, 26100 Cremona. Prop: Giancarlo Spotti. Tel: (0372) 23845. Fax: 413084. Est: 1986. Shop; open 9–12.45 and 3–7. Very large stock. Spec: violin–making; organs; Gregorian Chant; art; music; Cremona. CC: V; MC; EC; AE. Cata: 1 a year. Also, violin–making and organs and web site at: http://www.graffiti.it/tu. Corresp: French. Mem: A.L.A.I. VAT No: IT 006 853 301 93.

FLORENCE (FIRENZE)

ADC di Pierluigi Franchi, Via Castelfidardo 26, 50137 Firenze.

Studio Bibliografico Arno, via S. Spirito, 11, 50125 Firenze. Prop: Filippo Crocetti. Tel: (055) 287885. Est: 1991. Storeroom. Small general stock. Spec: alpinism/ mountaineering; antiquarian; bindings; children's; local history; illustrated; travel - general, Europe; wine. Cata: 2 a year. Corresp: Italian. Mem: A.L.A.I. VAT No: IT 043 263 404 88.

Studio Bibliografico "Bardi", via dei Bardi 23, 50125 Firenze. Prop: Andrea Conti. Tel: (055) 242892. Fax: 241999. Est: 1996. Storeroom; appointment necessary. Very small stock. Spec: antiquarian; manuscripts; incunabula; science; astronomy; occult; alchemy. PR: Lr.300,000–3,000,000. Cata: available every season. Corresp: Italian, French, German. VAT No: IT 047 329 004 87.

Libreria Antiquaria Cappellini s.a.s., Corso de' Tintori 27 R, 50122 Firenze. Tel: & Fax: (055) 240989. Est: 1976. Shop; open 9.30–1 and 3.30–7.30, closed Saturday afternoons. Very large stock. Spec: art; literature; history; local history; religion. Cata: 7 to 8 a year. Corresp: French. Mem: L.I.L.A.; A.L.A.I. VAT No: IT 011 592 504 87.

Libreria Chiari, Via Borgo Allegri, 16R, 50122 Firenze. Prop: Piero Chiari. Tel: (055) 245291. Fax: 2478881. Est: 1974. Shop; open 9.30–1 and 3.30–7.30, closed Monday morning in winter and Saturday morning in summer. Very large stock. Spec: archaeology; architecture; art; art history; bibliography; biography; classical studies; Egyptology; ethnology; general & local history; history of civilisation; humanities; limited editions; linguistics; literary criticism; literature; periodicals/magazines; philosophy; Oriental religion; social sciences; travel. PR: Lr.30,000–500,000. Cata: every 45 days. Also, a booksearch service and large print books. VAT No: IT 042 005 504 83.

Antica Libreria Antiquaria Luigi Gonnelli & Figli S.a.S., Via Ricasoli 14r, 50122 Firenze. Tel: (055) 216835. Fax: 2396812. Est: 1875. Shop; open Tuesday to Saturday 9–1 and 4–7.30. (closed Mondays and, in summer, Saturdays). Large stock. Spec: incunabula; manuscripts; classics; literature; science; occulta; travel; history; architecture; art; medicine. CC: V; AE. Cata: 3 a year. Corresp: French, Spanish. Mem: A.L.A.I. VAT No: IT 005 206 604 81.

Libreria Oreste Gozzini, Via Ricasoli 49 – 103r, 50122 Firenze. Prop: Pietro & Francesco Chellini. Tel: (055) 212433. Fax: 211105. E-Mail: gozzini@dada.it. Est: c.1850. Shop; open Monday to Saturday 9–12.30 & 3.30–7.30. Very large stock. Spec: art; fine arts; literature; law; economics. CC: V; MC; AE; D. Cata: 5 a year. Corresp: French, Spanish. Mem: A.L.A.I. VAT No: IT 036 629 504 88.

Libreria dello Studente, Via Laura 68a, 50121 Firenze.

Casa Editrice Olschki, Viuzzo del Pozzetto, (V. le Europa), 50126 Firenze. Prop: Alessandro Olschki. Tel: (055) 6530684. Fax: 6530214. Est: 1886. Private premises; open Monday to Friday 8.15–1 and 2.45–6. Very large stock. Spec: archaeology; art history; bibliography; history of civilization; humanities; literature; music; history of science. PR: Lr.25,000–1,000,000. CC: MC; EC; V. Also, Cata: 1 a year. publishing in the humanities. Corresp: Italian, French. Mem: A.I.E. VAT No: IT 003 954 304 81.

Opus Libri s.r.l., Via della Torretta 16, 50137 Firenze. Prop: Piero Riccetti. Tel: (055) 660833. Fax: 670604. Est: 1980. Private premises; appointment necessary. Large stock. Spec: archaeology; art; the arts; ceramics; classical studies; fine art; general, industrial and local history; literature; philosophy; science; sculpture. CC: V; CS; EC; MC. Cata: every 3 or 4 months. Corresp: Italian. VAT No: IT 030 860 304 87.

Libreria Antiquaria P. Pampaloni, Via dei Pucci, 4 (Pal. Pucci), 50125 Firenze.

Libreria G. Valleri, Via Ricasoli, 77R, 50122 Firenze.

Studio Bibliografico Vecchi Libri, Via dei Benci 20, 50122 Firenze. Prop: Pietro Crini. Tel: (055) 242768. Est: 1986. Storeroom; appointment necessary. Medium stock. Spec: topography; folklore; voyages. PR: £20–500. Cata: 2 a year. Corresp: French.

FOLIGNO

Editoriale Umbra S.a.S., Via Pignattara 40, 06034 Foligno.

GENOA (GENOVA)

Libreria Giuridica Ardy Bernardino, Piazza Sauli 4/2, 16123 Genova.

Libreria Antiquaria Dallai S.n.c. , Piazza de Marini 11–13 R, 16123 Genova. Prop: Giovanna and Norma Dallai. Tel: (010) 2472338. Est: 1939. Shop; open Tuesday to Saturday 9.30–12.15 & 4–7.15. Very small stock. Corresp: French, German.

GUSSAGO

"L'Arengario" Studio Bibliografico, Via Pratolungo, 192, 25061 Gussago (Brescia).

LODI

Studio Bibliografico Zazzera, Via Milite Ignoto 9, 20075 Lodi. Prop: Gianpiero Zazzera & Liz Marcucci Zazzera. Tel: (0371) 431103. Fax: 431102. Est: 1986. Private premises; appointment necessary. Small stock. Spec: gastronomy; oenology; science; medicine; natural history; books about books; printing; binding; voyages & discovery. Cata: 2 a year. Also, new bibliography and reference books. Mem: A.L.A.I.; I.L.A.B.

LUCCA

Libreria Musicale Italiana, P.O. Box 198, 55100 Lucca. Prop: Fino Massimo. Tel: (0583) 394464. Fax: 394469. Est: 1988. Storeroom; postal business only. Large stock. Spec: autographs; music. Cata: 3 a year on specialities. Also, publisher (musical editions). Corresp: Italian, French. Mem: A.I.E.; A.I.P.E. VAT No: IT 012 863 004 60.

LIM Antiquaria s.a.s., Via Arsina, 296/F, 55100 Lucca.

LURAGO MARINONE

Beccari - Antichità, Via Dante, 3, 22070 Lurago Marinone (Como).

MERAN (MERANO)

Athesiabuch, Lauben 186, 39012 Merano. *Also shops in:* Bozen, Brixen, Bruneck, Schlander *and* Sterzing (q.v.).

177

ITALY

MILAN (MILANO)

American Bookstore, Via Camperio, 16, 20123 Milano.

L'Archivolto, Via Marsala 2, 20121 Milano. Tel: (02) 6590842 or 29010444. Fax: 6595552. Est: 1981. Shop; open 10–1 and 3.30–7.30. Medium stock. Spec: architecture; design; garden architecture. PR: £50–5,000. CC: AE; DC; V; MC. Cata: 1 a year. Also, new books on architecture, publisher on architecture and a booksearch service. Corresp: French. Mem: A.L.A.I. VAT No: IT 022 401 301 59.

Studio Bibliografico Il Caffè di G. Bacigalupo, Via Eustachi, 7, 20129 Milano.

C.A. Chiesa – Libri Antichi, Via Bigli 11, 20121 Milano. Prop: Carlo Alberto Chiesa. Tel: (02) 798678. Fax: 76014542. Spec: old and rare; incunabula; 15th- to 19th-century first editions and illustrated. Mem: A.L.A.I.

Ex Libris Museum, Via G. Marconi, 36, 20080 Albairate, Milano. Prop: G. Mirabella. Tel: & Fax: (02) 94920542. Est: 1991. Storeroom. Very large stock. Cata: 2 a year. Mem: L.I.L.A.

Gallini – Libreria Musicale, Via Gorani 8, 20123 Milano. Prop: Annalisa Gusti Gallini. Tel: (02) 72000398. Shop; open Monday 3–7, Tuesday to Friday 10.30–12.30 & 3–7, and on Saturday by appointment. Medium stock. Spec: music; opera; books about music and musicians. Cata: 1 a year. Corresp: French, German, Spanish. Mem: L.I.L.A. VAT No: IT 093 017 801 52.

Piero Gribaudi Editore s.r.l., Via Costantino Baroni 190, I-20142 Milano.

Studio Bibliografico Kairos srl, Via Tartini, 38, 20158 Milano.

Libreria Antiquaria Il Labirinto, Via Spartaco 33, 20135 Milano.

Libreria Antiquaria '800 & 900, Riex S.r.l., Via Borromei, 11, 20123 Milano.

M'Arte s.r.l., Via Carlo Poerio 3, 20129 Milano. Prop: Luigi Majno. Tel: (02) 794034. Fax: 4390436. Est: 1968. Shop; open Tuesday to Friday 4–7 (and mornings by appointment), Saturday 10.30–1 and 4–7. Small stock. Spec: art; artist books. PR: £100–5,000. CC: V. Cata: 2 a year. Also, modern sculptures. Corresp: French. VAT No: IT 007 395 501 50. *London representative:* Miss Olimpia Theodoli, Georgian House, Flat 17, 10 Bury Street, London SW1Y 6AA. Tel: 0171-8397805; Fax: 8397905.

Libreria Malavasi s.a.s., Via Santa Tecla 2, 20122 Milano. Prop: Maurizio & Sergio Malavasi. Tel: (02) 804607. Fax: 864002. Est: 1940. Shop; open Monday 3.30–7.30, Tuesday to Saturday 9.30–1 & 3.30–7.30. Very large stock. Spec: bibliography; art; history and local history. Cata: 3 a year. Corresp: French. Mem: A.L.A.I.; L.I.L.A.

Banco Libri Mangiacasale Claudio, Largo Cairoli (Lato Foro Bonaparte), 20123 Milano. Tel: (02) 860769.

Libreria Antiquaria Gaetano Manusé, Via Hoepli 3, 20121 Milano.

Il Mercante di Stampe di Rosalba Mariani, Foro Buonaparte, 54, 20121 Milano.

C. Marzoli (La Bibliofila), Piazza Leonardo da Vinci, 3, 20133 Milano.

Libreria Antiquaria Mediolanum, Via Montebello 24, 20121 Milano.

Libreria Antiquaria Moretti, via Vittadini 3, 20136 Milano.

Moscova Libri E Robe s.n.c., Via della Moscova, NR. 15, 20121 Milano. Prop: Raffaella Zandonella & Lucia Moretti. Tel: (02) 6598209. Est: 1982. Shop; open Monday to Saturday 9.30–1.30 and 3.30–7.30. Medium stock. Spec: 19th & 20th century editions. PR: DM1–1,000. CC: AE; V; MC. Corresp: Italian, French, German.

Studio Bibliografico Roberto Orsini, via Candiani 18, 20158 Milano. Tel: & Fax: (02) 39322927. Est: 1987. Private premises; appointment necessary. Very small stock. Spec: early imprints; fine & rare; law; manuscripts; mathematics; science. PR: £100–4,000. Cata: 2 a year on general subjects. VAT No: IT 005 300 109 66.

Renzo Rizzi – Libri Antichi, Via Cernaia 4, 20121 Milano. Tel: (02) 29002705. Est: 1954. Storeroom; postal business only. Very small stock. Spec: palaeography; old manuscripts. Mem: A.L.A.I.

Libreria Rovello, Via Rovello, 1, 20121 Milano.

Sibrium – Libri e Manoscritti, Via Bigli 21, 20121 Milano. Prop: Dr. A. Martegani. Tel: (02) 76005969. Est: 1966. Office; appointment preferred. Medium stock. Spec: old and rare; science; manuscripts. PR: DM200 plus. Cata: periodically. Corresp: French, German. Mem: A.L.A.I.

Valeria Bella Stampe, Via S. Cecilia 2, 20122 Milano. Prop: Valeria Bella. Tel: (02) 76004413. Fax: 76006505. Est: 1987. Shop; open Monday 3–7 and Tuesday to Saturday 10–7. Cata: 1 a year. Corresp: French. Mem: A.L.A.I. VAT No: IT 085 902 701 56.

Libreria Stendhal di Oscar Tedeschi, Via del Don, 3, 20123 Milano.

Il Trovatore di Renata Vercesi, Via C. Poerio 3, 20129 Milano. Prop: Renata Vercesi. Tel: (02) 76001656. Est: 1982. Shop; open daily 9.30–12.30 and 3.30–7 (closed Monday morning). Spec: music and music literature. Cata: on request. Also, new books. Corresp: French, Spanish.

Paolo Zanetti, Via Rovelli, 1, 20121 Milano.

MODENA

Libreria Paolo Bongiorno, Via Lana, 72/2, 41100 Modena.

La Darsena, S.r.l., Piazzale S. Domenico, 2, 41100 Modena. Prop: Luciana Frigieri & Leonelli Siro. Tel: & Fax: (059) 219942. Shop; open 9.30–12.30 and 3.30–7.30. Very small stock. Spec: antiquarian; fine & rare; illustrated. Cata: 1 a year on general subjects. Corresp: French. VAT No: IT 016 357 503 65.

Libreria Antiquaria Govi, Casella Postale 321 – C, Via San Pietro 18, 41100 Modena. Tel: & Fax: (059) 225150. Est: 1973. Private premises; appointment necessary. Very small stock. Spec: early printed; medieval manuscripts. Cata: 2 a year. Corresp: French. Spanish. Mem: A.B.A. VAT No: IT 004 493 403 63.

Libreria Antiquaria Zanichelli, Via F. Selmi, 54, 41100 Modena.

NAPLES (NAPOLI)

Michele Ammendola, Studio Bibliografico, via S. Marcie No. 8, 80053 Castellammare di Stabia, Napoli.

Libreria Gaspare Casella, Via Carlo Poerio 92e/f, 80121 Napoli. Prop: Dott. Guido lo Schiavo. Tel: & Fax: (081) 7642627. Shop. Medium stock. Cata: 1 a year.

Libreria Antiquaria Colonnese, Via San Pietro a Majella 32–33, 80138 Napoli. Prop: Gaetano & Maria Colonnese. Tel: (081) 459858. Fax: 455420. Est: 1965. Shop; open Monday to Friday 9–1 and 4–7.30, Saturday 9–1. Medium stock. Spec: antiquarian, especially rare 17th–19th-century; 20th-century Italian literature; local history; art and curiosities; anthropology; children's; cinema/film; cookery/gastronomy; erotica; esoteric; fashion & costume; medicine; socialism; theatre. Cata: 4 a year. Corresp: French. Mem: A.L.A.I.; L.I.L.A. VAT No: IT 057 728 506 31.

Libreria Godot, Via Cosenza 67, Castellammare di Stabia, 80053 Napoli.

Studio Bibliografico B. Pucci, Via Ferdinando Russo, 31, (Posillipo), 80123 Napoli.

NEMBRO

Studio Bibliografico Naturalia, Via Vittoria 27, 24027 Nembro (BG). Prop: Renato Agazzi. Tel: & Fax: (035) 523110. Est: 1992. Private premises; postal business only. Very small stock. Spec: botany; entomology; geology; natural history; ornithology; palaeontology; zoology. PR: £15–4,000. Cata: 2 a year on general natural history, zoology, ornithology, entomology, botany, geology, palaeontology. Also, a booksearch service. Corresp: French. Mem: A.L.A.I. VAT No: IT 021 825 801 63.

NOVARA

Libreria Antiquaria La Tigre Di Carta, Piazza Tornielli Brusati 2, 28100 Novara. Prop: Marcioni Silvia. Tel: (0321) 391683. Fax: 627377. Est: 1984. Shop; open 4–8. Very small stock. Corresp: French.

PADUA (PADOVA)

Antiquariato Librario Bado & Mart, s.a.s., Via S. Francesco, 152, 35121 Padova.

ITALY

Libreria Sapienza, Via Zabarella, 34, 35121 Padova. Prop: Dr. Luigi Sapienza. Tel: & Fax: (049) 8758893. Est: 1994. Shop; open Tuesday to Saturday 10–12.30 and 4–7.30. Medium general stock. CC: AE; V; MC. Corresp: French, Italian. VAT No: IT 001 993 802 88.

PERUGIA

L'Amuleto S.A.S. di G. Monticelli & Co., Via Baldeschi 16, 06123 Perugia.

PISA

Libreria Antiquaria Andrea Vallerini, Via dei Mille, 7A/13, 56126 Pisa. Tel: (050) 555450. Fax: 562750. Est: 1975. Shop. Medium stock. Spec: literature; classics; old English books; early science; Italian local history; architecture; Americana; collectors' editions. CC: V; MC. Cata: 4 a year. Also, large print books. Corresp: French. Mem: A.L.A.I.; Associazione Librai Italiani. VAT No: IT 002 472 405 00.

RAVENNA

A.B. Antiquariato Brocchi SAS, Casella Postale 30, 48100 Ravenna. Prop: Adolfo Marcello Brocchi. Tel: (0544) 212252. Est: 1982. Shop at: Via Cairoli 6, 48100 Ravenna; open afternoons (closed Thursdays); and postal business. Large general stock. Spec: ecclesiastical history and architecture; first editions; general history; national history; illuminated manuscripts; incunabula; law; literature. Cata: 2 a year. Also, large print books, furniture and pictures. Corresp: Italian. Mem: A.L.A.I.; L.I.L.A.; L.I.L.A.B. VAT No: IT 008 162 503 93.

Studio Bibliografico Filippo Cristiano, Via S. Agata 13, 48100 Ravenna. Tel: & Fax: (0544) 32061. Open 3–7.30. Small stock. Spec: Italian literature. Cata: 2 a year.

REGGIO EMILIA

Libreria Antiquaria Prandi, Viale Timavo 75, 42100 Reggio Emilia.

RIVA DEL GARDA

Studio Bibliografico Benacense, Via Fiume, 2, 38066 Riva del Garda (Tn), Prop: Giupponi dr. Mario. Tel: & Fax: (0464) 556344. Private premises; appointment necessary. Medium general stock. PR: £200. Cata: 2 a year, on general ancient books, with a specific section on local history. VAT No: IT 013 209 802 28.

ROME (ROMA)

'900 La Tradiozione Moderna, Largo Camesena, 5, 00157 Roma. Prop: Ondine Montalant. Tel: (06) 41730101. Market stand and private premises; appointment necessary. Medium stock of only 20th century books. Spec: architecture; art; artists; avant–garde; decorative art; first editions; interior design; limited editions; literature; periodicals/magazines; politics; surrealism. PR: Lr.50,000–1,000,000. Cata: 1 a year on 20th-century art, literature, etc. Italian and European. Also, a booksearch service. Corresp: French, Italian.

Books on Italy, via dei Guibbonari 30, 00186 Roma. Prop: Louise McDermott. Tel: (06) 68805285. Est: 1986. Private premises; appointment necessary. Very small stock. Spec: Italy. PR: £2–400. Cata: 2 a year. VAT No: IT 089 009 905 84.

Ellediemme – Libri dal Mondo, P.O. Box 69, Poste S. Silvestro, via Baccina 30, 00184 Roma.

Ex-Libris, Via Dell' Umiltã, 77/A, 00187 Roma.

Fiammetta Soave – Libri Rari, Via Leccosa 4/6, 00186 Roma.

Libreria Carmen Rosetta Gullà, Via P.P. Bufalieri 15, 00124 Casal Palocco, Roma.

Hortus Musicus, Viale Liegi 7, 00198 Roma. Tel: (06) 8840230. Fax: 8559578. Est: 1968. Shop. Spec: academic/scholarly; antiquarian; antiques; ex-libris; music; musical instruments.

Konvolut s.a.s., Via Panama 18, 00198 Roma. Prop: Mirella Garofoli. Tel: (06) 8551848. Est: 1990. Private premises; open Tuesday to Saturday 10–1 and 5–7.30. Small stock. Spec: antiquarian; architecture; art; art history; art reference; artists; avant–garde; Catalogues Raisoneés; cinema/films; ex-libris; fine & rare; fine art; first editions; illustrated; limited editions; literary criticism; literature; literature in translation; music; periodicals/magazines; poetry; private press. PR: £30. Cata: 3 a year on specialities. Also, a booksearch service. Corresp: Italian, French.

Librars & Antiquaria s.r.l., Via Zanardelli 3/4, 00186 Roma. Tel: (06) 6875931. Est: 1976. Shop; open 9.30–1 and 5–8, Monday mornings closed. Medium stock. Spec: antiques; applied art; archaeology; architecture; art; art history; art reference; artists; the arts; carpets; ceramics; cinema; circus; conservation; dance; decorative art; fashion; glass; graphic art; iconography & many others. CC: AE; MC; EC; V; DC. Corresp: French, Italian. VAT No: IT 010 474 010 03.

La Linea D'Ombra Studio Bibliografico, Piazza Campitelli, 2, 00186 Roma.

Dana Lloyd Thomas, Viale Gramsci 80, 00015 Monterotondo (RM). Tel: (06) 90622008. Fax: 9068646. Est: 1994. Private premises; postal business only. Very small stock. Spec: esoteric; philosophy; history; Rome; Italy. PR: £5–200. Cata: 2 a year. Corresp: French, Italian, Spanish.

Organizzazione Libraria Maraldi, Viale Bastioni di Michelangelo 7/19, 00192 Roma.

Libreria Giá Nardecchia s.r.l., Via Revoltella 105–107, 00152 Roma. Tel: (06) 5373901. Fax: 5373902. Est: 1895. Shop; open Monday to Friday 9–6. Very large stock. Spec: old Italian books. Also, Italian periodicals. Corresp: German.

Studio Bibliografico Sonia Natale, Via Massaciuccoli, 51, 00199 Roma. Tel: (06) 86325576 or 8608520. Appointment necessary. Medium stock. Spec: architecture; children's; criminology; fine & rare; illustrated; Rome. Cata: 2 a year. Mem: A.L.A.I. VAT No: IT 084 094 605 84.

Open Door Bookshop, Via della Lungaretta 25, 00153 Roma. Prop: Nopar, Charles & Bandiera Carmelo. Est: 1976. Shop; open Tuesday to Saturday 10–1 and 4–8, Monday 4–8. Small general stock. Spec: antiquarian; antiques; applied art; archaeology; architecture; art; art history; astrology; cinema/films; detective, spy, thrillers; first editions; graphic art; foreign and national languages; literature; literature in translation; music; occult; parapsychology; religion; travel; women. PR: Lr.10,000–200,000. Corresp: Italian, German. VAT No: IT 010 404 710 03.

Libreria Antonio Pettini, 34, Via Monserrato, 00186 Roma. Tel: (06) 68308218. Fax: 68803104. E-Mail: MC3389@mc.link.it. Est: 1981. Private premises; open Monday to Friday 10–6. Very small stock. Spec: antiquarian; architecture; art; avant–garde; bindings. Mem: A.L.A.I.; L.I.L.A.

Libreria Antiquaria C.E. Rappaport, Via Sistina 23, 00187 Roma. Prop: Elisabeth & Bernard Seacombe. Tel: (06) 483826. Fax: 4818079 . Est: 1906. Shop; open Monday to Friday 10–1 & 3.30-7.30. Medium stock. Spec: medicine; science; fine arts; literature. Cata: 1 a year. Corresp: German, Italian. Mem: A.L.A.I.; A.B.A. (UK); V.D.A. (Germany).

Libreria Maresca Riccardi, Via Caposile, 2, 00195 Roma.

Libreria Scarpignato, Via Ripetta 156, 00186 Roma. Prop: Aldo Scarpignato. Tel: (06) 6875923. Fax: 6875760. Est: 1937. Shop; open Monday to Saturday 10–1 & 4.30–8. Medium stock. Spec: old and rare; art; illustrated; history; archaeology; literature; classics; natural history; architecture. Cata: 2 a year. Corresp: French, Spanish. Mem: A.L.A.I. VAT No: IT 082 301 905 82.

Studio Bibliografico Al Vascello di R. Palazzi, Via de' Maffei, 28, 00165 Roma.

ITALY

Studio Bibliografico, via Francesco Coletti 35, 00191 Roma. Prop: Dr. Vincenzo Montenegro. Tel: & Fax: (06) 3294848. Est: 1978. Private premises; open Monday to Saturday 10–1 and 4.30–7.30. Small stock. Spec: Fascism - War 1914–1918 and 1939–1945; applied art; architecture; art; art history; art reference; artists; decorative art; fine art; general, local and national history; military; war. Cata: 3 or 4 a year. Corresp: Italian. VAT No: IT 022 782 105 84.

SALA BOLOGNESE

Arnaldo Forni Editore s.r.l., Via Gramsci 164, 40010 Sala Bolognese. Prop: Guiseppina & Aurelia Forni. Tel: (051) 6814142 and 6814198. Fax: 6814672. Est: 1959. Appointment necessary. Very small stock. Spec: heraldry; music; cookery/gastronomy; folklore; numismatics; art; fine & rare; architecture. PR: Lr.18,000 and up. CC: V; DC; AE. Cata: 6 a year, issued by The Libreria Galliera & 1 every 2 years by A. Forni Publishing House. Also, specialist in anastatic reprints. Corresp: German, French, Italian, Spanish. VAT No: IT 005 028 212 00.

Libreria Galliera, Via Gramsci 164, 40010 Sala Bolognese.

SCHLANDER (SILANDRO)

Athesiabuch, Hauptstrasse 51, 39028 Silandro. *Also shops in:* Bozen, Brixen, Bruneck, Meran *and* Sterzing (q.v.).

SIENA

"Itinera", via Dei Pellegrini, 17, 53100 Siena. Prop: Duccio D'Aniello. Tel: (0577) 288939. Est: 1994. Shop; open Monday to Saturday 9.30–1 and 3–7.30. Very small stock. Spec: Siena and Tuscany; geography. CC: V; CS; EC; MC. Corresp: Italian.

STERZING (VIPITENO)

Athesiabuch, Alstadt 9, 39049 Vipiteno. *Also shops at:* Bozen, Brixen, Bruneck, Meran *and* Schlander (q.v.).

TRENTO

Libroteka di Oss Fabio, Via Mazzini 14, 38100 Trento. Tel: (0461) 238530. Fax: 930953. Est: 1985. Shop; open Monday 3–7.30 and Tuesday to Saturday 8–12 & 3–7.30. Medium stock. Spec: strip cartoons; children's; history. Also illustrated magazines. Cata: 3 to 6 a year.

TRIESTE

Libreria Giulia, Via Giulia 29/B, 34126 Trieste.

TURIN (TORINO)

L'Acquaforte, Via Principe Amedeo 25/c, 10123 Torino.

Bergoglio Libri d'Epoca, Via Moncalvo 53 bis, 10131 Torino. Prop: Letizia Benigni Bergoglio. Tel: (011) 8196890. Storeroom; postal business only. Medium stock. Spec: World War I & II; fine art; travel; medicine; occult; Italian antiquarian. Cata: 12 a year. Corresp: French.

Libreria Antiquaria Bourlot, Piazza San Carlo 183, 10123 Torino. Prop: Cesare Birocco. Tel: (011) 537405. Fax: 5613072. Shop; open 9.30–12.30 and 3.15–7.30. Very large general stock. PR: all prices. Also, large print books. Corresp: French. Mem: L.I.L.A.; A.L.A.I. VAT No: IT 011 029 000 14.

Adolfo Camusso, via Roma 11, 10081 Castellamonte, Torino. Tel: & Fax: (0124) 581848. Private premises; open Monday to Saturday 10–6. Medium stock. Spec: alpinism/mountaineering; art; artists; children's; periodicals/magazines; local topography; travel. PR: Lr.10,000–500,000. Also, a booksearch service. Corresp: French, Italian.

Libreria Antiquaria Il Cartiglio di Roberto Cena, Via Po 32d, 10123 Torino.

Galleria Gilibert, Galleria Subalpina, 17/19, 10123 Torino.

Studio Bibliografico Piero & Simonetta Gribaudi, Corso Galileo Ferraris, 67, 10128 Torino.

Libreria Arcimboldo di F. Freddi, Corso Moncalieri, 47/E, 10133 Torino.

Libreria Centrale S.N.C., via Nizza, 31, 10125 Torino.

Little Nemo Libreria Antiquaria, Casella Postale 680, 10100 Torino Centro. Prop: Sergio Pignatone. Tel: & Fax: (011) 8127089. E-Mail: Sergio.Pignatone @Torino.ALPcom.it. Est: 1989. Shop at: via Montebello 2/0 10124 Torino; open Monday to Friday afternoon 3.30–7.30, Saturday by appointment. Large stock. Spec: caricature; cartoons; children's books; cinema/films; comic books and annuals; comics; erotica; fables; detective, spy, thrillers; fantasy, horror; science fiction; fine & rare; illustrated; juvenile; periodicals/magazines; signed editions. PR: £100. Cata: 2 a year on children's illustrated books (1700–1960), Liberty & Art Decò Books, comics and original arts. Also, Internet: http://www.smart.it/Pignatone. Mem: A.L.A.I.

ITALY

Libreria Antiquaria Mantua, Via A. Doria, 6, 10123 Torino.

Old England Gallery, Via San Massimo, 42/A, 10123 Torino. Prop: Ilaria Daglio. Tel: (011) 8122021. Est: 1981. Shop; open 10–1, 3.30–7.15. Medium stock. Spec: cartography; botany; fashion; field sports and coaching; horse racing - equestrian; landscape; maritime/nautical; military. PR: £20–1,000. Also, large print books. Corresp: Italian, French. VAT No: IT 039 330 300 11

Giovanni Pasqua, Via Giacomo Balla 36, 10137 Torino. Tel: Fax: & Answering Machine: (011) 3081810. Mobile: (0330) 213720. Est: 1970. Private premises; appointment necessary. Very small stock. Spec: magic; conjuring; trick illusions; circus; magic lantern; cinema; amusements; recreation on physics; mathematics; chemistry. PR: Lr.10,000–200,000. Cata: list on request. Also, a booksearch service. Corresp: French, Spanish.

Libreria Antiquaria Peyrot, Piazza Savoia 8/G, 10122 Torino.

Libreria Antiquaria Piemontese, via Monte di Pietà 13/G, 10122 Torino. Prop: Marco Cicolini. Tel: & Fax: (011) 535472. Est: 1971. Shop. Small stock. PR: Lr.50,000–5,000,000. Cata: 1 a year. Corresp: French. Mem: A.L.A.I. VAT No: IT 057 121 400 10.

Libreria Antiquaria Arturo Pregliasco s.a.s., Via Accademia Albertina 3 bis, 10123 Torino. Tel: (011) 8177114. Fax: 8179214. Shop; open Monday to Saturday 9–12.30 and 3–7.30. Large stock. Spec: Italy; Italian books; manuscripts; autographs. Cata: 2 a year. Also, large print books. Corresp: Italian, French. Mem: L.I.L.A.; I.L.A.B.; A.L.A.I. VAT No: IT 040 919 830 010.

Libreria Antiquaria Soave, Via Po 48, 10123 Torino.

Libreria Antiquaria Il Vecchio Melo, Via San Dalmazzo, 6/C, 10122 Torino.

Libreria Antiquaria A. Viglongo di G. Spagarino, Via Genova, 266, 10127 Torino.

VARESE

Libreria Antiquaria E. Andreoli, Piazza Garibaldi 1, 21043 Castiglione Olona, Varese. Prop: Eduardo Andreoli. Tel: (0331) 858232. Est: 1950. Shop and market stand; open Monday to Saturday 10–6. Very large general stock. Corresp: French; Italian. VAT No: IT 019 882 701 36.

Luca Piatti - Libri E Oggetti D'Epoca, Postal Box 262, 21100 Varese. Prop: Luca Piatti. Tel: (0332) 320575; 310489 or (0337) 398148. Private premises and office; appointment necessary or postal business. Medium general stock. Cata: 4 a year. Corresp: Italian, French. VAT No: IT 021 167 501 22.

VENICE (VENEZIA)

Kleine Galerie del Prof. C. Gorini, San Marco, Calle delle Botteghe 2972, 30124 Venezia.

Lella & Gianni Morri, Giudecca, 699, 30133 Venezia. Tel: & Fax: (041) 5288006. Est: 1980. Private premises; appointment necessary. Very small stock. Spec: antiques; applied art; artists; carpets. CC: V; MC. Cata: 2 a year on antiquarian Japanese books. Mem: Booksellers Against The War. VAT No: IT 020 844 502 75.

VERCELLI

Studio Bibliografico Il Piacere e Il Dovere, Piazza Pajetta 8, 13100 Vercelli. Prop: Andrea Donati. Tel: (0161) 255126. Fax: 255662. Est: 1989. Shop; appointment necessary. Small stock. Spec: sea and navigation; mountaineering; aeronautics; hunting; sports; pastimes; handicraft; industry. CC: V; MC. Cata: 3 a year. Mem: A.L.A.I. VAT No: IT 014 091 500 24.

VERONA

Libreria Antiquaria Perini, Via A. Sciesa 11, 37122 Verona.

VICENZA

Il Libraio di C. Matteuzzi, Corso Fogazzaro 159, Vicenza. Prop: Carlo Matteuzzi. Tel: (0444) 545247. Est: 1979. Shop; open Tuesday to Saturday 10–12.30 and 4–7.30. Medium stock. Spec: Vicenza area. Corresp: French.

LIBRERIA ANTIQUARIA E. ANDREOLI
Piazza Garibaldi 1, 21043 Castiglione Olona, Varese
Tel: 0331 858232

LIECHTENSTEIN

Country dialling code: 4175 *Currency:* Swiss franc (Sfr)

RUGGELL

Topos Verlag A.G., Industriestrasse 105a, P.O. Box 551, 9491 Ruggell. Tel: (075) 3771111. Fax: 3771119. Est: 1977.

LUXEMBOURG

Country dialling code: 352 *Currency:* French franc (Ffr)

CHRISTNACH

Emile Borschette, 21 Fielserstroos, 7640-Christnach.

LUXEMBOURG

Arts & Livres, Librairie - Galerie, 34 Place Guillaume II, 1648-Luxembourg. Prop: Hans Fellner. Tel: & Fax: 220421. Est: 1990. Shop; open Tuesday to Saturday 2–6. Medium stock. Spec: art; autographs; fine & rare; local history; literature; voyages & discovery; Corresp: German, French, Dutch. VAT No: LU 155 709 48.

MALTA

Country dialling code: 356 *Currency:* Maltese pound (M£)

GOZO

Pomskizillious Museum of Toys, 10 Gnien Xibla Street, Xaghra, Gozo. Prop: Susan & Edwin Lowe. Tel: 562489 (museum). Est: 1992. Open April/May - Thursday, Friday & Saturday 11–1, June to mid October - Monday, Tuesday and Thursday to Saturday 10–12 and 3–6, winter - Saturdays only 11–1. Very small stock. PR: 85c–£M.85. Corresp: Maltese. Mem: P.B.F.A. (Porcupines in U.K.). VAT No: M 118 574 03.

LIJA

Peter A. Bologna – Rare Books, Melitensia Art Gallery, Transfiguration Avenue, Lija BZN 08. Prop: Peter Apap Bologna. Tel: 430338. Fax: 413297. Est: 1987. Shop; open Monday to Saturday 10–1 & 4–7.30. Very small stock. Spec: Melitensia (books about Malta); modern first editions.

MOSTA

Island Books, 4/1 St. Anthony Street, Mosta, MST 08. Prop: Liz Groves. Tel: 432774. Est: 1975. Private premises; open Saturday, Sunday and public holidays 9–5. Medium stock. Spec: Malta; English literature; literary criticism; philosophy. PR: £M1–500. Also, a booksearch service. VAT No: M 117 906 19.

ST. JULIANS

A. Micallef Grimaud, Clio, Trig il-Kuccard, St. Julians, SGN O2.

TARXIEN

N. & M. Borg, 62 Annunciation Street, PLA 04 Tarxien.

VALETTA

Collector's Den Ltd., Patros, Wignacourt Street, Birkirkara, BKR 08. Prop: Patrick & Rose Formosa. Tel: 231845. Fax: 440029. Est: 1994. Shop at: 122 Archbishop Street, Valletta, VLT 05; open Monday to Saturday 10–12.30, 5–6.30, Wednesday & Saturday 10–12.30, summer mornings only, August closed. Very small stock. Spec: Malta and Knights of Malta. PR: £M1–500. Also, large print books and antiques. Corresp: Italian, French.

VITTORIOSA

Paul Bezzina, 114 St. Lawrence Street, Vittoriosa. Tel: 665812. Private premises; appointment necessary. Spec: Maltese books; Malta and the Knights of Malta. Corresp: Italian, French.

NETHERLANDS

Country dialling code: 31 *Currency:* Florin or Guilder (Fl)

ALKMAAR

De Alkenaer, Ritsevoort 36, 1811 DP Alkmaar. Prop: J. Oyevaar. Tel: (072) 5111798. Est: 1982. Shop; open Monday to Saturday 11–6. Very large stock. Spec: literature in several languages; history; theology; travel; Indonesia; esoterics; children's; biology; maritime/nautical; psychology/psychiatry; science; technology. Corresp: all Western European languages.

AMERSFOORT

Antiquariaat T. Ezelsoor, Achter de Arnhemse Poortwal 35, 3811 LX Amersfoort. Prop: W.W. Rutgers & J.G.M. Steehouder. Tel: (033) 4621250. Fax: 4657214. Est: 1982. Shop; open daily 10–6. Very large stock of over 60,000. Spec: Dover Collection; history; biology; literature; art. PR: £1–5,000. Also, a booksearch service. Corresp: German, French. VAT No: NL 009 907 233 B01.

AMSTERDAM

A'dams Boek- & Prentenkabinet, Spuistraat 101, Amsterdam.

Antiquariaat Antiqua, Herengracht 159, 1015 BH Amsterdam. Prop: R. van der Peet. Tel: (020) 6245998. Est: 1960. Postal business only. Medium stock. Spec: musicology; philosophy; political economy; early science; travel; old and rare. Cata: 3 a year. Mem: N.V.A.

L'Art Médical, Hasebroekstraat 9, 1053 CL Amsterdam. Prop: Ms Annette Smit. Tel: (020) 6127253. Fax: 6129939. E-Mail: artmed@xs4all.nl. Est: 1973. Private premises; appointment necessary. Very small stock. Spec: old medical books; history of medicine; pharmacy. PR: Fl.50–5,000. CC: MC. Cata: 6 a year. Also, a booksearch service and web site at: http://www.xs4all.nl/~nan. Corresp: French, German. Mem: N.A.N.

Gebr. Bakker, 97 Gasthuismolensteeg 7, Amsterdam.

Beenders Boek, Jan van Galenstraat 161 hs., Amsterdam.

John Benjamins Antiquariat B.V., P.O. Box 75577, 1070 Amsterdam. Tel: (020) 6738156. Fax: 6739773. Est: 1964. Storeroom; appointment necessary. Stock of periodicals (especially in the liberal arts and social science). Cata: irregularly. Corresp: French, German, Italian, Spanish. Mem: N.V.A.

H. van den Berg, Rijnstraat 192 hs., Amsterdam.

Berg, Oude Schans 8, Amsterdam.

Boek & Glas, Agatha Dekenstraat 34 HS., Amsterdam. Prop: C. van der Linde. Tel: & Fax: (020) 6126673. E-Mail: boekglas@antiqbook.nl. Est: 1991. Shop; open Monday to Saturday 11–5. Medium stock. Spec: antiquarian; art; books about books; dictionaries; erotica; glass; Dutch literature; literature in translation in Dutch; history of medicine; poetry; printing; private press; sexology; typography. Cata: 4 a year. Also, bookbinding. Corresp: Dutch, French. Mem: N.A.N.

De Boekenboom, Spuistraat 230, Amsterdam.

Boekenkast–Triologo, Korte Koningstraat 8, Amsterdam.

Ton Bolland, Prinsengracht 493, 1016 HR Amsterdam. Tel: (020) 6221921. Fax: 6257912. Est: 1897. Shop; Large stock. Spec: humanism; Protestant and Roman Catholic theology; the Reformation and books 1500–1900. Cata: 2 a year. Corresp: German. Also, book auctioneers. VAT No: NL 16 42 698 B01.

Libreria Bonardi, Entrepotdok 26, 1018 AD Amsterdam. Prop: Marina Warners. Tel: (020) 6239844. Fax: 6223754. Est: 1977. Shop; open Tuesday to Friday 11–6, Saturday 11–5. Medium stock. Spec: Italian books. VAT No: NL 004 310 275 B01.

Book Traffic, Leliegracht 50, 1015 DH Amsterdam. Prop: Herb Lewitz. Tel: (020) 6204690. Est: 1988. Shop; open Monday to Friday 10–6, Saturday 11–6. Very large stock. Spec: English literature; science fiction; fantasy; art; travel; film. PR: Fl.5–100 plus. Corresp: German, French.

Antiquariaat Hieronymus Bosch, Leliegracht 36, 1015 DH Amsterdam. Prop: P.H. Kerssemakers. Tel: (020) 6237178. Est: 1970. Shop; open Monday to Saturday 11.30–5.30, (closed on Wednesday). Large stock. Spec: art history; ecclesiastical history & architecture; illuminated manuscripts; palaeography; Middle Ages (especially art and iconography). PR: £3–300. Cata: 6 to 8 a year on Middle Ages and Byzantium and Renaissance art. Also, a booksearch service. Corresp: French, German, Dutch.

Antiquariaat Brinkman, Singel 319, 1012 WJ Amsterdam. Prop: H. Brinkman & F. Rutten. Tel: (020) 6238353. Fax: 6207577. Shop; open Monday to Friday 10–5, Saturday 11–5. Spec: linguistics (English, German, Romance); history. Cata: 8 a year on specialities. Corresp: French, German. Mem: N.V.A.

Antiquariaat Broekema, P.O. Box 75880, 1070 AW Amsterdam. Prop: C. Broekema. Tel: (020) 6629510. Est: 1950. Private premises; appointment necessary. Very small stock. Spec: atlases; geography; cartography. Corresp: all European languages. Mem: I.L.A.B.; N.V.A. VAT No: NL 052 556 773 B01.

Charbo's Antiquariaat, Koninginneweg 79, 1075 CJ Amsterdam. Prop: R.H.W. Charbo. Tel: (020) 6761229. Fax: 6761726. Est: 1979. Shop; appointment necessary. Very large stock. Spec: ethnography; geography; history; topography; atlases, voyages and travel; colonial history, cultural history. PR: Fl.50–100. Cata: 8 to 10 a year. Also, a booksearch service. Corresp: German, French. VAT No: NL 070 226 325 B01.

Ciné-qua-non, Staalstraat 14, 1011 JL Amsterdam.

Antiquariaat Colombine, Ceintuurbaan 37, 1072 ET Amsterdam. Prop: J.C.H. Bloemgarten-Barends. Tel: & Fax: (020) 6621394. Est: 1983. Shop; open Tuesday to Saturday 10–6. Medium stock. Spec: antiquarian; history; Holocaust; literature; literature in translation; memoirs; politics; Jewish religion. PR: £10–100. Cata: 4 or 5 a year. Corresp: French, German.

Culturel, Gasthuismolensteeg 4, 1016 AN Amsterdam. Prop: I.U. Cramer-Verhaar. Tel: (020) 6248793. Est: 1986. Shop; open Monday to Saturday 11–6. Medium stock. Spec: Colonial; literature; local topography; World War II. PR: 50p– £20. Corresp: French, German, Dutch.

E.A.E. van Dishoeck, Raamsteeg 1, 1012 VZ Amsterdam. Prop: Eduard van Dishoeck. Tel: (020) 6247190. Fax: (035) 5316595. Est: 1981. Shop; open Tuesday to Friday 11.30–5 and, September to March, Saturday 11.30–4.30. Small stock. Spec: maritime; art; old and rare; Indonesia. PR: £10–1,000. Corresp: Dutch, French, German. VAT No: NL 072 522 240 B01.

van Duyvendijk & Brouwer, Nieuwe Spiegelstraat 46, 1017 DG Amsterdam. Prop: Pieke Van Duyvendijk & Jaap Brouwer. Tel: (020) 6248599. Fax: 6390533. Est: 1994. Shop; open 11–5. Medium stock. Spec: applied art; art reference. Corresp: French, Dutch. Mem: N.V.A.

E'soro Books, Box 1, Oudeman Huispoort, Amsterdam 1012 CN.

Egidius, Haarlemmerstraat 87, 1013 EL Amsterdam. Prop: J.J. Fictoor. Tel: (020) 6243255. Est: 1985. Shop and market stand; open 11–6. Medium stock. Spec: literature and art (mainly 20th century). Corresp: Dutch.

Antiquariaat S. Emmering B.V., Nieuwezijds Voorburgwal 304, 1012 RV Amsterdam.

Evenaar, Singel 348, Amsterdam.

Fa. J.H. Flint, Dikninge 119, 1083 VA Amsterdam. Prop: J.H. Flint & C.A. Hekma.
Tel: (020) 6423664. Fax: 6422751. Est: 1964. Storeroom; appointment
necessary. Very large stock. Spec: classical antiquity; philosophy; theology.
Cata: 15 a year on specialities plus history. Corresp: French, German. VAT
No: NL 049 826 505 B01.

Fragmenta Selecta Antiquariaat, KNSM-Laan 412, 1019 LN Amsterdam. Prop:
M.C. Hoogma & R. Stil. Tel: (020) 4185565. Fax: 4186288. Est: 1984. Private
premises; postal business only. Medium stock. Spec: classical (Greek and
Latin); philology; medieval and neo-Latin; ancient history and philosophy;
archaeology. Cata: 4 a year. Also, a booksearch service. Corresp: French,
German. VAT No: NL 006 786 091 B01.

Antiquariat De Friedesche Molen, Rosmarijnsteeg 6, 1012 RP Amsterdam. Prop:
Drs. Hein van Stekelenburg & Marion E. Greidanus. Tel: (020) 6255947. Est:
1980. Shop; open 12–6. Large stock. Spec: literature; exile literature; history of
science; old books in all fields; Judaica; travel; coffee. Cata: 1 a year on
German literature. VAT No: NL 064 034 859 B01.

E.A.G. Fukkink, Planciusstraat 26, Amsterdam.

van Gennep, Nieuwezijds Voorburgwal 330, Amsterdam.

A. Gerits and Son, B.V. Modern and Antiquarian Booksellers, Prinsengracht 445,
1016 HN Amsterdam. Prop: Anton & Arnoud Gerits. Tel: (020) 6272285. Fax:
6258970. Est: 1981. Shop: open Monday to Friday 9.30–5.30, and at other
times by appointment. Very large stock. Spec: humanities; social sciences. PR:
Fl.100–300,000 plus. Cata: 6 a year on specialities. Also, a booksearch service.
Mem: N.V.A.; S.L.A.M. Corresp: French, German. VAT No: NL 801 540 306
B01.

Antiquariaat Bart Gerritsma, Bakhuizen van den Brinkhof 37, 1065 BA Amsterdam.
Prop: Th. Gerritsma. Tel: & Fax: (020) 6141843. Est: 1984. Storeroom;
appointment necessary. Medium stock. Spec: alpinism/mountaineering;
autobiography; documents; ethnography; ethnology; newspapers; social
history; transport. PR: £25–350. Cata: 3 a year on specialities. Corresp:
French, German, Dutch, Japanese. VAT No: NL 074 234 559 B01.

Antiquariaat J. ter Gouw, Overtoom 480, 1054 JZ Amsterdam.

Bert en Reiny Hagen, Herenstraat 39, Amsterdam.

A. Haring, 3e Oosterparkstraat 44 hs. Amsterdam.

Humaniora Antiqua, Herengracht 242, 1016 BT Amsterdam.

NETHERLANDS

Indisch antiquariaat/uitgeverij Modjopahit, Burg. Hogguerstraat 253-8, Amsterdam.

Maarten J. Israel, P.O. Box 8, 1110 AA Diemen.

B.M. Israel, B.V., N.Z. Voorburgwal 264, 1012 RS Amsterdam. Tel: (020) 6247040. TA: Israelbook, Amsterdam. Fax: 6382355. (Print Room) 6225500. Est: 1899. Private premises, open Monday to Friday 9–1 & 2–5. Large general stock. Cata: 2 to 6 a year. Corresp: French, Dutch. Mem: N.V.A. VAT No: NL 003 894 289 B01.

Johan's Antiquariaat, Weissenbruchstraat 29, Amsterdam.

Peter de Jonge – Inter Antiquariat, Bernard Zweerskade, 18, 1077 TZ Amsterdam. Tel: (020) 6640841. Fax: 6641391. Spec: atlases; rare and fine. Also, large print books. VAT No: NL 051 723 967 B01.

Antiquariaat Junk, B.V., Van Eeghenstraat 129, 1071 GA Amsterdam. Prop: E.R. Schierenberg. Tel: (020) 6763185. Fax: 6751466. Est: 1899. Shop; open Monday to Friday 9–5.30. Spec: old and rare natural history and travel. Cata: 3 a year. Corresp: French, German. Mem: N.V.A.

Kapitein Rob, 2e Egelantiersdwarsstraat 7 hs, Amsterdam.

Antiquariaat de Kloof, Kloveniersburgwal 44, 1012 CW Amsterdam. Prop: J.G. Schokkenbroek. Tel: (020) 6223828. Fax: 6271395. E-Mail: kloof@xs4all.nl. Est: 1934. Shop; open Monday to Saturday 9–6, Sunday 1–5. Very large stock. Spec: theology; law; social sciences, economics; linguistics; novels in all languages; medicine; science. CC: V; EC: A; DC; AE. Cata: on law, economics and social sciences. Also, web site http://www.xs4all.nl/~kloof/ . Corresp: German, Dutch. VAT No: NL 087 344 646 B01.

Antiquariaat A. Kok en Zn., 14–18 Oude Hoogstraat, 1012 CE Amsterdam. Prop: A. & R. Kok. Tel: (020) 6231191. Fax: 6232809. Est: 1945. Shop; open Monday to Friday 9.30–6, Saturday 9.30–5. Very large stock. Spec: art; architecture; archaeology; natural history; ethnography. PR: Fl.1–125,000. Cata: 2 a year on biology, archaeology, art and architecture. Corresp: German. Mem: N.V.A. VAT No: NL 002 181 095 B01.

De Kookboekhandel, Runstraat 26, Amsterdam.

De Terechte Kronkel, P.O. Box 70118, Amsterdam.

Antiquariaat René Krul, P.O. Box 9951, 1006 AR Amsterdam.

Muziekantiquariaat G.N. Landré, 1e Anjeliersdwarsstraat 36, 1015 NR Amsterdam.

Ko van Leest, Banstraat 22, Amsterdam.

Antiquariat W.J. van Leeuwen, Binnenkant 17, Amsterdam.

Lorelei, Prinsengracht 495, Amsterdam.

Boekhandel Het Martyrium b.v., Van Baerlestraat, Amsterdam.

A. van de Meer, P.C. Hooftstraat 112, 1071 CD Amsterdam.

Antiquariat Pieter Mefferdt, Willemsparkweg 37, Amsterdam.

Minotaurus Boekwinkel, Sint Antoniesbreestraat 3d, P.O. Box 16477, 1001 RN Amsterdam.

Rudolf Muller International Booksellers BV, P.O. Box 9016, 1006 AA Amsterdam. Dir: R. Muller & C.M. Griffioen. Tel: (020) 6165955. Fax: 6838651. Est: 1969. Storeroom; appointment necessary. Small stock. Spec: geography; geology; earth sciences; history of cartography; 19th-century atlases. Cata: irregularly on cartography (historical & contemporary) and earth sciences. Also, new books on contemporary cartography and earth sciences. Corresp: French, German, Russian, Spanish.

Muziekbeurs Amsterdam, Trompenburgerstraat 111, Amsterdam.

Muziekmagazijn Opus 391, Rustenburgerstraat 391, 1072 GW Amsterdam. Prop: Anke J.C. Kuypers. Tel: (020) 6766415. Est: 1977. Shop; open Thursday to Saturday 10–8 & market stand; open Monday to Wednesday 10–5.30. Large stock. Spec: sheet music (esp. for small orchestras) and literature on music. PR: Fl.1–200. Also, records (78s, LPs and singles) and a booksearch service. Cata: 2 a year. Corresp: French, German.

V/h Gé Nabrink, Korte Korsjespoortsteeg 8, 1012 TC Amsterdam. Prop: K. Goulooze. Tel: (020) 6223058. Fax: 6245718. Est: 1924. Shop; open Monday to Friday 9–5, Saturday 10–2, (closed Wednesday afternoons). Very large stock. Spec: Orientalia (especially Indonesia). Cata: 12 a year on speciality. Also, new books and a booksearch service. Corresp: French, German. Mem: N.V.A.; I.L.A.B. VAT No: NL 008 694 734 B01.

Navigare Bookshop, Kattenburgerplein 1, 1018 KK Amsterdam. Prop: A.J. Hilgersom. Tel: (020) 6232059. Est: 1973. Shop; open 10–5, closed Monday. Medium stock. Spec: maritime/nautical. Also, a booksearch service. VAT No: NL 049 926 688 BO1.

Nijhof & Lee, Staalstraat 13a, 1011 JK Amsterdam. Prop: F.R. Nijhof & W.J. Lee. Tel: (020) 6203980. Fax: 6393294. Est: 1988. Shop; open Monday 12–6, Tuesday to Friday 9–6, Saturday 10–5.30. Medium stock. Spec: applied art; architecture; art; books about books; graphic art; interior design; typography. CC: MC; V; AE. Cata: 2 a year. Also, new books in the same fields. Corresp: German, French, Dutch. Mem: N.B.B. VAT No: NL 008 623 077 B01.

Leeshal Oost, Commelinstraat 53, Amsterdam.

Opbouw Art Books, Leliegracht 42, 1015 DH Amsterdam.

W. van Poelgeest b.v., Overtoom 85, 1054 HC Amsterdam, Tel: (020) 6163103. Est: 1928. Shop; open Wednesday to Friday 10.30–1 & 2–5.30, Saturday 10.30–4. *Also at:* O.Z. Voorburgwal 43, 1012 EJ Amsterdam. Tel: (020) 6221700; open Tuesday to Friday 9–5. VAT No: NL 67 84 677 B01 2300.

Boekhandel G. Postma, O.Z. Voorburgwal 249, 1012 EZ Amsterdam. Tel: (020) 6245781. Fax: 6241328. Est: 1948. Shop; open Monday to Friday 1–5. Medium stock. Spec: language; literature; art; books about books. Mem: N.V.A. VAT No: NL 052 845 291 B01.

Jacob E. van Ruller, Bloemstraat 171b, 1016 LA Amsterdam. Tel: (030) 2581069. Est: 1985. Private premises. Medium stock. Spec: World War II; Weiman Republic; National Socialism; Communism; The Sixties. PR: Fl.10–1,000. Cata: 2 a year. Also, a booksearch service. Corresp: German, French, Dutch.

Dieter Schierenberg, B.V., Prinsengracht 485–487, 1016 HP Amsterdam. Tel: (020) 6225730. Fax: 6265650. Est: 1975. Shop; appointment necessary. Very large stock, over 1,000,000. Spec: alpinism/mountaineering; animals; anthropology; beekeeping; biology; botany; colour–plate; earth sciences; ecology; entomology; ethnography; forestry; geography; geology; horticulture; microscopy; mineralogy; mining; natural history and sciences and many others. CC: AE; V. Cata: 3 a year. Corresp: French, German. Mem: I.L.A.B.; P.B.F.A. VAT No: NL 003 979 301 B01.

Antiquariaat Die Schmiede, Brouwersgracht 4, 1013 GW Amsterdam. Prop: A. & G. Leyerzapf. Tel: (020) 6250501. Fax: 6235470. Est: 1980. Shop; open Monday to Saturday 10–5. Small German language stock. Spec: fine printing; literature; private press; children's; Judaica; typography; book history and bibliography. Cata: 3 a year. Corresp: French, German. Mem: N.V.V.A.; V.D.A. VAT No: NL 005 911 710 B01.

Antiquariaat Schuhmacher, Geldersekade 107, 1011 EM Amsterdam. Prop: W. & M. Schuhmacher. Tel: (020) 6221604. Fax: 6206620. Est: 1952. Shop; open Monday to Saturday 11–6. Very large stock. Spec: Dutch literature, printing & language; avant–garde; German literature. PR: Fl.20–20,000. Cata: approximately 2 a year. Corresp: Dutch, German. Mem: N.V.A.; I.L.A.B. VAT No: NL 002 470 706 BO1.

Philip Silbernberg, Helstraat 74, Amsterdam.

Boekhandel J. de Slegte b.v., Kalverstraat 48–52, 1012 PE Amsterdam. Tel: (020) 6225933. Fax: 6241620. Est: 1900. Shop. Very large stock. Spec: art; colourplate; travels. Also, remainders. Corresp: German, French, Spanish. Mem: N.V.A. *Also shops at:* Rotterdam, Den Haag, Eindhoven, Utrecht, Arnhem, Groningen, Haarlem, Leiden, Enschede, Zwolle, Maastricht, Nijmegen, Antwerpen, Gent, Leuven, Brussels, Bruges, Hasselt (q.v.).

N. Smit, Gasthuismolensteeg 13, Amsterdam.

Antiquariaat Spinoza, Den Texstraat 26, 1017 ZB Amsterdam. Prop: Dr. W.J. Burgers. Tel: (020) 6242373. Fax: 6257540. E-Mail: spinoza@euronet.nl. Est: 1970. Storeroom and private premises; appointment necessary. Very large stock. Spec: bibles; Judaica; philosophy. Cata: 4 a year on Jewish history and literature, bibles, philosophy. Mem: N.V.A.; I.L.A.B. VAT No: NL 050 793 792 B01.

A.B.C. Staal, Staalstraat 11, Amsterdam.

Muziekhandel en - Antiquariaat Valerius, Koninginneweg 145, 1075 CM Amsterdam. Prop: Mr. Bert Uhlhorn & Mrs. Connie Bremer. Tel: (020) 6623629. Fax: 6648435. Est: 1985. Shop; open Monday to Friday 10–5. Medium stock. Spec: sheet music and music literature. PR: Ffr.10–500. CC: MC; V; AE; DC. Corresp: German, French. Mem: Dutch Music Federation (NMF). VAT No: NL 008 636 461 B01.

Antiquariaat Vrouwen in Druk, Postbus 3869, 1001 AR Amsterdam. Prop: Doris Hermanns. Tel: & Fax: (020) 6245003. E-Mail: vind@xs4all.nl. Est: 1984. Shop at: Westermarkt 5 1016 DH Amsterdam; open Tuesday to Saturday 11–6. Large stock. Spec: women's books in general; feminism; sexuality; English literature; biographies; travel; history; Dutch literature; Dutch poetry; Dutch children's. PR: Fl.5–500. Cata: 3 or 4 a year on suffragettes, Left Bank, Bloomsbury, lesbiana, travel. Also, a booksearch service and women's studies. Corresp: German, Dutch.

Wout Vuyk, Singel 383, Amsterdam.

Pampiere Wereld, Keizersgracht 428–432, Amsterdam.

Westman's Winkel, Korte Lijnbaanssteeg 1, Amsterdam.

APELDOORN

Scrinium v.o.f., Soerenseweg 49, 7314 JE Apeldoorn. Prop: Drs. Nelleke Dansen & Henk Waaijenberg. Tel: & Fax: (055) 3554292. E-Mail: scrinium@pi.net. Est: 1993. Private premises. Medium stock. Spec: exclusively classical antiquity. PR: Fl.1–1,000. CC: MC. Cata: 4 or 5 a year. Corresp: French, German. Mem: B.O.B. (Bond van handelare in Oude Boeken). VAT No: NL 801 561 966 B01.

H. de Weerd, Middellaan 34, 7314 GC Apeldoorn. Tel: (055) 3552181. Est: 1961. Storeroom & private premises; appointment necessary. Medium stock. Spec: aviation; marine; automobile; World War II. PR: £15. Also, a booksearch service. Corresp: French, German.

APPINGEDAM

Books Etc., Heiliggravenweg 15, 9901 CG Appingedam. Prop: B. Flikkema. Tel: (0596) 622546. Est: 1992. Private premises. Very small stock. Spec: theology, esp. Irvingism & Catholic Apostolic church. PR: £1–50. Cata: 1 a year. Also, Dutch theology booksearch. Corresp: Dutch, German.

ARNHEM

Gysbers en van Loon, Antiquarian & International Booksellers, Postbus 396, Bakkerstraat 7-7a, 6800 AJ Arnhem. Booksearch service. VAT No: NL 019 703 351 B01.

Peter van Os, Bakkerstraat 68, 6811 EK Arnhem. Tel: (085) 422009. Fax: 436418. Est: 1910. Shop; open Tuesday to Saturday 10–5. Stock includes important art periodicals and magazines. Cata: frequently.

Het Rijnoeverhuys, Antiquarian Bookshop & Publishers, Nieuwstad 20, 6811 BL Arnhem.

Boekhandel J. de Slegte b.v., Jansstraat 28, 6811 GJ Arnhem. Tel: (026) 4420597. Shop. General stock. *Also shops at:* Amsterdam, Rotterdam, The Hague, Eindhoven, Utrecht, Groningen, Haarlem, Leiden, Enschede, Zwolle, Maastricht, Nijmegen, Antwerp, Gent, Leuven, Brussels, Bruges, Hasselt (q.v.).

BARENDRECHT

Antiquariaat Batavia, Dorpsstraat 171, 2992 AA Barendrecht. Prop: Dr. G.C. Zijlmans. Tel: (0180) 619816. Fax: 615477. E-Mail: nan@antiqbook.nl. Est: 1985. Shop; open 10–5 (except Tuesdays). Large stock. Spec: South, East and Southeast Asia; Caribbean Area; Indonesia, Surinam and The Netherlands Antilles. PR: Fl.10–2,000. Cata: 3 a year. Also, a booksearch service. Corresp: Dutch, German. VAT No: NL 075 883 569 B01.

BARNEVELD

Antiquariaat Johan Beek, Graaf van Lyndenlaan 55, 3771 JB Barneveld. Tel: (03420) 15118. Fax: 21005. Est: 1957. Private premises; appointment necessary. Large stock. Spec: law; politics; history; economics; business history; political economics; philosophy; social sciences; social history. Cata: 2 or 3 a year. Also, a booksearch service. Corresp: French, German, Dutch. Mem: N.V.A.; I.L.A.B. VAT No: NL 056 561 283 B01.

BREDEVOORT

Ave, Landstraat 28, 7126 AS Bredevoort.

Antiquariaat Jan Bloemendaal, Landstraat 2E, 7126 AT Bredevoort. Tel: (0543) 451005. Est: 1992. Shop and storeroom; open any time. Large stock. Spec: genealogy. Also, a booksearch service. Corresp: Dutch, German, French, Spanish. VAT No: NL 776 88 673 B01.

De Boekenkring, Markt 4, 7126 AZ Bredevoort.

Bolwerk, Markt 5, 7126 AZ Bredevoort.

Das Kleine Deutsche Antiquariat, Thomas Jenisch, Koppelstraat 5, 7126 AE Bredevoort. *Also at:* Essen, Germany (q.v.).

"Emergo", 'tZand 21b, 7126 BG Bredevoort. Prop: Huitink Prinsen & Hyink Heezen. Tel: (0543) 452006. Shop. Medium stock. Spec: modern and antiquarian books written by women or about women (all kinds of subjects). Corresp: Dutch, German.

The English Bookshop, 'tZand 25, 7126 BG Bredevoort. Prop: Leonard Webb. Tel: (0544) 276703. Est: 1995. Shop; open Tuesday to Saturday 11–5. Medium stock. Spec: biography; literary criticism; literature; poetry. PR: £1–150. Corresp: Dutch.

Gemilang Antiquarian Booksellers, P.O. Box 26, 7126 ZG Bredevoort. Prop: Y.J. Heller & A.J. Land. Tel: (0543) 452325. Fax: 452300. E-Mail: booktown@ tref.nl. Est: 1982. Private premises; open 9am–10pm. Large stock. Spec: Insular Southeast Asia (Indonesia/Malaya/Singapore); costume; fashion; textiles (incl. non–Western). PR: £1–10,000. CC: AE; DC; V. Cata: 6 to 8 a year. Also, a booksearch service. Corresp: French, German. VAT No: NL 062 645 201 B01.

Dirkje van Gent, Boterstraat 7, 7126 BB Bredevoort. Tel: (0543) 451004. E-Mail: opletter@worldonline.nl. Est: 1994. Shop; open Monday to Saturday 11–5. Small stock. Spec: esoteric; mysticism; religion; spiritualism; philosophy; supernatural; typography. PR: Fl.30. Cata: 2 a year. Also, a booksearch service. Corresp: Dutch, French, German.

Het Oplettende Lezertje, Boterstraat 7, 7126 BB Bredevoort. E-Mail: opletter@ worldonline.nl. Est: 1986. Shop; open Thursday to Saturday 11–5. Medium stock. Spec: biology; books about books; children's colonial; general fiction; folklore; general & national history; Holocaust; illustrated; literature; literature in translation; Middle Ages; poetry; war. PR: Fl.25 and up. Also, a booksearch service. Corresp: French, Dutch, German.

Chris en Ineke Huis, Landstraat 13, 7126 AS Bredevoort.

De Kantlijn, 'tZand 25, 7126 BG Bredevoort. Prop: R.P. Wilstra. Tel: (0314) 363830 or (0543) 452320. Est: 1993. Open Tuesday to Saturday 12–5. Medium general stock. PR: Fl.4–1,000. Cata: 3 a year. Corresp: German, Dutch. VAT No: NL 122 927 175 B01.

Antiquariat Karla, Landstraat 4, 7126 AT Bredevoort. Tel: (0543) 452123. Shop; open Wednesday to Saturday 12–5 (in spring & summer). Medium stock. Spec: architecture; art; children's; education; feminism; general & women's fiction; first editions; foreign texts; history; Holocaust; foreign language; linguistics; literary criticism; philosophy; politics; psychoanalysis; psychology/psychiatry; socialism; theatre. PR: Fl.5–300. Cata: occasionally. Corresp: German, Dutch.

De Klarinet, Landstraat 4a, 7126 AT Bredevoort. Tel: (0543) 451717. Shop. General stock. Corresp: Dutch, German.

Stefan Krüger, Markt 1–II, 7126 Bredevoort.

Ovidius' Antiquarian Bookshop, Koppelstraat 9, 7162 AE, Bredevoort.

Pergamon, Landstr 12 and Koppelstraat 1, 7126 AT Bredevoort.

De Prins, Prinsenstraat 12, 7126 AX Bredevoort.

Richartz, Koppelstraat 5, 7126 AE Bredevoort.

Tahob, Misterstraat 17, 7126 CA Bredevoort.

Vrouwenindruk, Officierstraat 4, 7126 AN Bredevoort.

Waldo, Gasthuisstraat 9, 7126 BD Bredevoort.

BUSSUM

Carpinus Antiquariaat, Kerkstraat 26, 1404 HJ Bussum. Prop: A. van Geloven. Tel: (035) 6914996. Est: 1983. Premises; open Tuesday to Saturday 12–6. Large general stock. Spec: applied art; architecture; art; books about books; children's; esoteric; occult; poetry. PR: Fl.10–500. Cata: 3 a year. Also, a booksearch service. Corresp: German, French.

P.C. Notebaart, Postbus 280, 1400 AG Bussum. Tel: & Fax: (035) 6945801. Est: 1969. Private premises; postal business only. Small stock. Spec: old and rare Spanish and children's; surrealism. Cata: 4 a year on specialities. Corresp: German, French. Mem: N.V.A. VAT No: NL 052 034 057 B01.

CASTRICUM

Antiquariaat Bert Hagen, B.V., Molenweide 24, 1902 CH Castricum.

DE BEEK

Antiquariaat in de Roozetak, Rijksstraatweg 128A, 6573 DE De Beek.

DE MEERN

Euro Center (Horse Books), Zandweg 215, 3454 HE De Meern. Prop: P.A. Bogaard. Tel: (030) 6661696. Fax: 6621263. Est: 1966. Private premises; appointment necessary. Small stock. Spec: horses; driving; riding; trotting and related subjects in all languages. Also, new books, publisher and a booksearch service. Corresp: Dutch, German, French. VAT No: NL 029 344 049 B01.

DOORNSPIJK

Antiquariaat van Coevorden, Beukenlaan 3, 8085 RK Doornspijk. Prop: Joop W. van Coevorden. Tel: (0525) 661823. Fax: 662153. Est: 1968. Private premises; appointment necessary. Large stock. Spec: art; archaeology. PR: Fl.25–10,000. Mem: N.V.A. VAT No: NL 028 860 573 B01.

DORDRECHT

Antiquariaat Quist, Steegoversloot 42, 3311 PP Dordrecht. Prop: Ernie Quist. Tel: & Fax: (078) 6318867. Shop; open Wednesday to Saturday 12–6 and every first Sunday in the month. Small general stock. CC: AE; V; DC; MC. Corresp: German, Italian, French, Spanish. *Also at:* Nieuwe Binnenweg 110, 3015 BE Rotterdam (q.v.).

Antiquariaat J.P. van den Tol, Postbus 63, 3300 AB Dordrecht. Tel: (078) 6139522. Fax: 6317575. Est: 1921. Shop at: Steegoversloot 56, 3311 PP Dordrecht; open Tuesday to Saturday 11–5. Very large stock. Spec: old and rare religion; theology; history; topography. Cata: 5 a year on religion and theology. Also, new books. Corresp: German. Mem: N.V.A. VAT No: NL 036 054 495 B01.

DRIEBERGEN

Antiquariaat Anna, Prins Hendriklaan 1, 3972 EV Driebergen. Prop: D.T.S. Hovinga. Tel: (0343) 514200. Fax: 512474. Shop; appointment necessary. Medium stock. Spec: children's. VAT No: NL 028 229 551 B01.

EINDHOVEN

Eppo Superstrip Speciaalzaak, Kleine Berg 33, 5611 JS Eindhoven. Prop: Jos & Mari Huddleston Slater. Tel: (040) 2441882. Fax: 2735873. Est: 1978. Shop; open Tuesday to Thursday 11–6, Friday 11–9, Saturday 11–5. Very large stock. Spec: comic books and annuals; comics; games; wargames. Also, new comic books, all comic art, Also, new comic books, all comic art, originals, drawings, ornaments, etc. and a booksearch service. Corresp: German, French. VAT No: NL 080 678 579 B01.

Antikwariaat Max Silverenberg, Kleine Berg 81, 5611 JT Eindhoven. Tel: (040) 2432064. Fax: 2462879. Est: 1976. Private premises; appointment necessary. Small stock. Spec: topography; travel - Middle East; art; Judaica; The Orient; Cata: 2 to 4 a year on specialities. Also, large print books and auctions twice a year. Corresp: French, German, Turkish, Dutch. VAT No: NL 069 665 722 B01.

Boekhandel J. de Slegte b.v., Rechtestraat 36A, 5611 GP Eindhoven. Tel: (040) 2447419 . Shop. General stock. *Also shops at:* Amsterdam, Rotterdam, Den Haag, Utrecht, Arnhem, Groningen, Haarlem, Leiden, Enschede, Zwolle, Maastricht, Nijmegen, Antwerp, Gent, Leuven, Brussels, Bruges, Hasselt (q.v.).

ENSCHEDE

Boekhandel J. de Slegte b.v., Marktstraat 13, 7511 GC Enschede. Tel: (053) 4319200. Shop. General stock. *Also shops at:* Amsterdam, Rotterdam, Den Haag, Eindhoven, Utrecht, Arnhem, Groningen, Haarlem, Leiden, Zwolle, Maastricht, Nijmegen, Antwerp, Gent, Leuven, Brussels, Bruges, Hasselt (q.v.).

FRANEKER

T. Wever B.V., P.O. Box 59, 8800 AB Franeker. Tel: (0517) 393147. Fax: 395450. Est: 1926. Shop at: Zilverstraat 4–14, 8801 KC; open Monday to Friday 9–5. Very large stock. Spec: (only) theology; philosophy. CC: MC; V. Cata: 4 a year. Also, new books on theology and a booksearch service. Corresp: German. Mem: Vereeniging ter Bevordering van de Belangen des Boekhandels.

GELDROP

Paulus Swaen Old Maps and Prints, Hofstraat 19, Postbus 317, 5660 AH Geldrop. Prop: P.W.A. Joppen. Tel: (06) 53195323 or Tel: & Fax: (040) 2853571. Est: 1978. Shop; appointment necessary. Small stock. Spec: atlases/cartography; maritime/nautical; general topography; travel - Asia; V.O.C. (Dutch East India Company). PR: £200 and up. Cata: 5 a year. Also, globes. Corresp: Dutch, German. Mem: N.V.A.; I.L.A.B. VAT No: NL 020 688 854 B01.

GOUDA

Antiquariaat Coornhert, Walestraat 24, 2801 PV Gouda. Prop: H. de Kleer. Tel: (0182) 528732. Est: 1984. Shop; open Wednesday to Saturday 2–6. Medium stock. Spec: illustrated; fine & rare; antiquarian. PR: Fl.100–3,000. CC: EC; DC; AE. Cata: 1 a year. Corresp: Dutch, German, French. VAT No: NL 790 326 79 B01.

GRAVE

Alfa Antiquarian Booksellers, Postbus 26, 5360 AA Grave. Prop: Leo Kerssemakers. Tel: (0486) 473966. Est: 1970. Private premises; appointment necessary. Medium stock. Spec: the Middle Ages and Renaissance; old and rare. Cata: 1 a year on medieval subjects. Also, a booksearch service and large print books. Corresp: French, German, Spanish, Italian. Mem: N.V.A. VAT No: NL 803 493 502 B01.

GRONINGEN

Isis, Folkingestraat 20, 9711 JW Groningen. Prop: E.M.H. Belt & T.G.J. Butterhof. Tel: (050) 3184233. Fax: 3112298. Est: 1984. Shop; open Monday 1–6, Tuesday, Wednesday and Friday 10–6, Thursday 10–9, Saturday 10–5. Large stock. Spec: philosophy; German literature; religion; esoteric; antiquarian; history; psychology/psychiatry. Cata: 1 a year on philosophy. Also, a booksearch service. Corresp: German.

Boekhandel J. de Slegte b.v., Herestraat 33, 9711 LB Groningen. Tel: (050) 3121422. Shop. General stock. *Also shops at:* Amsterdam, Rotterdam, The Hague, Eindhoven, Utrecht, Arnhem, Haarlem, Leiden, Enschede, Zwolle, Maastricht, Nijmegen, Antwerp, Gent, Leuven, Brussels, Bruges, Hasselt (q.v.).

Antiquariaat Sphinx, Nieuwe Boteringestraat 56, 9712 PN Groningen. Prop: F. Elzer & H.B.F. Prins. Tel: (050) 3137237. Est: 1982. Shop; open Monday to Friday 11–6, Saturday 11–5. Large stock. Spec: history; literature; occult. Cata: 1 or 2 a year on history. Also, a booksearch service. Corresp: French, German.

Timbuctoo, Turftorenstraat 16, Groningen. Prop: A.M.J. Groenhuysen & R.P. 't Riet. Tel: (050) 3143162. Est: 1983. Shop; open Tuesday to Saturday 12–6; and market stand, open Friday at Amsterdam Spuimarkt. Medium stock. Spec: general fiction; gardening; horticulture; philosophy; travel. PR: £5–100. Cata: irregularly on gardening. Corresp: German, French.

HAARLEM

Lourens Jansz. Coster, Postbus 5196, 2000 GD Haarlem. Prop: M.C. de Vries. Tel: (023) 5424878. Est: 1984. Private premises. Small stock. Spec: general & local topography; sport; decorative art; foreign & national culture. PR: £2–1,000. Corresp: German.

Bubb Kuyper, Jansweg 39, 2011 KM Haarlem. Prop: F.W. Kuyper. Tel: (023) 5323986. Fax: 5323893. Est: 1978. Private premises; open Monday to Friday 9–5. Very small stock. Spec: bibliography; typography; old and rare; illustrated. Cata: 2 a year. Also, book and print auctioneers. Corresp: French, German. Mem: N.V.A. VAT No: NL 800 403 381 B01.

Versandantiquariat Helmut Rödner, Postbus 9700, 2003 LS Haarlem. Tel: (023) 5354807. Fax: 5367101. Est: 1990. Storeroom and private premises; appointment necessary. Medium stock. Spec: 20th century German books; academic/scholarly; architecture; art; caricature; cinema/films; foreign culture; erotica; feminism; first editions; Holocaust; homosexuality; literature; media; pacifism; photography; politics; psychoanalysis; radical issues; sexology; social history. PR: DM80–500. Cata: 2 a year. Also, a booksearch service and direct offers. Corresp: German, French, Dutch. Mem: Kamer van Krophandel Haarlem. VAT No: NL 048 306 472 B01.

Boekhandel J. de Slegte b.v., Grote Houtstraat 100, 2011 SR Haarlem. Tel: (023) 5315250. Shop. General stock. *Also shops at:* Amsterdam, Rotterdam, The Hague, Eindhoven, Utrecht, Arnhem, Groningen, Leiden, Enschede, Zwolle, Maastricht, Nijmegen, Antwerp, Gent, Leuven, Brussels, Bruges, Hasselt (q.v.).

A.G. van der Steur Historisch Antiquariaat, Kruisstraat 3, 2011 PV Haarlem. Tel: (023) 5311470 or 5324237. Fax: 5420670. Est: 1989. Shop; open Wednesday to Saturday 11–5.30. Very large stock. Spec: antiquarian; archives; fine and rare; genealogy; heraldry; local and national history; manuscripts. Cata: 1 or 2 a year on specialities. Mem: N.V.V.A.; I.L.A.B. VAT No: NL 0032 281 055 B01.

THE HAGUE (DEN HAAG)

Muziekhandel Albersen & Co., B.V., Groot Hertoginnelaan 182, 2517 EV den Haag. Prop: Jan & Herman Albersen. Tel: (070) 3456000. Fax: 3614528. Est: 1928. Shop; open Tuesday to Saturday 9–5. Very large stock. Spec: music and books about music. PR: Fl.1–5,000. CC: All. Also, over 20,000 classical CDs. Corresp: Dutch, German, French. VAT No: NL 005 609 471 B02. *Also at:* Theresiastraat 55, 2593 AA den Haag.

Apollo Art Books, P.O. Box 96826, 2509 JE den Haag. Prop: Jac. Hundepool. Tel: (070) 3451765. Fax: 3563122. Est: 1986. Shop at: Frederikstraat 22, 2514 LK The Hague; open daily 12–6 and a market stand in Voorhout - Sundays May to September. Medium stock. Spec: antiquarian; antiques; applied art; archaeology; architecture; art; art history; art reference; artists; carpets; Catalogues Raisonées; ceramics; collecting; decorative art; dictionaries; glass; jewellery; lace; needlework; sculpture; porcelain; silver; furniture; painting; clocks. PR: Fl.10–1,000. Also, a booksearch service. Corresp: German, French, Dutch.

Juridisch Antiquariaat A. Jongbloed & Zoon, Noordeinde 39, 2514 GC den Haag. Prop: A.K. Jongbloed. Tel: (070) 3560277. Fax: 3455870. E-Mail: jbl@tip.nl. Est: 1926. Shop; open Monday to Friday 9–5.30 and Saturday 9–4. Medium stock. Spec: law. Cata: 1 a year. Also, new law books. Mem: N.V.A.

Fa. Loose, Papestraat 3, 2513 AV den Haag. Prop: R. & J. Loose. Tel: (070) 3460404. Est: 1946. Shop; open Tuesday to Friday 9.30–6, Saturday 9.30–5. Medium stock. Spec: children's; topography; pre-1860 illustrated; almanacs. PR: 50p–£1,000. Corresp: French, German. Mem: N.V.A.

Boekhandel J. de Slegte b.v., Spuistraat 21, 2511 BC den Haag. Tel: (070) 3639712. Shop. General stock. *Also shops at:* Amsterdam, Rotterdam, Eindhoven, Utrecht, Arnhem, Groningen, Haarlem, Leiden, Enschede, Zwolle, Maastricht, Nijmegen, Antwerp, Gent, Leuven, Brussels, Bruges, Hasselt (q.v.).

Sumba Indah, Prinsestraat 86, 2561 TX den Haag. Prop: Mr. J.G.W. Bavelaar. Tel: (0654) 765560. Est: 1980. Shop; open daily 11–6 (except on Sundays). Spec: Indonesia; maritime/nautical. PR: Fl.30–1,000. Also, Indonesian traditional textiles. Corresp: French, German, Indonesian. Mem: B.O.B.

R.G. Ulrich Cathay Books, Dalveen 83, 2544 SC den Haag. Tel: & Fax: (070) 3214123. Est: 1970. Private premises; appointment necessary. Medium stock. Spec: China. PR: Fl.20–2,000. Cata: 4 a year on speciality. Also, new books on speciality. Corresp: German.. VAT No: NL 055 437 382 B01.

J.A. Vloemans, Anna Paulownastraat 10, 2518 BE den Haag. Tel: (070) 3607886. Fax: 3450365. E-Mail: vloebook@euronet.nl. Est: 1932. Appointment necessary. Spec: 20th century architecture; avant–garde. Cata: 6 a year. Corresp: French, German. Mem: I.L.A.B.; N.V.V.A.; V.D.A. VAT No: NL 036 863 312 B01.

HARLINGEN

Antiquariaat de Robijn, Rommelhaven 26, 8861 AS Harlingen. Prop: J.R.P. Ferwerda & H.E.M. Beerling. Tel: (0517) 414357. Est: 1981. Shop; open Saturday 12.30–5 and at other times by appointment. Medium stock. Spec: children's; illustrated; old comics. Cata: 4 a year. Corresp: German.

HEEMSTEDE

A. van der Marel, Jacob van Ruisdaellaan 30, 2102 AP Heemstede.

HELVOIRT

Ben Hoepelman, Eikendonk 11, 5268 LB Helvoirt. Prop: Ben & Eva Hoepelman Tel: (0411) 641212. Fax: 643131. Est: 1985. Private premises; open Monday to Friday 10–6. Spec: atlases/cartography; illustrated botanical. Corresp: German, Dutch. Mem: N.V.V.A. VAT No: NL 803 146 590 B01.

HILVERSUM

Antiquariaat Frans Melk, Havenstraat 13, 1211 KG Hilversum. Booksearch service.

HONTENISSE

Antiquariaat Secundus, Notendyk 7, 4583 SV Ter Hole. (•) Prop: P.F.W.H. Everaers. Tel: (0114) 314209. Est: 1993. Storeroom and private premises; hours on request. Large stock. Spec: antiquarian; art; art history; artists; children's; fables; fine & rare; fine art; fine printing; first editions; folklore; local history; illustrated; juvenile; national languages; limited editions; literature; poetry; signed editions; local topography. PR: DM1–1,000. Cata: 2 a year. Also, a booksearch service, publisher of "De Maelstede" and publicist. Corresp: French, German, Dutch. Mem: C.R.K. 207238. VAT No: NL 771 543 32 B01.

LEIDEN

Antiquariaat Aioloz, Botermarkt 8, 2311 EM Leiden. Prop: Piet & Monique van Winden. Tel: (071) 5140907. Fax: 5128498. Shop; open Friday 12–5, Saturday 10–5. Large stock. Spec: modern art; photography; literature; antiquarian. PR: Fl.4–20,000. Cata: 6 a year. Corresp: French, German. Mem: I.L.A.B.; N.V.A.

Anthro-Books, Breestraat 113a, 2311 CL Leiden. Prop: C.G. Uhlenbeck. Tel: (071) 5143552. Fax: 5141488. E-Mail: ukiyoe@xs4all.nl. *Also at:* Hotei Japanese Prints *and* Ukiyo-É Leiden. (q.v.).

Burgersdijk & Niermans, Nieuwsteeg 1, 2311 RW Leiden. Prop: Drs. A.W. de Bruin & Drs. A.D. Steenkamp. Tel: (071) 5121067. Fax: 5130461. Est: 1894. Shop; open Monday to Friday 9–6, Saturday 11–5. Medium stock. Spec: antiquarian; archaeology; books about books; classical studies; general fiction; first editions; literature; philosophy; Jewish religion; travel. PR: DM1–1,000. CC: EC; MC; V. Cata: 8 a year. Also, auction sales twice a year. Corresp: French, German, Dutch. Mem: I.L.A.D.; N.V.V.A. VAT No: NL 005 804 814 B01.

Hotei Japanese Prints, Breestraat 113A, 2311 CL Leiden. Prop: G.C. Uhlenbeck. Tel: (071) 5143552 or 5124459. Fax: 5141488 or 5123855. E-Mail: ukiyoe@xs4all.nl. Est: 1982. Shop; open Saturday 11–4 and by appointment. Large stock. Spec: Japanese illustrated. PR: Fl.200–90,000. CC: V; JCB; MC; AE; EC. Cata: 2 a year. Also, Japanese paintings. Mem: I.L.A.B. VAT No: NL 031 913 064 B01. *See also:* Ukiyo-É Books, *and* Anthro-Books, Leiden (q.v.).

Antiquariaat Hans Kretzschmar, Jan Vossensteeg 63, 2312 WC Leiden. Tel: (071) 5131727. E-Mail: hkboek@xs4all.nl. Est: 1979. Shop; open daily 10–6, Thursday evening 6–9, and Saturday market stand. Small general stock. Spec: art; printing; travel; typography; natural history; voyages & discovery. PR: Fl.1–3,000. Corresp: German, Swedish, Dutch.

Het Oosters Antiquarium BV, Nieuwe Rijn 2, 2312 JB Leiden. Prop: R. Smitskamp. Tel: (071) 5149305. Fax: 5127542. E-Mail: oriental@dsl.nl. Est: 1683. Shop; open Tuesday to Friday 10–5. Very large stock. Spec: bibles; classical studies; fine & rare; Jewish religion; Oriental religion; travel - Asia and Middle East. CC: All. Cata: 6 a year. Corresp: any. Mem: N.V.A. VAT No: NL 050 935 422 B01.

Boekhandel J. de Slegte b.v., Breestraat 73, 2311 CJ Leiden. Tel: (071) 5122007. Shop. General stock. *Also shops at:* Amsterdam, Rotterdam, The Hague, Eindhoven, Utrecht, Arnhem, Groningen, Haarlem, Enschede, Zwolle, Maastricht, Nijmegen, Antwerp, Gent, Leuven, Brussels, Bruges, Hasselt (q.v.).

NETHERLANDS

Ukiyo-É Books, Breestraat 113a, 2311 CL Leiden. Prop: C.G. Uhlenbeck. Tel: (071) 5143552. Fax: 5141488. E-Mail: ukiyoe@xs4all.nl. Shop; open Saturday 11–4 and by appointment. *See also:* Hotei Japanese Prints *and* Anthro-Books, Leiden. (q.v.).

LEIDSCHENDAM

Ludwig Rosenthal's Antiquariaat, Park Leeuwenberghlaan 1, 2267 BM Leidschendam. Prop: Edith Petten–Rosenthal. Tel: (070) 3193049. Fax: 3194731. Est: 1859. Private premises; appointment necessary. Medium stock. Spec: architecture; bibliography; bindings; early imprints; fables; fine & rare; humanism; illustrated; incunabula; mathematics; miniature books; music; numismatics; occult; philosophy; science; theology; typography; emblems; Hebrew imprints. PR: Fl.1,000–40,000. Cata: 2 or 3 a year. Corresp: Dutch, German, French. Mem: I.L.A.B.; V.D.A. ev; N.V.A. VAT No: NL 081 981 557 B01.

MAASTRICHT

Boekhandel J. de Slegte b.v., Grote Staat 53, 6211 CV Maastricht. Tel: (043) 3217296. Shop. General stock. *Also shops at:* Amsterdam, Rotterdam, The Hague, Eindhoven, Utrecht, Arnhem, Groningen, Haarlem, Leiden, Enschede, Zwolle, Nijmegen, Antwerp, Gent, Leuven, Brussels, Bruges, Hasselt (q.v.).

MIDDELBURG

De Boekenbeurs, Turfkaai 33, 4331 JV Middleburg. Booksearch service.

NAARDEN

Anton W. van Bekhoven – Antiquarian Bookseller and Publisher, Nieuwe Haven 27a, 1411 SG Naarden. Tel: (035) 6947638. Fax: 6940551. Est: 1965. Shop; appointment necessary. Very large stock. Spec: art; art history; architecture; history; Middle Ages; philosophy; bibliography; typography. PR: Fl.50–2,000. Cata: 4 a year on art, art history, bibliography, art periodicals and Portuguese history. Also, periodicals, new books and a booksearch service. Corresp: German. Mem: Vereeninging ter Bevordering van de Belangen des Boekhandels.

NIEUWKOOP

Antiquariaat de Graaf, Postbus 6, 2420 AA Niewkoop. Prop: B. de Graaf. Tel: (0172) 571461. TA: Degraaf, Nieuwkoop. Fax: 572231. Est: 1959. Private premises; appointment necessary. Medium stock. Spec: humanism, the Reformation and books printed 1500 to 1700. Cata: 3 a year. Also, new books and publishing. Corresp: French, German, Italian. Mem: N.V.A. VAT No: NL 024 597 181 B01.

NIJMEGEN

De Keerkring, Postbus 1359, 6501 BJ Nijmegen.

Boekhandel J. de Slegte b.v., Molenstraat 54, 6511 HG Nijmegen. Tel: (024) 3238293. Shop. General stock. *Also shops at:* Amsterdam, Rotterdam, The Hague, Eindhoven, Utrecht, Arnhem, Groningen, Haarlem, Leiden, Enschede, Zwolle, Maastricht, Antwerp, Gent, Leuven, Brussels, Bruges, Hasselt. (q.v.).

Antiquariaat Verzameld Werk, Van Welderenstraat 97, 6511 ME Nijmegen.

OSS

Knuf, Frits – Antiquarian Books, P.O.Box 780, 5340 AT Oss. Prop: A. van Elferen-Boerakker. Tel: (0412) 626072. Fax: 638755. Private premises. Medium stock. Spec: bibliography; bindings; books about books; calligraphy; palaeography; paper–making; printing; typography; books about manuscripts, incunabula, book collecting and history of book trade. Cata: approximately 8 a year. Corresp: Dutch, German, French. Mem: N.V.V.A. VAT No: NL 150 526 192 B01.

OVERASSELT

Postantiquariaat Onademi, Kruisbergsestraat 57, 6611 AH Overasselt. Prop: Mr. E. Diersmann. Tel: (024) 6222606. Est: 1990. Private premises; postal business only. Very small stock. Spec: 19th century Protestant theology. PR: Fl.10–300. Cata: occasionally. Also, a booksearch service. Corresp: German. VAT No: NL 123 226 545 B01

ROERMOND

Boekhandel Boom, Neerstraat 31, 6041 KA Roermond.

Calliope, P.O. Box 1189, 6040 KD Roermond. Prop: J. Lommertzen. Tel: & Fax: (0475) 317284. E-Mail: jooplomm@ilimbug.nl. Est: 1971. Storeroom; appointment necessary. Large stock. Spec: classical studies; cookery/ gastronomy; economics; education; law; literature; social sciences; general history. Cata: periodically. Also, a booksearch service.

't Ezelsoortje, Bakkerstraat 30, 6041 JR Roermond. Prop: P.M.R. Hoeberechts & G.J. Dethmers. Tel: (0475) 333782. Fax: 311682. Est: 1978. Shop; open Monday 1–6, Tuesday to Friday 10–6, Saturday 10–5. Medium stock. Spec: Limburg area topography; modern literature; art; applied arts. PR: Fl.2–800. Cata: 2 a year. Also, old & new comics, secondhand records and compact discs, and a booksearch service. Corresp: French, German. VAT No: NL 006 664 829 B01.

ROTTERDAM

Atlas, Zaagmolenstraat 152, 3035 HJ Rotterdam. Prop: Mrs. E. de Leeuwe. Tel: & Fax: (010) 4673783. Est: 1967. Shop; open Wednesday to Friday 12–6, Saturday 12–5. Large general stock. Corresp: French, German.

Cremers & Beereboom Books, P.O. Box 4041, 3006 AA Rotterdam. Tel: & Fax: (010) 4653837. E-Mail: cremers@xs4all.nl. Private premises. Small stock. Spec: art; books about books; fine art; fine printing; photography. VAT No: NL 767 658 91 B02.

Kiefhoek, Hr. Arnoldstraat 33, Rotterdam. Prop: P.J. Seij & P. Franke. Tel: (010) 4233129. Est: 1996. Shop; open Thursday to Saturday 12–5.30. Medium stock. Spec: history of World War II; Holocaust; children's before 1960 (mostly Dutch). PR: Fl.10–100. Cata: 2 to 5 a year. Also, a booksearch service. Corresp: German, French, Dutch.

Lindenberg Boeken & Muziek, Slaak 4–14, 3061 CS Rotterdam. Prop: P. Lindenberg. Tel: (010) 4111607. Fax: 4136682. Est: 1949. Shop; open Monday 1.30–5.30, Tuesday to Thursday 9–5.30, Friday 9–9, Saturday 9–5. Very large stock. Spec: theology; philosophy; church history. Cata: 1 a year on theology, church history and pre–1800 books. Also, new books and music.

Antiquariaat Quist, Nieuwe Binnenweg 110, 3015 BE Rotterdam. Prop: Ernie Quist. Tel: & Fax: (010) 4364398. Est: 1989. Shop; open Tuesday to Saturday 11–6. Medium stock. Spec: antiquarian; bibles. CC: AE; V; DC; MC. Also, a booksearch service. Corresp: Spanish, Italian, French, German. *Also at:* Steegoversloot 42, 3311 PP Dordrecht (q.v.).

Boekhandel J. de Slegte b.v., 3012 AE Rotterdam, Coolsingel 83. Tel: (010) 4138305. Shop. General stock. *Also shops at:* Amsterdam, The Hague, Eindhoven, Utrecht, Arnhem, Groningen, Haarlem, Leiden, Enschede, Zwolle, Maastricht, Nijmegen, Antwerp, Gent, Leuven, Brussels, Bruges, Hasselt (q.v).

'sHERTOGENBOSCH

Antiquariaat Brabant, Lange Putstraat 14, 5211 KN 'sHertogenbosch.

Antiquariaat Lilith, Rompertpark 93, 5233 RK 'sHertogenbosch. Prop: W.J.M. van Eck. Tel: & Fax: (073) 6425968. Est: 1992. Private premises. Medium stock. Spec: psychology; psychiatry; Dutch literature between 1880–1940; music. PR: Fl.10–1,000. Cata: 4 a year. Also, a booksearch service. Corresp: German, Dutch. VAT No: NL 783 74 960 B01.

Antiquariaat Luïscius, Verwersstraat 40, 5211 NX 'sHertogenbosch. Prop: Henk van Stipriaan. Tel: (073) 6136359. Fax: 6136354. Est: 1974. Shop; open Tuesday to Sunday 11–5. Medium stock. Spec: art; graphic art. PR: £10–1,000. CC: All. Also, a booksearch service. Corresp: French, German, Italian. VAT No: NL 663 066 15 B01.

SOMEREN

Boekhandel van de Moosdijk B.V., Collectors Books, Wilhelminaplein 8, 5711 EK Someren. Prop: W.A. Willems-Van de Moosdijk. Tel: (0493) 496370. Fax: 493549. E-Mail: moosbk@pi.net. Est: 1979. Shop; open daily 9–6, except Monday 10–6, Saturdays 9–5. Large stock. Spec: antiques; art; circus; collecting; dolls; fairgrounds; military; textiles and many others as listed in the speciality index. Cata: only on new books. Corresp: German, French, Dutch. Mem: Vereniging Voor de Boekhandel. VAT No: NL 007 800 836 B02.

TILBURG

Antiquariaat de Rijzende Zon, Poststraat 8, 5038 DH Tilburg. Prop: Thomas Leeuwenberg. Tel: (013) 5360337. Fax: 5361450. Est: 1971. Shop. Medium stock. Spec: Orientalia; Scandinavica; Brabantica; ethnology; exotic. Cata: thematic 1 a year. Corresp: any. Mem: N.V.A. VAT No: NL 098 896 726 B01.

Antiquariaat de Schaduw, Nieuwlandstraat 23–25, 5038 SL Tilburg. Prop: Corrie and Kees Kolen. Tel: (013) 5431229. Est: 1976. Shop; open Wednesday to Saturday 12–6. Very large stock. Spec: antiquarian; bibles; classical studies; countries & continents; ecclesiastical history & architecture; fine & rare; general & national history; Christian religion; general & local topography; travel. Corresp: French, German.

UTRECHT

Boekhandel–Antiquariaat Aleph, Vismarkt 9, 3511 KR Utrecht. Prop: Jan van Hassel. Tel: (030) 2322069. Fax: 2318797. Est: 1986. Shop; open Monday 1–6, Tuesday and Wednesday 11–6, Thursday 11–9, Friday 11–6, Saturday 10–5. Large stock. Spec: art history; Dutch and Flemish art; architecture; photography. Cata: periodically. Corresp: German, French, Italian. VAT No: NL 075 134 548 B01.

J.L. Beijers, B.V., Achter Sint Pieter 140, 3512 HT Utrecht. Prop: E. & N. Franco. Tel: (030) 2310958. TA: Bookbee, Utrecht. Fax: 2312061. Est: 1865. Private premises; open Monday to Friday 8.30–5. Large stock. Spec: early; illustrated; history of ideas. Cata: occasionally. Also, book auctioneers. Corresp: German, French. Mem: N.V.A.

Gert Jan Bestebreurtje, P.O. Box 364, 3500 AJ Utrecht. Tel: (030) 2319286. Fax: 2343362. Est: 1981. Shop at: Brigittenstraat 2, (corner Nieuwegracht 42), 3512 KK Utrecht; open Monday to Friday 9–6, Saturday by appointment only. Medium stock. Spec: old and rare books, travel and exploration; history of the Dutch Colonies. Cata: 5 a year on travel, VOC and Indonesia. Mem: N.V.A.

Antiquariaat Tjerk de Boer, Springweg 7a, 3511 VH Utrecht. Tel: (030) 2328888. Fax: 2300582. Est: 1984. Shop; open Monday to Friday 12–6, Thursday 7–9, Saturday 11–5. Medium stock. Spec: history; architecture; fine and rare. CC: AE; EC; V; DC; JCB. Cata: 1 or 2 a year on history and architecture. Also, a booksearch service. Corresp: French, German. VAT No: NL 075 312 530 B01.

Eureka Booksellers, Nachtegaalstraat 28, 3581 AJ Utrecht. Prop: Siebold T. Tromp. Tel: (030) 2340169. Fax: 2364563. E-Mail: eureka @ knoware.nl. Est: 1981. Shop; open Monday to Friday 11–6, Saturday 9–5 and storeroom; appointment necessary. Very large stock of 50,000 books. Spec: English and French books; literature; esotericism. Cata: several a year on specific subjects. Corresp: French. VAT No: NL 072 982 937 B01.

Forum Antiquarian Booksellers BV, "Westrenen", 3997 MS 't Goy - Houten, Utrecht. Prop: Sebastiaan S. Hesselink. Tel: (030) 6011955. Fax: 6011813. Est: 1970. Private premises; appointment necessary. Large stock. Spec: manuscripts; rare and old books on all subjects. CC: all major. PR: £100–100,000. Cata: 3 a year on general subjects. Also, a booksearch service and publishers of bibliography. Corresp: French, German, Spanish, Italian. Mem: N.V.A.; I.L.A.B. VAT No: NL 007 076 514 B02.

Boekhandel J. de Slegte b.v., Oude Gracht 121, 3511 AH Utrecht. Tel: (030) 2313001. Shop; open 9.30–6. Very large general stock. Also, a booksearch service and remainders. Mem: N.V.A. *Also shops at:* Amsterdam, Rotterdam, The Hague, Eindhoven, Arnhem, Groningen, Haarlem, Leiden, Enschede, Zwolle, Maastricht, Nijmegen, Antwerpen, Gent, Leuven, Brussels, Bruges, Hasselt (q.v.).

Antiquariaat André Swertz bv, Postbus 85054, 3508 AB Utrecht. Tel: (030) 520169. Fax: 522900. Est: 1976. Appointment necessary. Spec: literary first editions; art; typography; private presses. Cata: 6 a year. Corresp: German, French. Mem: N.V.A.

VENLO

Antiquariaat Lambiek Coopmans, H. Kiespenninckstr. 2, 5912 EA Venlo. Tel: (077) 3515583. Est: 1979. Private premises; appointment necessary. Medium stock. Spec: literature; popular; children's; dictionaries; fine & rare; illustrated; all books in Dutch, pre 1850. PR: £30–1,000. Corresp: Dutch, German, French.

VINKEVEEN

Dat Narrenschyp, Loopveltweg 39, 3645 WK Vinkeveen. Prop: Th. Rienks. Tel: (0297) 264633 or (0512) 461752. Est: 1939. Shop at: 8 Nieuwenhuisweg 112, Nybeets 9245 VP; appointment necessary. Medium stock. Spec: Amsterdam and Friesland; topography; old books; theology. Cata: 1 or 2 a year on specialities. Corresp: French, German, Dutch. Mem: B.V.B. VAT No: NL 300 9684 5000.

VLISSINGEN

Bellamy v.o.f., Bellamypark 50–52, 4381 CK Vlissingen. Prop: J. Metman & J.L. Metman-Kok. Tel: (0118) 418410. Est: 1981. Shop; open Monday to Thursday 9–6, Friday 9–9, Saturday 9–5. Small general stock. PR: Fl.1–500. Corresp: German. VAT No: NL 935 084 6B01.

L.M.C. Nierynck, Verdilaan 85, 4384 LD Vlissingen. Tel: & Fax: (0118) 470172. Private premises; appointment necessary. Spec: 16th- to 19th-century newspapers.

VOORBURG

Antiquariaat Papyrus, Prinses Mariannelaan 106, 2275 BK Voorburg. Prop: Rita Colognola. Tel: & Fax: (070) 3868504. Est: 1991. Private premises; appointment necessary. Small stock. Spec: science (natural, exact and applied); music; architecture; military. PR: Fl.10–6,000. Cata: 1 a year. Corresp: French, Italian, Dutch. Mem: N.V.A. VAT No: NL 196 851 348 B01.

ZANDVOORT

E.J. Bonset, Patrijzenstraat 8, Postbus 136, 2040 AC Zandvoort.

ZELHEM

Christian S. Koenig, Frans Halsstraat 3, 7021 DL Zelhem.

ZIEST

Internatonaal Antiquariaat P. van Vliet, Parklaan 17, 3701 CE Zeist. Prop: Dr. P. van Vliet. Tel: & Fax: (030) 6911222. Est: 1988. Private premises; open 9–6. Large stock. Spec: academic/scholarly; art history; atlases; cartography; biology; fine & rare; first editions; travel guides; history; illustrated; foreign languages; limited editions; literature; manuscripts; natural history; natural sciences; railways; science; history of science; signed editions; travel. PR: DM50–10,000. Cata: 4 a year. Corresp: Dutch, German, French, Spanish, Italian, Portuguese. VAT No: NL 051 162 763 B01.

ZUTPHEN

Matthys de Jongh, Coehoornsingel 28/A, 7201 AC Zutphen. Tel: (0575) 543136. Fax: 543182. Est: 1975. Private premises; appointment necessary. Very large stock. Spec: social history; economics. Corresp: German.

Antiquariaat de Stokroos, Achterhoven 3, 7205 AH Zutphen. Prop: H. Lichthart–Baumans. Tel: & Fax: (0575) 512658. Est: 1990. Market stand and storeroom; appointment necessary. Medium stock. Spec: animals; archaeology; beekeeping; biology; botany; ecology; entomology; forestry; gardening; geology; herbalism; horticulture; landscape; microscopy; natural history; ornithology; palaeontology; whaling; zoology. PR: Fl.1–1,000. Cata: 4 a year. corresp: German, Dutch, French. Mem: Kuk Zutphen. VAT No: NL 513 637 68 B01.

ZWOLLE

Antiquariaat Theo de Boer, P.O. Box 1114, 8001 BC Zwolle. Prop: Drs. T.S.T. de Boer. Tel: (038) 217524. Fax: 221867. Est: 1978. Storeroom at: Terborchstraat 10, 8011 GG Zwolle; appointment necessary. Medium stock. Spec: history of medicine and science; pharmacy; dentistry; physics; chemistry; mathematics; biology; technology; Dutch topography; Japan. PR: Fl.60–20,000. Cata: 6 a year, and computer access allows immediate answer to any query. Corresp: Dutch, French, German. Mem: N.V.V.A. (I.L.A.B.). VAT No: NL 078 617 042 B01.

Boekhandel J. de Slegte b.v., Melmarkt 10, 8011 MC Zwolle. Tel: (038) 4214408. Shop. General stock. *Also shops at:* Amsterdam, Rotterdam, The Hague, Eindhoven, Utrecht, Arnhem, Groningen, Haarlem, Leiden, Enschede, Maastricht, Nijmegen, Antwerp, Gent, Leuven, Brussels, Bruges, Hasselt. (q.v.)

NORWAY

Country dialling code: 47 *Currency:* Norwegian krone (NKr)

BERGEN

Eikens Antikvariat, P.O. Box 973, 5001 Bergen.

GRIMSTAD

Thorsens Antikvariat, Gartnerimyra 35, 4890 Grimstad. Prop: Frode Thorsen. Tel: & Fax: 37044392. Shop; appointment necessary. Large stock. Spec: maritime/ nautical; local topography; whaling. Cata: 6 a year. Also, a booksearch service. Mem: N.A.B.F. VAT No: 295 325 08.

OSLO

J.W. Cappelens Antikvariat, Universitetsgt. 20, 0162 Oslo. Prop: Jörgen W. Cappelens. Manager: Idar Nilstad. Tel: 22421570. Fax: 22423545. Est: 1829. Shop; open Monday to Friday 10–5, Saturday 10–2. Very large general stock. Spec: old and rare; travel; topography. CC: V; AE; DC; MC; JCB. Cata: 8 a year. Mem: N.A.B.F. VAT No: 291 858 75.

Damms Antikvariat A/S, Tollbugt. 25, 0157 Oslo. Prop: Claes Nyegaard. Tel: & Fax: 22410402. Est: 1843. Shop. Very large stock. Spec: old and rare; topography; atlases. PR: NKr.50–500,000. Mem: N.A.B.F.

Lucky Eddie, Trondheimsv 8, 0560 Oslo. Tel: 22381290. Est: 1984. Shop; open Monday to Friday 10–5, Saturday 10–2.30. Small stock. Spec: cinema/film; comic books and annuals; comics; periodicals/magazines. PR: £1–50. Also, records and CDs. Corresp: Norwegian.

Majorstuen Antikvariat, Vibesgt. 15, 0356 Oslo 3.

Vinderen Antikvariat, Slemdalsveien 63, 0373 Oslo 3. Prop: Helge Rønnevig Johnsen. Tel: 02148075. Est: 1980. Shop; open Monday to Friday 11.30–5, Saturday 11.30–2.30. Medium stock. Corresp: German, French. Mem: N.A.B.F.

TRONDHEIM

Adamstuen Antikvariat, Kongensgt. 68, 7012 Trondheim.

Wangsmo Antikvariat AS, Postboks 4700, 7002 Trondheim. Prop: Vidar Rudolf Wangsmo. Tel: 73524455. Est: 1978. Shop at: Vår Frue Strete 1, Trondheim; open Monday to Friday 10–5 (Thursday 10–6), Saturday 10–2. Very large stock. Spec: topography. Cata: 18 a year. Mem: N.A.B.F. VAT No: 974 401 819.

POLAND

Country dialling code: 48 *Currency:* Zloty (PLN)

BIALYSTOK

Antykwariat, ul. lipowa 18, 15-428 Bialystok. Prop: Dom Ksiazki. Tel: (085) 52-38-71. Est: 1950. Shop; open 10–6. Medium general stock. PR: about 50p–£100. Mem: Stowarzyszenie Ksiegarzy Polskich (Society of Polish Book Dealers).

CRACOW (KRAKÓW)

Antiquariat Grafika, ul. Juliusza Lea 7A/9, 30-046 Kraków. Prop: Nina & Tomasz Maczugowie. Tel: & Fax: (012) 34-26-50. Private premises; appointment necessary. Small stock. Spec: art; atlases/cartography; bibliography; books about books; Poland, Germany and France; Polish history; illustrated; reference; books in Polish, German, French and English; graphic art; travel - Europe (Poland & Russia). Cata: 4 a year on specialities. Also, a booksearch service. Corresp: Polish, Russian.

Antykwariat "Silva Rerum", ul Stolarska 8-10, 31-043 Kraków.

Antykwariat Stefan Kamiński, ul. Sw Jana 3, 31-017 Kraków.

GDAŃSK

Antykwariat Naukowy im. A. Krawczyńskiego, Szeroka 74/76, 80–835 Gdańsk.

GDYNIA

Antykwariat Polipol, ul. Świetojańska 83, Gdynia. Prop: Skawomir Szymański. Tel: (058) 20-56-67. Est: 1992. Shop; open Monday to Friday 11–7, Saturday 10–2. Medium stock. Spec: academic/scholarly; antiquarian; art; dictionaries; encyclopedias; science fiction; general history; foreign languages; literature; medicine; military; mind, body & spirit; music; natural history; philosophy; psychology/psychiatry; religion; science; technical; war; zoology. PR: $1–25. Corresp: Polish.

LÓDŹ

Antykwariat Naukowy, ul. Piotrkowska 85, 90–420 Lódź. Prop: J.W. Plóciennik and M. Sobczak. Tel: & Fax: (042) 33-18-91. Est: 1990. Shop; open Monday to Friday 10–6, Saturday 10–3. Large general stock. PR: PLN 10–1,000. Cata: 3 a year. Also, a booksearch service and book auctions. Corresp: German, French, Russian.

POLAND

OŚWIECIM

Galician Books, State Museum Auschwitz, Birkenau, ul.Wiezniow Oswiecimia 20, 32–603 Oświecim. Prop: Slawomir Jan Staszak. Tel: & Fax: (033) 43-25-43; 43-20-22 Ext. 212. Est: 1990. Shop at: Harmeze 129, 32–600 Oświecim; open Monday to Saturday 9–3. Medium stock. Spec: Holocaust; Judaica; gypsies; bibliographies; books about books; Central–East Europe - history, ethnography, art and culture. PR: £1–500. CC: AE; V; MC; JCB; DC; CJ. Cata: irregularly (quarterly). Also, a booksearch service, large print books, sculpture and periodicals, old and new. Corresp: German, Polish.

POZNAŃ

Antykwariat im. Y. Zupańskiego, Stary Rynek 53/54, 61–772 Poznań.

SZCZECIN

Antykwariat–Ksiegarnia, ul. Slaska 43, 70–431 Szczecin. Prop: Jacek Galkowski & Andrzey Grodecki. Tel: (091) 88-31-23. Est: 1982. Shop; open Monday to Friday 10–6, Saturday 10–3. Medium stock. Spec: cookery; dictionaries; encyclopaedias; general fiction; science fiction; graphic art in books; general & local history; poetry. PR: £1–100. Corresp: Polish, German, Russian.

WARSAW

Antykwariat J.R. Kubicki, ul. Hoza 27a, Warszaw. Prop: Józef Roch Kubicki. Tel: (02) 629-04-20. Est: 1945. Shop; open Monday to Friday 11–7, Saturday 10–2. Small general stock. Corresp: Polish, Russian.

PORTUGAL

Country dialling code: 351   *Currency:* Portuguese escudo (PE)

LISBON (LISBOA)

Livraria Camões, Rua da Misericordia 137–141, 1200 Lisboa.

Livraria Antiga do Carmo, Calçada do Carmo, 50, 1200 Lisboa.

Antiquário do Chiado, Rua Anchieta 7, 1200 Lisboa.

Livraria Ferin, Rua Nova do Almada 70–74, 1200 Lisboa. Prop: Dias Pinheiro. Tel: (01) 3424422 or 3467084. Fax: 3471101. Est: 1840. Shop; open 9.30–6.30. Small stock. Spec: history; biographies; cartography; artists; architecture; heraldry; genealogy. PR: £1.80–100. CC: V; MC. Also, a booksearch service, large print books, a subscription agency and art gallery. Corresp: French. Mem: A.P.E.L. (Portuguese Publishers and Booksellers' Assoc.). VAT No: PT 500 426 021.

Loja das Colecções, R. da Misericórdia, 147, 1200 Lisboa. Prop: José Manuel Castanheira da Silveira. Tel: & Fax: (01) 3463057. Est: 1985. Shop; open 10–1 and 2.30–7. Medium stock. Spec: advertising; the arts; cinema/films; collecting; comics; ex-libris; literature. Corresp: French, Spanish. VAT No: PT 804 706 344.

Livraria Moreira e Almeida, Rue Anchieta 7, 1200 Lisboa.

Livraria D. Pedro V, Rua D. Pedro V 16, 1200 Lisboa.

A. Tavares de Carvalho, Avenida da Republica 46–3, 1000 Lisboa.

J.A. Telles da Sylva, Rua Laura Alves 19 – 3 Esq, 1000 Lisboa. Prop: Herdeiros (Heirs) de J.A. Telles da Sylva. Tel: (01) 7978754. Fax: 7971535. Est: 1966. Shop; open Monday to Friday 10–1.30 & 3–6. Medium stock. Spec: Portuguese and Spanish travels; Braziliana; fine books. Cata: 24 a year. Also, new books. Corresp: French, Spanish. Mem: A.B.A. (United Kingdom). VAT No: PT 900 464 771.

223

PORTO

Candelabro, Rua da Conceição 3-27-29, 4050 Porto. Prop: Maria Beatriz Rêgo de Oliveira Barros. Tel: (02) 2002449. Shop; open Monday to Friday 9–12 & 2.30–7. Small general stock. Spec: antiquarian; antiques; architecture; art history; bibliography; Catalogues Raisoneés; illustrated; literature. CC: MC; V. Corresp: French.

Esquina – Livraria Lda., Rua Afonso Lopes Vieira 126, (AO Foco), 4100 Porto. Prop: Luis Barroso. Tel: & Fax: (02) 6065314. Est: 1980. Shop; open (except in July and August) Monday to Friday 10–1 & 2.30–7.30, Saturday 10–1. Small stock. Spec: art; genealogy; literature. Also, a booksearch service. Corresp: French, Spanish. Mem: Associação Portuguesa dos Editores e Livreiros.

SPAIN

Country dialling code: 34 *Currency:* Peseta (Ptas)

ALICANTE

Librería Lux, S.C., Calle Mayor 33, 03002 Alicante.

BARCELONA

Librería Novecientos, C/ Libreteria 10–12, 08002 Barcelona.

Puvill Libros S.A., Boters 10 i Palla 29–31, 08003 Barcelona.

Salas Llibreteria, L/Unio, 3, 08001 Barcelona. Prop: Manel Gràcia. Tel: & Fax: (93) 318-72-92. Open Monday to Friday 11–2 and 3–8. Medium general stock. Spec: paperback English books. CC: V; MC; JCB. Also, a booksearch service. Mem: Gremi Llibreters de Vell De Catalunya.

Librería Fernando Selvaggio, C/ Frenería 12, 08002 Barcelona. Tel: (93) 315-15-56. Shop; open Monday to Saturday 10-2 & 4-8. Medium general stock. Spec: geography; chemistry; physics; medicine; literature. Cata: 2 a year. Corresp: Italian, French. Mem: Gremio de Libreros de Cataluña.

BILBAO

Librería Boulandier, Juan de Ajuriaguerra, 52, 48009 Bilbao. Prop: Francisco Javier Boulandier. Tel: (94) 424-10-72. Est: 1991. Shop; open 11–2 and 5–8. Medium stock with specialities. Cata: 4 a year on general subjects and Basque culture and literature. Corresp: all languages. Mem: LIBRIS - A.I.L.A. VAT No: ES 305 530 90M.

Libros y Grabados Antiguos, Apartado Postal 364, Oficina Principal, 48001 Bilbao.

LAS PALMAS

Adolf M. Hakkert, Calle Alfambra 26, 35010 Las Palmas. Prop: Adolf M. Hakkert & W. Kos. Tel: (928) 27-73-50. Est: 1952. Very small general stock. Spec: classical philology; ancient history; Byzantium. Corresp: German. VAT No: ES X01 422 78T.

LEÓN

La Trastienda – Libros de Lance, Mariano D. Berrueta 11, 24003 León.

MADRID

Guillermo Blázquez - Libros Antiquos, Carrera de San Jerónimo, 44, ÎB, 28014 Madrid. Tel: & Fax: (91) 429-36-38. Est: 1966. Private premises; appointment necessary. Large stock. Spec: antiquarian; architecture; autographs; early imprints; national history; illuminated manuscripts; illustrated; incunabula; law; limited editions; literature; fine & rare; politics; travel - Americas. Ptas.10,000–1,000,000. Cata: 1 a year. Also, large print books and publisher. Corresp: Spanish. Mem: A.I.L.A.; I.L.A.B. VAT No: ES 005 485 82D.

Librería Dedalus – Humanidades Hispanoamérica, Apartado 50791, 28080 Madrid. Prop: Gustavo Peña Arévalo. Tel: & Fax: (91) 528-48-74. Est: 1983. Shop at: C.Marqués de Toca, 12, 28012 Madrid; open Monday to Friday 12–2 and 5–8, Saturday 11–2. Large stock. Spec: art; bibliography; ethnography; ethnology; philosophy; travel - Americas; literature; 20th century Spanish history. CC: V. Cata: 4 a year. Corresp: French. Also, large print books. Mem: Gremio de Librerosde Madrid.Libris.

El Filobiblión, Calle de la Cruz Verde 14, 28004 Madrid.

Frame, c/ General Pardiñas 69, 28006 Madrid. Prop: J. Armero. Tel: (1) 411-33-62. Fax: 564-15-20. E-Mail: armero@mailhost.navtaies. Est: 1973. Shop; open Monday to Friday 10–2 and 5–8.30, Saturday 10–2. Very small stock. Spec: antiquarian; atlases; cartography; travel. CC: V; AE. Also, large print books. Corresp: Spanish, French. VAT No: ES B28 344 893.

Librería Gulliver, C/ León 32, 28014 Madrid.

Llorente – Libros, Desengaño Nro. 13, 3̂ H, 28004 Madrid.

Libros Madrid, Apartado de Correos 156.111, 28080 Madrid. Prop: J. Miguel Madrid Antonaya. Tel: & Fax: (91) 518-02-35. Est: 1985. Private premises and storeroom at: San Leon 7, 28011 Madrid; appointment necessary. Large general stock. Spec: Spanish history; literature; erotica; philosophy; occult; religion; ex-libris; bibliography; pharmacy/pharmacology; antiquarian; erotica; esoteric; general fiction; first editions; herbalism; homeopathy; hydrography; mysticism; paleography; parapsychology and others. Cata: 6 a year. Corresp: Portuguese, Italian, French. Mem: Libris; A.I.L.A. Gremio Madrileño. VAT No: ES 138 456 6N.

Mexico – Librerias Anticuarias, C/Huertas 17y20, 28012 Madrid.

Miranda – Libros, Calle San Pedro 7, 28014 Madrid. Prop: Miguel Miranda Miravet. Tel: (91) 429-45-76. Fax: 429-26-84. Est: 1950. Shop; open 10–3 & 5.30–8.30. Very large stock. Spec: 19th- and 20th-century political; history; economics; literature; America; the Golden Age; philosophy; arts; science; theatre; medicine. PR: £10–200. CC: V; MC; EC. Cata: 6 a year, up to date general list or by subject. Also, a booksearch service and antique book fairs in May and October. Corresp: French, Italian. Mem: Cámara Oficial del Libro; Gremio de Libreros Anticuarios de Madrid. VAT No: ES 507 946 25E.

Librería Para Bibliofilos Luis Bardon, Plaza de San Martin 3, Apartade de Correos 7029, 28013 Madrid. Prop: Luis Bardon Mesa. Tel: (341) 521-55-14. Fax: 521-55-14. Est: 1945. Shop; open Monday to Friday 10.30–1.30 and 5–8. Very large stock. Spec: antiquarian; Spanish books; early imprints; fine & rare; history; illuminated manuscripts; illustrated; literature; travel. PR: Ptas.10,000–1,000,000. CC: V; MC; DC. Cata: 2 a year. Corresp: Spanish, French. Mem: A.B.A.; A.I.L.A. VAT No: ES 001 970 37 2P.

Librería del Prado, Calle Prado 5, 28014 Madrid.

Jose Porrua Turonzas, Cea Bermúdez, 10, 28003 Madrid.

MATARÓ

Rogés Llibres, Carretera de Mata 23, 08304 Mataró-Catalunya. Prop: Francesc Rogés Falguera. Tel: (93) 796-06-19. Fax: 796-49-82. E-Mail: mataro@seker .es. Est: 1980. Shop; open Monday to Saturday 4–8. Very large stock. Spec: jazz; Catalan. Cata: 4 a year. Also, a booksearch service, bookbinding and Internet: http://www.seker.es/scap/comprar/roges.htm.

PALMA DE MALLORCA

Fiol – Llibres, OMS 45a, 07003 Palma de Mallorca. Prop: Catalina Fiol Guiscafré. Tel: (971) 72-14-28. Est: 1950. Shop; open Monday to Friday 10–1.30 & 5–8, Saturday 10–1.30. Large stock. Spec: rare books on the western Mediterranean; Spanish and English 20th-century.

SANTANDER

Carmichael Alonso Libros, 69694 Lloreda de Cayóon, Cantabria. (•) Tel: (42) 55-57-53. Est: 1993. Private premises; appointment necessary. Small stock. Spec: Garćia Lorca and The Generación del 27; academic/scholarly; avant–garde; art (20th century Spanish); literature; literature in translation; poetry (20th century Spanish). PR: Ptas.2,000–200,000. Cata: 3 a year. Corresp: Spanish, French.

SARAGOSSA (ZARAGOZA)

Librería Hesperia, Plaza de los Sitios 10, (Apartado Postal 272), Zaragoza. Prop: Luis Marquina y Marín. Tel: (76) 23-53-67. Fax: 22-28-30. Est: 1953. Shop; open evenings Monday to Friday. Very large stock. Spec: old and rare Hispanica; Americana. Cata: 2 a year. Also, new books. Corresp: French, Italian. Mem: A.B.A. (U.K.). VAT No: ES 172 249 54R.

Pons – Librería Especializada, P: de Fernando el Católico 37, P.O. Box 648, 50006 Zaragoza. Prop: Juan F. Pons. Tel: (76) 35-90-37. Fax: 35-60-72. E-Mail: lpns@parser.es. Est: 1951. Shop; open 9–1 & 4–7. Small stock. Spec: mathematics; library sciences; bibliography. CC: V. Cata: 4 a year. Also, back sets of academic journals and a booksearch service. Corresp: French, Italian, Spanish. VAT No: ES 178 239 27P.

SEVILLE (SEVILLA)

Librería Renacimiento, Mateos Gago 27, 41004 Sevilla. Prop: Abelardo Linares. Tel: (05) 421-56-64 or 422-07-28. Fax: 456-47-29. Est: 1974. Shop; open 10–2 and 4.30–8.30. Large general stock of over 1,000,000. Spec: Spanish literature; Latin America; first editions; literary criticism; art; bibliography; general fiction; national history; literature; literature in translation; poetry; travel - Americas. PR: Ptas.500–300,000. Cata: 12 a year. Corresp: Spanish, French Mem: A.I.L.A.

VIGO

Librería Anticuaria el Mar y la Alameda, Marqués de Valladares 12, Ofic. 11–12, 36201 Vigo. Prop: Los Amigos del Mar y la Alameda. Tel: (986) 43-41-24. Est: 1982. Private premises. Medium general stock. PR: £5–2,500. Cata: 2 a year. Also, a booksearch service. Corresp: Spanish, Portuguese, Italian.

VILANOVA I LA GELTRÚ

La Ploma – Llibreria de Vell, C/ de l'Argentería 8, 08800 Vilanova i la Geltrú (Barcelona). Prop: Pere J. Ruiz de Casteñede Verde. Tel: (93) 893-16-23. Est: 1980. Shop; open Monday to Saturday (winter) 7–9 pm, (summer) 6.30–9.30 pm. Medium general stock. Spec: literature; poetry; history; bibliography; monographs; gastronomy; cookery; wine. Corresp: Catalan, French, Italian. Mem: Gremi de Llibreters de Vell de Catalunya.

SWEDEN

Country dialling code: 46   Currency: Swedish krona (SKr)

ESLÖV

Antikvariat Crafoord, Kastberga Mansion, Box 40, 24121 Eslöv.

Gunnar Johanson–Thor, Nämndemansvägen 5, 241 37 Eslöv.

FÄRILA

Hälsinglands Antikvariat, Härjedalsvägen 12, 820 41 Färila.

FALKÖPING

Antikvariat Carl Hellmor, Hasselgatan 10, (S. Bestorp), P.a Box 644, 521 21 Falköping.

GOTHENBURG (GÖTEBORG)

Antiquaria AB, Kristinelundsgatan 7, 411 37 Göteborg. Prop: Sten Ringselle & Lillemor Eriksson. Tel: & Fax: (031) 16-14-15. Est: 1978. Shop; open Monday to Friday 10–6, Saturday 10–2. Large stock. Spec: fine and rare; Lapponice. Cata: 2 to 4 a year. Mem: S.A.F.; I.L.A.B. VAT No: SE 556 453 389 001.

Antikvariat Olivia Dal, Gibraltargatan 10, 411 32 Göteborg. Prop: Connoisseur Bokhandel AB. Tel: (031) 11-89-75. Fax: 19-54-18. Est: 1987. Private premises; postal business only. Very small stock. Spec: genealogy - Swedish only. PR: SKr.50–10,000. Cata: 3 a year on speciality. Corresp: French, German. *See also:* Bohusläns Antikvariat, Skärhamn; Kokbokhandeln AB *and* Thulin & Ohlson Antikvarisk Bokhandel AB, Gothenburg (q.v.).

Kokbokhandeln AB, P.O. Box 24116, 400 22 Göteborg. Prop: Connoisseur Bokhandel AB. Tel: & Fax: (031) 20-10-96. E-Mail: cookbook@ connoisseur.se. Est: 1982. Shop at: Skånegatan 20; open Tuesday to Thursday 11–6, Saturday 11–6 or by appointment. Large stock. Spec: cookery; tobacco; wine; beer and related subjects. PR: SKr.100–100,000. Cata: 4 to 6 a year from SKr.50–400. Also, new cookery books. Corresp: French, German, Scandinavian. VAT No: SE 556 470 076 201. *See also:* Bohusläns Antikvariat, Skärhamn; Antikvariat Olivia Dal *and* Thulin & Ohlson Antikvarisk Bokhandel AB, Gothenburg (q.v.).

Lundquists Antikvariat, Geijersgatan 5, 411 34 Göteborg.

Thulin & Ohlson Antikvarisk Bokhandel AB, P.O. Box 24116, 400 22 Göteborg. Prop: Connoisseur Bokhandel AB. Tel: & Fax: (31) 20-10-96. E-Mail: T&O@Connoisseur.se. Est: 1918. Storeroom; open Tuesday to Thursday 11–6 or by appointment, closed during the summer. Medium stock. Spec: nautical; travel; voyages; Swedish East India Company; Sweden. PR: SKr.100–50,000. Cata: 4 a year. Corresp: French, German, Scandinavian. VAT No: SE 556 470 076 201. *See also:* Bohusläns Antikvariat, Skärhamn; Kokbokhandeln AB *and* Antikvariat Olivia Dal, Gothenburg (q.v.).

HÖGANÄS

Lundgrens Antikvariat, Köpmansgatan 5, 263 38 Höganäs.

JÄRPÅS

Andreassons Antikvariat, Höra Stommen, 531 94 Järpås. Prop: Bo Andreasson. Tel: 51-09-17-83. Est: 1976. Private premises; appointment necessary. Small stock. Spec: bibliography; fine & rare books; philosophy; reference; theology. Cata: 2 to 4 a year. Mem: Svenska Antikvariatfreningen. VAT No: SE 44 10 17 5410.

KARLSTAD

Harvigs Antikvariat, P.O. Box 189, 651 05 Karlstad. Prop: Hans Harvig. Est: 1983. Private premises. Medium general stock. Spec: art; decorative art; graphic art; topography. CC: Yes. Cata: 4 a year. Corresp: German, French, Swedish. Mem: Svenska Antikvariat Forningen (I.L.A.B.).

Karlstads Antikvariat, Kungsgatan 2, P.O. Box 509, 651 11 Karlstad.

LIDINGÖ

Enhörningen Antikvariat, Stockholmsvägen 60, 181 42 Lidingö. Prop: Bo Löwenström. Tel: (08) 767-64-11. Fax: 766-10-57. Est: 1973. Shop; open Monday to Friday 1–6, Saturday 10–2. Very large stock. Also, printed music, Swedish autographed music and sheet music. Mem: S.A.F.; I.L.A.B.; Svenska Musikbibl.föreningen; A.I.B.M.

LUND

Åkarps Antikvariat, Box 1129, Klostergaten 11, 221 04 Lund.

SWEDEN

Umeå Antikvariat Roger Jacobsson, Klostergatan 11, 22222 Lund. Tel: (046) 14-91-33. Fax: (090) 14-80-55. Est: 1972. Private premises; appointment necessary. Large stock. Spec: Lapland and Northern Scandinavia; books about books (book history); travel. PR: £10–3,000. Cata: 2 to 4 a year. Corresp: any Scandinavian language. Mem: Svenska Antikvariat Föreningen; I.L.A.B. VAT No: SE 254 709 300 190.

MALMÖ

Lengertz' Antikvariat, Regementsgatan 56 A, 217 48 Malmö

Rogers Antikvariat, Bergsgatan 4, 211 54 Malmö.

ÖREBRO

Bergslagens Antikvariat, Box 208, 701 44 Örebro.

ÖSTERBYMO

Thulins Antikvariat AB, 570 60 Österbymo. Prop: R. Du Rietz. Tel: (0140) 83-021. Fax: 83-027. Appointment necessary. Medium stock. Spec: old and rare. Cata: 6 a year.

SKÄRHAMN

Bohusläns Antikvariat, P.O. Box 98, 440 60 Skärhamn. Prop: Connoisseur Bokhandel AB. Tel: (304) 67-12-64. Fax: (31) 19-54-18. Est: 1989. Private premises; postal business only and shop at: Södra Hammen; open Saturday 10–2 during winter and every day from June to August. Small stock. Spec: maritime/nautical. PR: SKr.50–20,000. Cata: 3 a year, on speciality. *See also:* Kokbokhandeln AB; Thulin & Ohlson Antikvarisk Bokhandel AB *and* Antikvariat Olivia Dal, Gothenburg (q.v.).

Hyrrokkin (Booksellers) AB, Box 111, 440 60 Skärhamn.

STOCKHOLM

ANDRA, Rörstrandsgatan 25, 11340 Stockholm. Tel: (08) 31-07-07. Fax: 31-41-62. Shop; open 2–6.30. Small stock. Spec: 20th-century books; art; music; film; theatre; philosophy; literature; jazz records. VAT No: SE 401 113 1218.

Antikvariat Antiqua, Karlavägen 12, 114 31 Stockholm. Prop: Ulf Egelius. Tel: & Fax: (08) 10-09-96. Est: 1980. Shop; open Tuesday to Friday 1–6. Large stock. Spec: applied art; architecture; fine art; antiquities. Cata: 1 or 2 a year on specialities. Corresp: French, German. Mem: S.A.F. VAT No: SE 451 124 051 901.

Aspingtons Antikvariat, Västerlånggatan 54, 111 29 Stockholm. Prop: Mats Aspington. Tel: (08) 20-11-00. Fax: 20-52-00. Shop; open Monday to Friday 10–6 and Saturday 10–2. General stock. Mem: S.A.F.

Antiquariat Athenaeum, Skeppargatan 56, 114 59 Stockholm. Prop: Dr. Wolf A. Terner. Tel: & Fax: (08) 667-78-40. Est: 1980. Shop; open Monday to Friday 11–1 and 3–6, Saturday 11–1. Large stock. Spec: history; memoirs; biographies; voyages; natural history. CC: V; MC; EC; E; JCB; EDC. Corresp: French, German, Swedish. Mem: S.A.F.; I.L.A.B. VAT No: SE 400 523 921 701.

Björck och Börjesson, Odengatan 23, 114 24 Stockholm.

Antikvariat Bokslussen, Götgatan 17 (T-banan Slussen), Box 15102, 104 65 Stockholm.

Central Antikvariatet, Drottninggatan 73 B, 111 36 Stockholm. Tel: (08) 411-91-36. Fax: 20-93-08. E-Mail: mats@centralant.se. Shop; open Monday to Friday 10–6, Saturday 11–3. Very large stock. Spec: geography; music; travel. CC: V; MC; AE. Cata: 4 a year. Mem: S.A.F.; I.L.A.B. VAT No: SE 370 101 001 301.

ERA Antikvariat, Box 45511, 104 30 Stockholm.

Antikvariat Erato, Norrtullsgatan 13, Box 6329, 102 35 Stockholm.

Evas Antikvariat, Ringvägen 143, 116 61 Stockholm.

Grafik–Antikvariatet, P.O. Box 2271, 103 16 Stockholm.

Halléns Antikvariat, Tegnérgatan 17, 111 40 Stockholm.

Jones Antikvariat, Norrtullsgatan 3, 113 29 Stockholm.

Konst–Bibliofilen, P.O. Box 2042, 103 11 Stockholm. Prop: Stefan Schueler. Tel: & Fax: (08) 21-27-68. Est: 1972. Shop at: Västerlånggatan 6, Stockholm; open Monday to Friday 9.30–5. Small stock. Spec: art. Cata: 4 a year. Also, new art books. Corresp: German, French.

Leopold's Antikvariat, Box 7769, 103 96 Stockholm. Prop: Owe Leopold. Tel: (08) 21-34-20. Est: 1978. Shop at: Regeringsgatan 54; open Tuesday to Friday 11–6, Saturday 11–3. Small stock. Spec: philately.

Libris Antikvariat, Nybrogatan 64, P.O. Box 5123, 102 43 Stockholm.

Mats Rehnström, Box 16394, 10327 Stockholm. Tel: (08) 411-92-24. Fax: 411-94-61. E-Mail: rehnstroem@stockholm.mail.telia.com. Est: 1991. Shop at: Jakobsgatan 27; open Thursdays 3–6.30 or by appointment. Small stock. Spec: (mostly Swedish books) autographs; bibliography; books about books; documents; fine & rare; manuscripts; printing. PR: £10–5,000. Cata: 4 a year. Corresp: German. Mem: S.A.F.; I.L.A.B. VAT No: SE 660 227 101 401.

Rönnells Antikvariat AB, Birger Jarlsgatan 32, 114 29 Stockholm.

Ryös Antikvariat AB, Hantverkargatan 21, 112 21 Stockholm. Tel: & Fax: (08) 654-80-86. Est: 1977. Shop. Large stock. Spec: art; first editions. Cata: 4 or 5 a year. Mem: S.A.F.

Sörhuus Antikvariat, Riddargatan 3A, 11535 Stockholm.

Ulf Ström, Wahlbergsgatan 10, 121 38 Johanneshov. (•) Tel: & Fax: (08) 600-34-52. Est: 1991. Private premises; appointment necessary. Very small stock. Spec: Olympic Games; F.I.F.A. World Cup. Corresp: German. VAT No: SE 571 119 783 901.

Antikvariat Blå Tornet, P.O. Box 45198, 10430 Stockholm. Tel: (08) 20-21-43. Est: 1967. Shop; open Monday to Friday 10–6, Saturday 11–3. Medium stock. Spec: Strindbergiana.

Karna Wachtmeister Bildantikvariat, Storgatan 1/IV, 114 44 Stockholm.

SUNDSVALL

Sundsvalls Antikvariat AB, Kyrkogatan 5, 852 31 Sundsvall.

UMEÅ

Antikvariat Bocum, Via Esplanaden 6, Box 4102, 904 04 Umeä. Prop: Björn Olofsson. Tel: & Fax: (090) 12-15-77. Est: 1990. Shop; open Monday to Friday 12–6, Saturday 11–3. Large stock. Spec: atlases/cartography; bibliography; books about books; calligraphy; local history; paper–making; printing; local topography; travel - Polar, Europe; typography. PR: £1–100. Cata: 2 to 4 a year. Mem: S.A.F.; I.L.A.B.; L.I.L.A.

Antikvariat Bothnia, AB, Kullavägen 73, 903 62 Umeå. Prop: Jan Berglund. Tel: & Fax: (090) 14-89-90. Est: 1986. Shop; appointment necessary. Medium stock. Spec: topography; ethnography; Lapland and Northern Scandinavia; Polar regions; ethnology; travel - Polar; whaling. Cata: 4 a year on specialities. Also, a booksearch service. Mem: S.A.F.

UPPSALA

Eva Bergströms Antikvariat, Ö. Slottsgatan 14c, 753 10 Uppsala.

Antikvariat Ola Eng, S:t Johannesgatan 27, P.a. Kyrkogatan 23, 753 12 Uppsala.

Antikvariat Claes Olofsson, Dragarbrunnsgatan 53, 753 20 Uppsala.

Redins Antikvariat, Box 15049, 750 15 Uppsala. Prop: Johan & Kerry Redin. Tel: (018) 10-71-00. Fax: 71-10-14. Est: 1974. Shop at: Drottninggatan 11, S-753 10 Uppsala; open 11–6. Very large stock. Spec: national history; foreign and national languages; theology. CC: V; MC. Cata: 4 or 5 a year on specialities and local topography. Corresp: German. Mem: I.L.A.B.; S.A.F.

SWITZERLAND

Country dialling code: 41 *Currency:* Swiss franc (Sfr)

BADEN

Mittlere Mühle, Kronengasse 35, 5400 Baden.

BASLE (BASEL)

Buchantiquariat "Am Rhein", Kartausgasse 1, P.O. Box 46, 4005 Basel. Prop: Georg J. Beran. Tel: (061) 692-62-84. Fax: 692-62-63. E-Mail: 100660.1674@ compuserve.com. Est: 1983. Storeroom; appointment necessary. Medium stock. Spec: illustrated; German literature and philosophy; history of art; architecture; regional history; travel; science; Czech Avantgarde. PR: Sfr.10– 10,000. CC: V; MC; AE. Cata: 2 a year Sfr.10 each. Also, book fairs in Germany and in the U.S. Corresp: German, Czech. Mem: V.E.B.U.K.U.; V.D.A.

Erasmushaus–Haus der Bücher AG, Bäumleingasse 18, 4051 Basel. Man: Mr. Timur Yüksel. Tel: (061) 272-30-88. Fax: 272-30-41. E-Mail: hdb@erasmushaus.ch. Est: 1800. Appointment necessary. Large stock. Spec: autographs; fine and rare; fine art; first editions; literature. Cata: 4 a year. Also, auction sales. Corresp: German, French, Italian. Mem: I.L.A.B./Syndicat Suisse.

Antiquariat Gerber AG, Schneidergasse 18, 4001 Basel.

Antiquariat Hupfer und Bieri, St. Alban–Berg 2A, 4052 Basel.

Moirandat Company AG, Rotbergerstrasse 6, 4011 Basel. Prop: Alain François Moirandat. Tel: (061) 281-37-73. Fax: 281-38-72. E-Mail: moi@iprolink.ch. Private premises; appointment necessary. Very small stock. Spec: autographs; the arts; fine printing; history of ideas; fine & rare. PR: Sfr.200–20,000. Cata: 2 or 3 a year. Corresp: French, German, Italian. Mem: V.E.B.U.K.U.; V.D.A.

Antiquariat & Edition Oriflamme, Postfach 4065, 4002 Basel. Prop: Martin P. Steiner. Tel: & Fax: (061) 313-20-00. Est: 1984. Private premises; open Monday to Friday 9–11 & 2.30–midnight. Small stock. Spec: general history 1740–1950; literature; poetry 1100–1970; alchemy; Masonry; Rosicrusians; Heraldics; old printings 1500–1740; and others. PR: Sfr.10–8,000. Also, microfilms, translating from English & French into German and German editions of above books. Mem: World Trade Centre Club, Jacees International (Senator) and Basel Chamber of Commerce.

Antiquariat Dr. Karl Ruetz, Ahornstrasse 25, Postfach, 4009 Basel. Tel: (061) 302-53-28. Fax: 302-53-52. Est: 1987. Shop; appointment necessary. Small stock. Spec: animals; architecture; art; astronomy; bibles; botany; children's; early imprints; entomology; fine printing; first editions; history; incunabula; literature; natural history; private press; travel; zoology. PR: Sfr.100–25,000. Cata: 2 year. Corresp: German, French, Italian, Spanish, Arabic. Mem: V.E.B.U.K.U.; I.L.A.B.; V.D.A.

Schlöhlein GmbH, Schützenmattstrasse 15, 4003 Basel. Prop: Heinz Kyburz & Marianne Wehrli. Tel: (061) 261-43-17. Fax: 261-45-95. Shop. Medium stock. Spec: music. Mem: S.L.A.C.E.S.

Antiquariat A. Thomi, Möresbergerstr. 48/50, 4057 Basel. Tel: & Fax: (061) 692-69-25. Est: 1984. Shop; appointment necessary. Small stock. Spec: art; children's; ex–libris; history; literature; literature in translation; photography. PR: DM1–1,000. Cata: 3 a year. Corresp: German, French.

BERN

Comenius Antiquariat, Rathausgasse 28 - Postfach, 3000 Bern 8. Prop: Samuel Hess & Jörg Zoller. Tel: & Fax: (031) 312-16-04. E-Mail: shess@access.ch. Est: 1989. Shop; open Tuesday to Friday 11–6, Saturday 9–4. Large stock. Spec: history of civilization; literature; martial arts; philosophy; politics; psychoanalysis; psychology/psychiatry; general religion; socialism and anarchism. PR: £8. Cata: 15 to 20 a year on specialities. Also, martial arts/Aikido/Zen. Corresp: German, French. Mem: Vereinigung der Buchantiquare und Kupferstich-handler in der Schweiz.

Hegnauer und Schwarzenbach, Kramgasse 16, 3011 Bern. Prop: Eduard Hegnauer & Christoph Schwarzenbach. Tel: (031) 311-64-15 or 311-74-00. Fax: 311-96-53. Est: 1944. Shop; open Tuesday to Friday 9–6.30, Saturday 9–4. Very large general stock. Also, a booksearch service. Corresp: German, French, Italian. Mem: S.L.A.C.E.S.

Galerie Hofer, Münstergasse 56, 3011 Bern. Prop: Roland & Marta Hofer. Tel: (031) 311-78-97. Est: 1973. Shop; open Thursday to Friday 1.45–6.30, Saturday 9–12 and 1.30–4. Medium stock. Spec: atlases/cartography; decorative art; botany; early imprints; local topography. Corresp: German. Mem: V.E.B.U.K.U.

Antiquariat Iberia, Hirschengraben 6, 3001 Bern. Prop: Jaime Romagosa. Tel: (031) 381-59-43. Est: 1950. Shop; open Tuesday to Friday 9–12.15 & 2–6.30, Saturday 9–12.15 and 2–4. Medium stock. Spec: literature (especially Spanish); philosophy. Cata: irregularly on Spanish books. Also, new Spanish books. Corresp: Spanish. Mem: S.L.A.C.E.S.

Antiquar und Universitäts–Buchhändler Kampf, Ob. Wehrliweg 2, 3074 Muri b. Bern. Tel: (031) 951-55-80. Private premises; appointment necessary. Medium general stock. PR: DM1–1,000. Cata: 1 a year. Also, a booksearch service and large print books. Corresp: Russian, Polish, Scandinavian, German, French. Mem: V.E.B.U.K.U.; L.I.L.A.; S.B.V.V.

Galerie Kornfeld, Laupenstrasse 41, 3008 Bern.

Herbert Lang & Cie AG, Münzgraben 2, 3011 Bern.

Pulitzer Gallery & Knöll AG, Junkerngasse 17, 3011 Bern. Prop: Elsbeth Haudenschild. Tel: (031) 311-93-33. Fax: 312-29-76. Est: 1962. Shop; open during normal business hours. Small stock. Spec: Helvetica. Mem: S.L.A.C.E.S. *Also at:* Galerie Pulitzer & Knöll AG, Kramgasse 62, Bern. VAT No: 122 261.

Buchantiquariat Daniel Thierstein, Gerechtigektsgasse 60, 3011 Bern. Tel: (031) 312 37 11. Est: 1988. Shop; open Tuesday to Friday 11–6.30, Saturday 10–4. Small stock. Spec: literature; 20th-century art; architecture; philosophy. Mem: V.E.B.U.K.U.; I.L.A.B. *Also at:* Schmiedengasse 60, 2502 Biel. (q.v.).

Alexander Wild, Wissenschaftliches Antiquariat, Rathausgasse 30, 3011 Bern.

BERNEX

L'Exemplaire, 27, chemin des Rouettes, 1233 Bernex.

BIEL (BIENNE)

Buchantiquariat Daniel Thierstein, Schmiedengasse 6, 2502 Biel. Tel: & Fax: (032) 323-29-37. Est: 1988. Shop; open Tuesday to Friday 1.30–6.30, Saturday 10–4. Small stock. Spec: literature; 20th-century art; architecture; philosophy. Mem: V.E.B.U.K.U.; I.L.A.B. *Also at:* Gerechtigkeitsgasse 60, 3011 Bern (q.v.).

CHERNEX SUR MONTREUX

Serge Paratte, Le Couvent, 1822 Chernex sur Montreux.

CHUR

Antiquariat Narrenschiff, Karlihofplatz 1, 7000 Chur. Prop: Walter Lietha. Tel: (081) 252-10-81. Fax: 252-10-03. Est: 1976. Shop and storeroom; open Monday 1.30–6.30, Tuesday to Friday 8–6.30 and Saturday 8–4. Very large stock. Spec: rare; Raetica; first editions; art; illustrated. PR: Sfr.1–1,000. CC: V; EC; T. Cata: 2 a year. Also, a booksearch service and new books. Corresp: Italian, French, Dutch, Portuguese. *Also at:* Rabengasse 10, 7000 Chur.

CULLY

Librairie du Grand-Chêne, Place d'Armes, C.P. 39, 1096 Cully. Prop: E. Abravanel. Tel: (021) 799-25-21. Shop; open Wednesday to Saturday 3–6. Small stock. Spec: antiquarian; artists; books about books; illustrated; letters; literary criticism; music; poetry; private press; theatre; French and German books. Cata: 4 a year on French books and 1 a year on German books - Rilke, Stendhal, Goethe, also on general subjects. Also, a booksearch service on French books only. Corresp: French, German. Mem: I.L.A.B.; V.E.B.U.K.U.

FRIBOURG

Alstadt Antiquariat, rue des Alpes 5, 1700 Fribourg. Prop: B.A. Harteveld. Tel: (037) 322-38-08. Fax: 322-88-93. Est: 1977. Shop; open Tuesday to Saturday 9–6.30. Very large stock. Spec: antiquarian; topography; medical; sciences; Helvetica; humanities in all languages. PR: Sfr.20–2,000. Cata: 8 a year. Corresp: all modern languages. Mem: I.L.A.B.; V.E.B.E.K.L.I.

Librairie Intermède Belleroche S.A., Place Notre Dame 6, Fribourg 1700.

GENEVA (GENÈVE)

L'Autographe S.A., 1 rue des Barrières, 1204 Genève. Prop: Renato Saggiori, Expert International. Tel: (022) 348-77-55. Fax: 349-86-74. Est: 1958. Storeroom; appointment necessary. Very large stock. Spec: autographs (on books, letters, photos etc.). PR: Sfr.20–150,000 plus. Cata: 3 or 4 a year (mail bid auctions and fixed price). Corresp: French, Italian, German. Mem: L.I.L.A.; Syndicat Suisse des Libraires; Association Genevoise des Antiquaires; Manuscript Society; U.A.C.C.

Edwin Engelberts, Grand–Rue 3, 1204 Genève.

Librairie J.-J. Faure, La Part du Rêve, Case Postale 5604, 1211 Genève 11. Prop: Jean-Jacques Faure. Tel: (022) 320-87-59. Est: 1974. Shop at: rue Leschot 4, 1205 Genève; open Monday to Friday 2–6.30. Large stock. Spec: first editions; illustrated (19th and 20th century painters); fine arts; gastronomy; oenology. PR: SFr.10–20,000. Cata: 4 a year. Also, literary, artists' and musical autographs and large print books. Corresp: French. Mem: S.L.A.C.E.S.

Librairie Jullien, Bourg du Four 32, Case Postale 3401, 1211 Genève 3. Prop: Jacques Matile. Tel: (022) 310-36-70. Est: 1839. Shop; open 8.30–12 and 2–6.30, closed Monday mornings and Saturdays at 5. Medium stock. Spec: anthropology; archaeology; art; countries - Switzerland (Geneva), France (Savoie); Egyptology; local and general history; horology; French literature; Christian and general religion. PR: Sfr.25. CC: V; EC; AE; DC. Cata: irregularly. Corresp: French, German. Mem: Société des Libraires et Editeurs de la Suisse Romande and Schweizenischer Buchhändler- und Verleger- Verband.

Librairie Montparnasse, 39 Grand'Rue, 1204 Genève. Prop: Monique Huguenin. Tel: (22) 311-67-19. Fax: 312-30-47. Shop; open 10–12 and 2–6.30. Very small stock. Spec: literature; science; voyages & discovery. Cata: 2 a year on general subjects. Mem: Amor Librorum.

Librairie Quentin (Molènes S.A.), 9–11 place de la Fusterie, 1204 Genève. Prop: Jacques T. & Ghislaine Quentin. Tel: (022) 311-14-33 Fax: 781-46-59. Est: 1979. Shop; appointment necessary. Small stock. Spec: illuminated manuscripts; old and rare; 15th- to 20th-century. Cata: 1 a year. Also, contemporary illustrated books. Mem: I.L.A.B.

Librairie Werner Skorianetz, Case Postale 5128, 1211 Genève 11. Tel: (022) 32-80-67. Fax: 800-17-03. Est: 1976. Shop at: 4, Place Neuve, 1204 Genève; open Monday 1.30–6.30, Tuesday to Friday 10–12 and 1.30–6.30. Small stock. Spec: art; autographs; bibliography; children's; cookery/gastronomy; dance; feminism; first editions; geography; history; humanities; literature; natural sciences; philosophy; photography; psychology/psychiatry; travel. PR: Ffr.50–5,000. CC: V; MC. Cata: 3 a year. Corresp: French, German. Mem: I.L.A.B.; S.L.A.C.E.S. VAT No: CH 280 404.

HERISAU

Naturwissenschaftl. Versandantiquariat Thomas Ruckstuhl, Ifangstrasse 19, 9100 Herisau. Tel: & Fax: (071) 351-30-11. Private premises. Spec: rare books on natural history, especially entomology. Cata: lists on demand.

HILTERFINGEN

Daniel Lehmann, Kirchgässli 17, 3652 Hilterfingen. Tel: & Fax: (033) 243-29-84. Est: 1980. Shop and private premises; appointment necessary. Large stock. Spec: aviation; ballooning; railways; fashion & costume. PR: various. CC: EC. Cata: 4 a year, 2 on aeronautica and 2 on railwayana. Corresp: German.

HINTERKAPPELEN

Volkoff & Von Hohenlohe, Postfach 140, 3032 Hinterkappelen.

LAUSANNE

Librairie Lehmann, Rue Cité-Derrière 10, 1005 Lausanne. Tel: (021) 311-80-21. Fax: 311-80-20. Est: 1980. Shop. Medium stock. PR: Sfr.500–10,000. CC: V; AE; EC. Corresp: German, French, Italian.

OH 7e Ciel, Academie 4, 1005 Lausanne. Prop: Aline Doerig & Yves Gindrat. Tel: (021) 329-09-06. Fax: 329-09-11. Est: 1988. Shop; open during normal business hours. Medium stock. Spec: applied art; architecture; art; art history; art reference; artists; the arts; authors - Brassens, Cendrars, Cocteau, Michaux, Picasso, Queneau, Simenon, Vian; autographs; avant–garde; bibliography; Catalogues Raisonées; children's; cinema/films; decorative art; erotica; detective/spy/thrillers; romance; science fiction; fine & rare; fine art; fine printing; foreign texts; illustrated; limited editions; literature; literature in translation; painting; photography; poetry; sculpture; signed editions; surrealism; theatre. Cata: on 20th century art and literature, illustrated and signed books, and first editions, 6 a year. Also, a booksearch service and Constitution de fonds consacré à des personnalités. Corresp: French. Mem: S.L.A.C.E.S.

Librairie R.J. Ségalat, 4 rue de la Pontaise, C.P. 244, 1018 Lausanne 18. Tel: (021) 648-36-01. Fax: 648-25-85. Est: 1980. Shop; open Monday to Saturday 9–12 & 2–6.30. Medium stock. Spec: academic/scholarly; antiques; limited editions; literature; illustrated; transport. CC: V. Cata: 4 a year on literature, Helvetica, art, philosophy and illustrated. Also, a booksearch service. Corresp: French, German. Mem: S.L.A.C.E.S; L.I.L.A.

LUCERNE (LUZERN)

"Allerdings" Antiquariat, Murbacerstrasse 17, 6003 Luzern. Prop: Egli Joseph & André Graf. Tel: (041) 210-10-25. Est: 1994. Shop; open Monday to Friday afternoon, Saturday 10–4. Small stock. Spec: art; general fiction; first editions; local & national history; literature; philosophy; poetry; Christian religion. PR: Ffr.10–1,000. Also, a booksearch service. Corresp: German, French.

Galerie Fischer, Haldenstrasse 19, 6006 Luzern.

Gilhofer & Ranschburg GmbH, Truellhofstrasse 20a, 6004 Luzern. Prop: Axel Erdmann. Tel: (041) 240-10-15. Fax: 240-50-01. Est: 1924. Shop; appointment preferred. Very small stock. Spec: incunabula; the 16th century; history of science and medicine. PR: Sfr.500–100,000. Cata: 2 a year. Mem: S.L.A.C.E.S.

Antiquariat & Buchhandlung Niels Hagenbuch, Postfach 3120, 6002 Luzern. Tel: & Fax: (041) 210-08-52. E-Mail: hagenb@centralnet.ch. Est: 1993. Private premises; Very small general stock. PR: Sfr. 10–1,000. Cata: 2 a year. Also, a booksearch service. Corresp: German, French.

Antiquariat Scientia Curiosa, Burgerstrasse 31, 6003 Luzern.

Buch– und Kunstantiquariat Die Wolkenpumpe, Steinenstrasse 2, Postfach 58, 6000 Luzern 10. Prop: Daniel Segmüller & Ruth Seiler. Tel: (041) 410-18-84. Fax: 420-48-84. Est: 1989. Shop; open Friday 10–6, Saturday 10–4 and by request. Small stock. Spec: Expressionism; Dadaism; concret and visual poetry; Hans Arp; experimental literature; art; artists; autographs; avant–garde; Catalogues Raisonées; early imprints; fine & rare; first editions; illustrated; limited editions; natural sciences; poetry; signed editions; surrealism; typography. PR: Sfr.100– 50,000. Cata: 1 or 2 a year. Corresp: German, French, Italian. Mem: S.B.V.V.

LUGANO

Bredford Libri Rari S.A., 2, via Molinazzo, 6900 Lugano. Prop: Dr. Francesco Radaeli. Tel: (091) 970-20-81. Fax: 970-26-24. Est: 1988. Storeroom and private premises; open Monday to Friday 9–12.30 and 2–6. Small stock. Spec: Italian 15th–18th century fine and rare. Corresp: Italian, French. Mem: A.L.A.I.; S.L.A.C.E.S.; L.I.L.A.

Libreria Antiquaria La Fiera del Libro, Via Marconi 2, 6900 Lugano.

Fuchs & Reposo Librairie WEGA, Via Nassa 21, 6900 Lugano. Prop: Riccardo, Susanne and Sibylle Reposo. Tel: (091) 923-16-06. Est: 1935. Shop; open Monday to Friday 8.30–12 & 2–6.30, Saturday 8.30–12. Small stock. Spec: art. Mem: S.B.V.V.; A.L.S.I.; V.E.B.U.K.U.; S.B.G.; B.Z.

MÜHLEBERG

Büchersuchdienst M. Ramseier, Mösliweg 2, 3203 Mühleberg.

NEUHAUSEN

Antiquariat Bücherwurm, Bahnhofstrasse 8, 8212 Neuhausen. Prop: Gert & Regina Heil. Tel: & Fax: (052) 672-55-27. Est: 1984. Shop and storeroom; open Thursday to Saturday. Very large general stock. Spec: exile literature. Also, a booksearch service and new books. Corresp: French, German. Mem: S.B.V.V./ B.B.D.S. (Union of the Swiss Book Trade).

RAMSEN

Antiquariat Bibermühle AG, Bibermühle 1, 8262 Ramsen. Prop: Heribert Tenschert. Tel: (052) 741-13-21. Fax: 741-48-89. Est: 1983. Private premises; open 8–12 and 1–5. Large stock. Spec: bibles; bindings; book of hours; books about books; botany; illuminated manuscripts; illustrated; incunabula; limited editions; private press; travel. PR: Sfr.100–500,000. Cata: 3 a year. Corresp: German, French, Italian. Mem: I.L.A.B.; V.D.A.; V.E.B.U.K.U. VAT No: DE 128 402 011.

RICHTERSWIL

Robert Hirt, Dorfstrasse 34, 8805 Richterswill.

ST. PREX

Françoise Bloch (Succ. of Félix Bloch), P.O. Box 58, 1162 St. Prex. Tel: (021) 806-16-62. Fax: 806-30-59. Est: 1973. Private premises; appointment necessary. Small stock. Spec: medicine; natural sciences; psychology/psychiatry. PR: Sfr.20–6,000. CC: EC; V; MC. Cata: 1 or 2 a year. Also, a booksearch service. Corresp: German, French. Mem: S.L.A.C.E.S.; S.L.E.S.R.

SOLOTHURN

Antiquariat am Marktplatz, Marktplatz 47, 4500 Solothurn. Prop: Paul L. Feser, lic.phil. Tel: (065) 23-68-08 or 21-47-77. Est: 1985. Shop; open Tuesday and Wednesday 2–6.30, Saturday 2–5. Very large stock. Spec: alpinism/mountaineering; national culture; travel guides; literature (Swiss); philately; travel. PR: Sfr.10–1,000. CC: Keine CC. Corresp: German, French.

TAGELSWANGEN

Antiquariat Struchen & Co., Riestr. 3, 8317 Tagelswangen. Tel: (052) 343-53-31. Fax: 343-49-30. Shop; appointment necessary. Medium stock. PR: DM1–1,000. Corresp: Spanish, German.

WINTERTHUR

Versandantiquariat Henry Müller, Arbergstr. 17, Postfach 228, 8405 Winterthur. Tel: (052) 232-99-03. Fax: 233-67-80. Storeroom; appointment necessary. Very small general stock. Corresp: German.

ZÜRICH

Altstadt Antiquariat, Oberdorfstrasse 10, 8001 Zürich.

Antiquariat Im Seefeld, Seefeldstrasse 189, 8008 Zürich. Prop: Ernst Jetzer, Taja & Ursula Gut & Christine Viccelli. Tel: & Fax: (01) 381-81-51. E-Mail: 100553.652@compuserve.com. Est: 1979. Shop; open Monday to Friday 10–6.30, Saturday 10–4. Large stock. Spec: architecture; art; art history; artists; cookery/gastronomy; dance; esoteric; general fiction; health; history; foreign languages; literature; literature in translation; music; occult; philosophy; photography; psychology/psychiatry; travel. PR: Sfr.1–1,000. CC: AE; EC; MC; DC; V. Also, secondhand records and CDs (classical/jazz/rock). Corresp: German, French, Italian, Norwegian. Mem: S.B.V.V.

Hans Bolliger, Bücher & Graphik, Gegründet 1970, Lenggstrasse 14, 8008 Zürich.

EOS Books & Prints, Kirchgasse 22, 8024 Zürich. Prop: Marcus & Gertrud Benz. Tel: (01) 261-57-50. Fax: 932-59 25. E-Mail: 100626.2627@compuserve.com. Est: 1985. Shop; open Tuesday to Friday 11–6, Saturday 10–4. Medium stock. Spec: pre-1850 illustrated; medicine; natural history; travel; children's; German and French literature; La Fontaine. Cata: 6 to 10 a year. Also, a booksearch service, large print books and Home Page: http://www.iprolink.ch/eos/. Mem: S.L.A.C.E.S.

Buch- u. Grafik–Antiquariat Falk & Falk, Kirchgasse 28, 8001 Zürich. Tel: (01) 262-56-57. Fax: 261-62-02. Est: 1982. Shop; open Tuesday to Saturday 8–12 and 2–6. Small stock. Spec: alchemy; alpinism/mountaineering; antiquarian; art history; atlases; cartography; bibles; bindings; books about books; cookery/gastronomy; early imprints; first editions; illuminated manuscripts; illustrated; incunabula; limited editions; medicine; natural history; history of science; topography; travel. PR: Sfr.50–10,000. CC: V; MC; EC; AE; DC. Cata: 2 a year. Corresp: German.

Flühmann Rare Books, Restelbergstrasse 82, 8044 Zürich. Prop: Adrian Flühmann. Tel: (01) 350-14-41. Fax: 350-14-43. E-Mail: adrianf@eunet.ch. Est: 1993. Private premises; open Monday to Friday 10–12 and 2–6. Very small stock. Spec: bindings; fine & rare; first editions; illustrated; literature. PR: £100–100,000. Cata: 2 a year. Corresp: French, German, Italian. Mem: V.E.B.U.K.U.

Bibliotheca Gastronomica, Winzerstrasse 5, 8049 Zürich. Prop: Hans Weiss. Tel: (01) 341-97-84. Fax: 341-97-90. Est: 1977. Private premises. Medium stock. Spec: food and drink and related gastronomy. CC: V; AE; MC; EC. Cata: 3 a year. Corresp: German, French, Italian.

Das Gute Buch, Rosengasse 10, 8001 Zürich.

Klio Antiquariat, Zähringerstrasse 41, P.O.B. 699, 8025 Zürich. Prop: C. von der Crone, Dr. K. Linow & C. Heiniger. Tel: (01) 251-42-12. Fax: 251-86-12. Est: 1989. Shop; open Tuesday to Friday 11–6.30, Saturday 11–4. Medium stock. General stock at Zäringerstrasse 41, and specialised stock at Zäringerstrasse 45, 8025 Zürich. Spec: philosophy; history; ethnology; general fiction; literary criticism; mathematics; politics; psychology/psychiatry; religion; theatre. PR: Sfr.1–3,000. Corresp: German, French. Mem: I.L.A.B.

August Laube, Inh. Laube & Co., Buch- und Kunstantiquariat, Trittligasse 19, 8001 Zürich. Tel: (01) 251-85-50. Fax: 252-75-27. Est: 1922. Shop; open Monday to Friday 9–6. Medium stock. Spec: rare illustrated books from 15th–19th century. Cata: 1 a year on Swiss topography views. Corresp: German, French. Mem: V.E.B.U.K.U.; S.L.A.C.E.S.

Angela Muhrer, Dufourstrasse 134, 8008 Zurich.

Antiquariat Peter Petrej, Sonneggstrasse 29, 8006 Zürich. Tel: & Fax: (01) 251-36-08. Est: 1993. Shop; open Tuesday to Friday 11–6.30, Saturday 10–4. Large stock. Spec: alpinism/mountaineering; architecture; art; art history; avant-garde; books about books; cartoons; children's; erotica; feminism; first editions; illustrated; photography; private press; psychoanalysis; psychology/psychiatry; Jewish religion; socialism; general travel; typography. PR: Ffr.10–1,000. Cata: 2 to 4 a year. Also, a booksearch service. Corresp: French, German.

Hans Rohr, Oberdorferstrasse 5, 8024 Zürich 1. Tel: (01) 251-36-36. Fax: 251-33-44. Est: 1921. Shop. Very large stock. Spec: classical philology; philosophy; psychology; literature; films; Helvetica. Also new books and a booksearch service in German language only. Mem: S.L.A.C.E.S. *Also at:* Torgasse 4, Zürich.

Jörg Schäfer, Alfred-Escher–Strasse 76, 8002 Zürich. Tel: (01) 202-69-75. Fax: 201-05-38. Est: 1971. Shop; appointment necessary. Spec: 15th- and 16th-century books; illustrated; history of science. Cata: 3 a year. Mem: S.L.A.C.E.S.; V.D.A. (Germany).

SWITZERLAND

Buchantiquariat Schöni AG, Adlikerstrasse 246, 8105 Regensdorf. (•) Prop: Allan P. Schöni. Tel: (01) 870-01-02. Fax: 870-05-15. E-Mail: 101555,3403@compuserve.com. Est: 1984. Shop; appointment necessary. Small stock. Spec: natural history; botany; zoology; applied sciences; travel; costumes; fashion; children's; rare books. PR: Sfr.500–100,000. CC: AE; MC; V. Mem: I.L.A.B.; V.E.B.U.K.U.

Hellmut Schumann AG, Rämistrasse 25, 8024 Zürich. Prop: Hans Neubauer (Manager). Tel: (01) 251-02-72. Fax: 252-79-61. E-Mail: 101737.1631@compuserve.com. Est: 1828. Shop; open Tuesday to Friday 9–6, Saturday 9–4. Large stock. Spec: old and rare. CC: V. Cata: 3 a year. Corresp: German, French, Italian. Mem: I.L.A.B.; V.E.B.U.K.U.

René Simmermacher AG, Kirchgasse 25, 8024 Zürich.

Travel Book Shop, Rindermarkt 20, 8001 Zürich. Prop: Gisela Treichler. Tel: (01) 252-38-83. Fax: 252-38-32. Est: 1976. Shop; open Monday 1–6.30, Tuesday to Friday 9–6.30, Saturday 9–4. Very large stock. Spec: travel; culture; cooking; art; guide books; handicrafts; reliefs; picture books. CC: V; MC; EC; AE. Also, globes worldwide. Corresp: German, French, Italian, Spanish, Hebrew, Hindi. Mem: Swiss Book Sellers Association.

Gerhard Zähringer, Bücher und Graphik, Froschaugasse 5, 8001 Zürich. Tel: (01) 252-36-66. Fax: 252-36-54. Est: 1977. Shop (Antiquariat und Galerie); open Tuesday to Friday 10–6, Saturday 10–4. Large stock. Spec: books about books; Catalogues Raisonées; fine art; fine printing; illustrated; limited editions; private press; typography; bookbinding, marbling & artists books. Cata: 2 a year on 20th-century private press and artists books, illustrated, finely printed books, fine & decorative arts, bookbinding, marbling and papermaking. Also, a booksearch service and special exhibitions of 20th-century & contemporary art. Mem: I.L.A.B.

ZUG

Antiquariat Fatzer, Unter Alstadt 11, 6301 Zug. Prop: B. Fatzer. Tel: & Fax: (041) 710-95-80. Est: 1990. Shop; open Wednesday to Saturday 10–12 and 1.30–5.30. Medium stock. Spec: Alpine books; Helvetica; art; first editions; travel. PR: DM20–5,000. CC: V; EC. Cata: 6 a year. Corresp: German, French. Mem: S.B.V.V.

TURKEY

Country dialling code: 90 *Currency:* Turkish lira (Tl)

ANKARA

Sanat Kitabevi, Karanfil Sokaği, Birlik Is Merkezi 5/2, 06650 Kizilay, Ankara. Prop: Ahmet Yüksel. Tel: & Fax: (312) 418-62-03. Est: 1986. Shop; open daily 10–7, except Sunday. Very large stock. Spec: academic/scholarly; anthropology; antiquarian; archaeology; architecture; archives; art history; bibliography; cookery/gastronomy; dictionaries; geography; local history; history of civilisation; manuscripts; memoirs; periodicals/magazines; local topography; Middle East; Ottoman Empire. PR: £5–500. Also, auctions, publishing, periodicals, a booksearch service and Web Site at: http:\\www.wec.net. com.tr\kebikec. Corresp: Turkish.

ANTALYA

Owl Book Shop, Akar Cesme Sokaği 21, 07100 Antalya. Prop: Kemal Özkurt. Tel: (242) 243-57-18. Est: 1990. Shop; open daily 10–1 and 3–7. Small general stock. Spec: literature. PR: £1–100. Corresp: Turkish.

ISTANBUL

Rifat Behar, Cemal Sahir Caddesi A7/1, 80300 Gayrettepe, Istanbul. Tel: (212) 267-24-63. Fax: 272-68-03. Est: 1995. Private premises; postal business only. Very small stock. Spec: travel; history. Also, a booksearch service. Corresp: Turkish.

Denizler Kitapevi, Istiklal Cad., Galatasaray Istiklal Cad., Galatasaray Ishani, 16 Beyoglu, Istanbul. Prop: M. Turgay Erol & Ugur Kogulu. Tel: & Fax: (212) 252-40-94. Est: 1996. Shop and storeroom; open 10.30–7. Small stock. Spec: maritime/nautical; atlases; cartography; military; zoology; botany; natural history; ship modelling. PR: £1–1,000. CC: V. Cata: 1 a year. Also, a booksearch service and provide an information service to researches related to all aspects of maritime. Corresp: German. Mem: Istanbul Chamber of Commerce.

Eren Yayincilik ve Kitapçilik Ltd., Sofyali Sokaği 34, 80050 Beyoğlu–Istanbul. Tel: (212) 251-28-58 or 252-05-60. Fax: 243-30-16. Very large stock. CC: MC; V; EC; A. Cata: 1 a year. Also, a booksearch service and large print books. Mem: Istanbul Chamber of Commerce.

Hisar Kitabevi, Sahne Sok, Aslihan Pasaji 17/47 Galatasaray, Istanbul. Prop: Orhan Devret. Tel: (212) 249-01-60. Est: 1994. Shop; open Monday to Saturday 12–8. Medium general stock. Spec: literature; history; fine arts etc.

Isis, Semsibey Sokaği 10, 81210 Beylerbeyi, Istanbul. Prop: S. Kuneralp & S. Helvaciğolu. Tel: (216) 321-38-51. Fax: 321-86-66. Est: 1983. Storeroom; open weekdays 9–5. Large stock. Spec: Turkey; national culture; national history; national languages. PR: US$ 5–100. Cata: 4 a year. Also, a booksearch service and library suppliers. Corresp: French, German.

Narteks Kitap, Asli Han Pasaji 46, 80060 Galatasaray, Istanbul. Prop: Sitki Altuner. Tel: (212) 245-48-54. Est: 1995. Shop; open Monday to Saturday 1–7.30. Large general stock. Spec: general and local history; fine arts; literature; periodicals; English, French, German and Greek books. Also, a booksearch service.

Librairie de Péra – Beyoğlu Kitapçilik Ltd., Galip Dede Caddesi 22 Tünel, 80050 Istanbul.

Arsiv Sahaf, Dereçikmazi Sokaği 20/5, 80840 Ortaköy, Istanbul. Prop: Naim Dikli. Tel: (212) 227-40-76. Est: 1985. Shop; open 10.30–8. Very large stock. Spec: antiquarian; archaeology; architecture; art; biography; classical studies; dictionaries; general fiction; first editions; history; foreign & national languages; limited editions; literature; literature in translation; periodicals/magazines; philosophy; politics; signed editions; travel - Middle East. PR: DM1–1,000.

Sahaf Dil–Tarih, Dr Esat Isik Caddesi 18/A, 81300 Kadiköy, Istanbul. Prop: Sami Önal. Tel: (216) 345-10-79. Fax: 345-88-28. Est: 1983. Shop; open Monday to Saturday 9–6.30. Very large stock. Spec: (in Turkish and deal with the subject from a Turkish point of view) architecture; art history; atlases; cartography; autobiography; biography; calligraphy; Turkey; diaries; dictionaries; encyclopaedias; fine & rare; geography; national history; literature; memoirs; military; monographs; periodicals/magazines; poetry; politics. Cata: 2 a year. Also, a booksearch service. Corresp: French, Turkish.

Sahaf Pegasus, P.O. Box 404, Kadiköy, 81300 Istanbul. Prop: Mrs. Refika. Tel: (216) 349-17-02. Fax: 348-98-29. Est: 1990. Shop; open weekends and by appointment and postal business. Medium stock. Spec: Ottoman Empire; Turkey; Islam; (comprising civilisation, culture, history, music, folklore etc.) and also interests on Kurdish features. PR: DM10–100. CC: MC; V. Cata: 3 a year. Also, a booksearch and photocopying service. Corresp: any language. Mem: Sahaflar Dernegi (Antiquarian Booksellers Association, Istanbul). VAT No: 309 002 0580.

Simurg, Hâsnun Galip Sokaği 2/A, 80060 Beyoğlu, Istanbul. Prop: Ibrahim Yilmaz. Tel: (212) 243-63-77. Fax: 243-38-48. Est: 1987. Shop; open Monday to Sunday 9–8. Very large general stock. CC: V; MC. Also, a booksearch service and large print books. Corresp: French, German, Greek.

IZMIR

Eski Kitapgilik, 1757. Sokak 1, 35530 Karsiyaka, Izmir. Prop: Sabri Gûrbûzer. Tel: (232) 342-02-26. Est: 1991. Shop; open every day for 12 hours. Medium stock. Spec: handwritten books; history. PR: up to £180,000. Corresp: German.

Hisaronu Sahafiye, Kizlaragasi Han P.35, Hisaronu 35210, Izmir. Prop: Ali Haydar Toprak. Tel: (232) 441-03-76. Fax: 441-93-07. Est: 1995. Shop; open Monday to Saturday 9.30–7. Small stock. Spec: archaeology; architecture; art; art history; art reference; artists; calligraphy; carpets; national culture; fine art; folklore; history; illuminated manuscripts; national languages; magic & conjuring; manuscripts; mysticism; painting; poetry; Oriental religion; sculpture. PR: £5–200. CC: V. Cata: 9 a year. Also, calligraphy and miniature artist. Corresp: German, French, Italian. Mem: Chamber of Book Dealers.

Kitap–Bank, 1714 Sokak 18, 35600 Karsiyaka, Izmir. Prop: Hakan Palabiyik. Tel: (232) 368-05-28. Market stand and storeroom; open every day except Sunday 8.30–8.30. Very large general stock. PR: DM1–1,000. Also, a booksearch service and large print books.

Sahaf, 871 SK. No: 19/P-57, Kizlarağasi Hani, Izmir. Prop: Giğgem (Erkal) Ipek. Tel: (232) 425-91-51. Fax: 425-50-63. Est: 1995. Shop; open 6 days a week (except Sunday) 9–6. Small stock. Spec: astrology; atlases; early imprints; encyclopaedias; law; travel - Middle East; music - old Turkish; numismatics; first editions; manuscripts; pharmacy; railways; Oriental religion; history; guides. PR: DM1–6,000. Also, large print books. VAT No: 479 000 5406.

ALPHABETICAL INDEX BY NAME OF BUSINESS

These are presented in two sections, Business and Proprietor. Those businesses typeset in italics means that the entry contains only their name and address.

251

INDEX OF DEALERS WITH E-MAIL NUMBERS

ALPHABETICAL INDEX BY NAME OF PROPRIETOR

This index shows all proprietors cross referenced to their business, the country and the page references on which complete details are shown.

SPECIALITY INDEX

ANTIQUARIAN

ANTIQUES

APICULTURE

APPLIED ART

ARACHNOLOGY

ARCHAEOLOGY

ARCHITECTURE

SPECIALITY INDEX

ARCHIVES

SPECIALITY INDEX

AUTHORS

– BAEDEKER, KARL

– BEHMER, MARCUS

– BRASSENS

– CARMEN, SYLVA

– CENDRARS, BLAISE

– COCTEAU, JEAN

– GREY, ZANE

– HEINE, HEINRICH

– HERMINE, DAVID

– HESSE, HERMANN

– LORCA, GARCÍA

– LOTI, PIERRE

– MAXIMILIAN ZU WIED

– MAY, KARL

– MICHAUX, FRANÇOIS

AUTOMOBILIA/AUTOMOTIVE

AVANT–GARDE

BINDINGS

BIOGRAPHY

BIOLOGY

BOOK OF HOURS

BOOKS ABOUT BOOKS

BOTANY

BROADCASTING

BUSINESS STUDIES

SPECIALITY INDEX

CINEMA/FILMS

CIRCUS

SPECIALITY INDEX

COUNTRIES & REGIONS
– GENERAL

– AFRICA

– ALGERIA

– ASIA

– AUSTRIA

– BAHAMAS, THE

– BELGIUM

– CARIBBEAN, THE

– CENTRAL EAST EUROPE

– CHINA

– CYPRUS

– CZECH REPUBLIC

DESIGN

DIARIES

DICTIONARIES

DIRECTORIES

DOCUMENTS

DOGS

DOMESTICITY

EARLY IMPRINTS

EDUCATION & SCHOOL

EGYPTOLOGY

EMBLEMATA

EMBROIDERY

ENCYCLOPAEDIAS

SPECIALITY INDEX

FINE ART

FLOWER ARRANGING

FOLKLORE

GEOGRAPHY

GEOLOGY

– ANCIENT

– MIDDLE AGES (THE)

SPECIALITY INDEX

SPECIALITY INDEX

ILLUSTRATED

INCUNABULA

INDUSTRY

SPECIALITY INDEX

– NATIONAL

LAW

LITERATURE IN TRANSLATION

MAGIC & CONJURING

MANUSCRIPTS

MARITIME/NAUTICAL

MATHEMATICS

SPECIALITY INDEX

SPECIALITY INDEX

NATURAL SCIENCES

NAVIGATION

NEEDLEWORK

NEWSPAPERS

SPECIALITY INDEX

PUBLIC HOUSES

PUBLISHERS

PUPPETS & MARIONETTES

RADICAL ISSUES

RAILWAYS

REFERENCE

RELIGION
– GENERAL

– CHRISTIAN

– JEWISH

SPECIALITY INDEX

SPECIALITY INDEX

TOWN PLANNING

TOYS

TRADES & PROFESSIONS

TRANSPORT

– POLAR

– MIDDLE EAST

SPECIALITY INDEX

WAR

– GENERAL

– WORLD WAR I

– WORLD WAR II

WARGAMES

SPECIALITY INDEX

BOOKSEARCH SERVICE

BOOKSEARCH SERVICE

LARGE PRINT BOOKS

DISPLAYED ADVERTISEMENTS
Index of Advertisers